THE GREATEST TOIL EVER STORIED

If you are busy (!) and have time to read only one book on missions history this year, make it this gem. With the glad tidings of Christmas and Easter in their hearts, and with the love of God compelling, small numbers of missionaries set sail to "advance the gospel in the regions beyond." In Arabia, Turkey, and Persia missionaries endured more hardships, suffered the death of more children, and laid down their lives in greater numbers than we who have made some attempt in recent years to follow the trail they blazed. It is not for us to judge those missionaries who came before us—they were made of sterner stuff—but there are lessons to learn, cautionary tales. When one reads Henry Riggs' thoughtful, heartfelt examination of his own missionary life in Turkey and Lebanon and Jerusalem, which Livingstone incudes in an appendix, one feels empowered to keep telling the message to those who need it most, and to stand on the shoulders of giants. As Greg Livingstone has said, "It's too soon to celebrate, too soon to quit."

— BOB BLINCOE, FRONTIERS US PRESIDENT EMERITUS

Greg Livingstone, along with his Research Associates, have produced a ground breaking historical overview of evangelistic efforts among Muslims in Turkey, Persia and the Middle East. Perhaps never before has so much information on this subject been brought to publication.

It is heartrending to read of the dedication of hundreds who went forth to toil and persevere through innumerable obstacles and then see only trickles of converts, many of whom, under intense family pressure revert to Islamic faith.

The reader will be surprised to read how many of the pioneer missionaries were women. Greg points out that their witness usually brought little tangible fruit. One can only salute these soldiers of the cross who labored in a male dominated culture.

Livingstone has lived with his 'magnificent obsession' throughout his extremely productive life. His founding of FRONTIERS allowed for hundreds of visionaries to flow forth to every majority Muslim nation in the world.

Kudos to my good friend, Greg, for producing a work that will help new recruits learn from past unheralded heroes. Their successes and failures will be a guide for all to ponder.

— PHIL PARSHALL, SIM

I cannot recommend too highly the outstanding new work by Dr. Greg Livingstone, The Greatest Toil Ever Storied: Reflections on Protestant Mission to Muslims, Volume 1: Turkey, Persia, Mesopotamia, and the Arab World 1800-1978. Dr. Livingstone has combined an amazing breadth of historic detail and personal experience with a concern for their application to current missions work. This volume should be required reading for anyone desiring to serve God in the Muslim world, so that they might take advantage of the hard lessons learned by those who have given their lives to that work.

— TIM LEWIS, CEO TELOS FELLOWSHIP, FRONTIERS INTERNATIONAL DIRECTOR EMERITUS, FRONTIERS SENIOR STRATEGIST

I have known of Greg Livingstone since the early 1990s, and have been honored to know him more personally over that last 4 years. Anything coming from the heart and pen of this catalytic servant of Jesus is worth the reader's time and prayerful engagement!

— KEVIN HIGGINS, FRONTIER VENTURES GENERAL DIRECTOR

THE GREATEST TOIL EVER STORIED

THE GREATEST TOIL EVER STORIED

REFLECTIONS ON EARLY PROTESTANT MISSION TO MUSLIMS VOLUME 1: TURKEY, PERSIA, MESOPOTAMIA, AND THE ARAB WORLD 1800-1978

GREG LIVINGSTONE, DOCTOR OF MISSIOLOGY

MOF PUBLISHING

ISBN 978-0-9958951-7-1 (print); 978-0-9958951-8-8 (e-book)

Published by MOF Publishing; info@mofpublishing.com; https://mofpublishing.com

MOF PUBLISHING

THE GREATEST TOIL EVER STORIED

REFLECTIONS ON EARLY PROTESTANT MISSION TO MUSLIMS VOLUME 1: TURKEY, PERSIA, MESOPOTAMIA, AND THE ARAB WORLD 1800-1978

GREG LIVINGSTONE, DOCTOR OF MISSIOLOGY

MOF PUBLISHING

ISBN 978-0-9958951-7-1 (print); 978-0-9958951-8-8 (e-book)

Published by MOF Publishing; info@mofpublishing.com; https://mofpublishing.com

MOF PUBLISHING

CONTENTS

WHY THIS BOOK: AN INTRODUCTION

I'd like to think this isn't so much a book as a love letter from an 80-year-old veteran of the Cross to his family in Christ Jesus and especially to and for Christ's ambassadors to the Muslim world. Muslims today are 24% of the men, women and children on the planet and, through little fault of their own, are locked into Satan's masterpiece, "without hope and without God" according to the Lord Jesus and his Apostles (Eph. 2:12).

Some clichés endure for generations because they are so poignantly vital. This book is based on one: "Those who are ignorant of history are in danger of repeating it." These reflections, looking back on the faithfulness of the pioneering ground-breakers, is all about asking that question: OF WHAT IN THE PAST SHOULD WE BE AWARE? We pose this question so that the making of disciples of the Lord Jesus among followers of the false prophet can be done more fruitfully, i.e. "fruit that lasts" (John 15:16).

These bits of mission history were originally envisioned to highlight efforts of the Lord's servants, up until 1978, across all the countries dominated by Muslim peoples. However, many will be disappointed that what you have before you is only *Volume One: Turkey, Persia, Mesopotamia, and the Arab World.* Future volumes await someone else to utilize our notes which will incubate reflection regarding the history of Protestant ministry among those other Muslim peoples.

It will be obvious to a more gifted historian of Protestant Mission among Muslim peoples that this present volume serves as only a small representative of the many more faithful servants of Christ, brothers and sisters who very likely heard "well done, good and faithful servant" on the day of their Homecoming. The Lord God has had many more unsung and unmentioned heroes than are highlighted in this review. Not a few laid down their lives before they saw even one Muslim become a true disciple of Isa Al Masih (Jesus the Messiah). Thankfully, we are promised by the Lord Jesus Himself: "The sowers and the reapers will rejoice together" (John 4:36).

Sadly there have been many others, including ourselves, who were either unprepared, lacking in appropriate gifting, or without a large enough team. I am strongly convinced (and the record shows) that having co-workers with complementary gifting is a key to greater fruitfulness.

May these vignettes be utilized to cause fruitful reflection on the efforts of those who preceded us. By so doing, you are more likely to have a significant role in seeing a lasting remnant of worshipers enjoying Christ's Kingdom for Eternity.

It is my hope and prayer that you will be inspired by those who went before us, and that through the reflection questions you will be able to evaluate present ministries, avoid mistakes of the past, and be encouraged to experiment with what has not yet been attempted. To benefit most from these historical glimpses, take time to write out your own reflections on what you read. Never stop asking, "What can we learn from the past, so that we can become maximally fruitful?"

Disclaimer: I am neither a historian, nor the son of a historian, nor an exciting writer. No small effort has been made toward accuracy, but to provide actual quotes from the missionaries and their reporters, the literary level of the writing suffered. If some reporting causes your nose to wrinkle, look it up yourself.

Signed: The smiling author,

Greg Livingstone

P.S. If you're one of those persons who seldom read beyond page 20 of a book, skip down to the amazing foresightful report by Henry Riggs of Turkey (Appendix 1).

DEDICATION

To the servants of Jesus Christ who are, in obedience to their King of Kings, faithfully persevering at their assigned posts from Mauritania to Mindanao; from the Comoros to Kolkata and Kashgar.

These pages are a gift for a very special band of servants of the Lord Jesus Christ. It is a love offering for those who have embarked on a gigantic enterprise (I call it the most vital rescue operation on the earth). Most, even church people, who profess to believe the Bible is authentic communication from the Creator, silently suppose it (if they think about it at all) as probably an exercise in futility: introducing Muslim men and women to our God and Savior, the Lord Jesus Christ. I'm sure you realize you qualify as peculiar and out of step with the world; for that matter, also with most church attenders. You are scrambling to maintain residency among Muslim peoples who don't particularly want you there. If they think about it at all, indeed, your message is not worthy of consideration. It doesn't feel good to not be appreciated, or worse to be perceived by your Muslim neighbors as an influence from Satan!

Still, you men and women open your Bibles daily and remind yourselves: "God said it, I believe it, that settles it." You are God's ambassadors to a stubborn people, commissioned both by your church(es) back home, but more importantly, by The Creator Himself, to take up residence among a Muslim people where Christ is not known, loved or followed. Constantly remind yourselves that the God who sent you there will somehow utilize you to provide the Bread of Life to those blindly adhering to a false prophet. May you, like the Master who beckons you to follow Him, miraculously feed five thousand with what often feels like only a little bread and a few dry fish.

In these pages I've endeavored to relate actual events by real missionaries in real time, i.e not simply pass on third-hand stories. All sources are listed in the bibliography, which itself can lead the reader into goldmines of mission history. May you, the Lord's servants of today, be bolstered to "run the race to win" (1 Cor. 9:24), taking courage from those who ran before you, "of whom the world was not worthy" (Heb. 11:38). They are now among "that great audience of witnesses" (Heb. 12:1) cheering you on in your race. May the joy and wisdom of the One True God be your strength as you are faithfully "manning a lighthouse" in the dense fog blinding Muslim peoples.

Additionally, I do not forget you who with concern, prayer, finances, and much encouragement bolster this special band of servants. Yours is a significant Kingdom contribution in itself, and this book is also dedicated to you.

ACKNOWLEDGMENTS

For as long as I can remember (it has been over fifty-five years since my 23-year old self flew overseas from Wheaton College by propeller plane to "win the Muslims"), I have been asking God and His servants: "How can we do it more fruitfully?" His answer has been to link my heart with His missionaries to the Muslims, who since the Protestant era of mission began have gone before us, taking on the greatest challenge on earth for Christ's Great Commission: the Muslim peoples.

Thank you George Verwer, Dale Rhoton, Ralph Winter, Norm Lewis, William Miller, Don McCurry, Phil Parshall, Christy Wilson Jr., Warren Chastain, Francis Schaeffer, Francis Steele, John Piper, Tim Lewis, and many more (who don't want their names in print), who have been God's instruments to help me love God with my heart AND mind, and be moved with compassion, that a remnant from every Muslim people might join us and forever give glory to their God and Savior Jesus Christ.

I am also eager on "that Day" to sit at the table with you Henry Martyn, Anthony Norris, Samuel Zwemer, Henry Jessop, and the rest of God's apostolic band sent to the Muslims, not to ignore Saul of Tarsus, David Livingstone, Hudson Taylor, and the rest of the innumerable "pace setters" for THE NAME.

I will be grateful for Eternity how You, Lord Jesus, have kept me and my precious wife Sally pressing on toward the goal of His High calling since 1959. In regard to this book, Sally contributed significantly by ransacking countless books and resources to help me find anything which described what Christians have attempted among Muslims in the pursuit of what The Apostle Paul described as being sent "to open their eyes and turn them from darkness to light, from the power of Satan to God (Himself) so that they may receive forgiveness of their sins and take their place with all those who are made holy by their faith in Christ," entering into the Kingdom of God's beloved Son. (Acts 26:18; Col. 1:13).

However, this book would have never seen the light of day without the arduous efforts for two and a half years of my beloved journeyman teammate, Ben Childs. Ben had to wade through and organize twelve years of transcribed notes (thank you to Pauline Jagger, Greg Salazar and those other transcribers whose names I cannot remember), plus research ministries of the past alluded to by others. Ben stuck with me and the research through all those many months when we were trying to practice what we're writing about; struggling alongside our MBB colleague Amjad and Dr. Christian Puritz in an effort to birth a house church among Pakistani Muslims in England.

May these glimpses of those who went before cause God's reinforcements to be stimulated further (and wiser) toward the accomplishment of the promised turning of a remnant from all Muslim peoples into the everlasting Kingdom of the One True God (c.f. Rev. 5:7; 7:9).

Yours to have Muslim-background friends welcome us into eternal dwellings (Luke 16:9),

Greg Livingstone

HISTORICAL EVENTS AFFECTING MINISTRY TO MUSLIMS: A TIMETABLE

1793 - William Carey, father of Protestant missions (outside the West), arrives in India.

1799 - Founding of the CMS (Church Missionary Society) in England by evangelical Anglicans.

1800 - There are fewer than 100 Protestant missionaries ministering outside the West. By 1900, there were about 45, though only a tiny proportion would focus on ministry to Muslims.

1804 - The British and Foreign Bible Society is founded, sparking the greatest Bible translation and distribution in history.

1805 - Henry Martyn takes a job as chaplain to the British living in India, thereby obtaining residency and the opportunity to work with Urdu-speaking Muslims when off-duty.

1815 - Founding of the Coptic (Egyptian, not Arab) Protestant Church.

1817 - Robert Moffat, father-in-law of David Livingstone, arrives in Botswana from South Africa.

1818 - The first Protestant missionaries from the London Missionary Society reach Madagascar.

1819 - CMS lasts only two years in Egypt. It is restarted in 1930 and continues work until 1950.

1820 - American Board of Commissioners (Presbyterians & Congregationalists) arrive in Turkey [Smyrna].

1826 - Basel Mission sends workers from Switzerland and Germany to the Caucasus of Russia, but almost immediately shift from Muslim Turkish people to the Greeks, Assyrians, and Armenians.

1827 - John Darby births the Christian (Plymouth) Brethren who send out Anthony Norris Groves as the first Protestant missionary to Baghdad.

1830 - France colonizes Algeria and beyond in Africa.

1839 - The Sultan of Turkey temporarily allows Protestant missionaries to evangelize, leading to the first dozen known Turkish MBBs.

1846 - The Orthodox Church in the Ottoman Empire excommunicates Armenian evangelicals discipled by American Presbyterians.

1849 - David Livingstone begins 27-year effort to open central Africa to Christianity, commerce, and civilization.

1850 - Joseph Wolff travels from Jerusalem to Bukhara, Jedda and throughout Mesopotamia to evangelize Jewish people.

1857 - MBB Wallayat Ali martyred in Sepoy Mutiny [India].

1860 - Druze Muslims massacre Catholics and Orthodox in Syria. Mary Whately founds schools for poor Muslim boys and girls in Egypt.

1861-1865 - Civil War in the United States causing almost one million deaths. Massive response to "revival meetings" in the USA leads to many offering to serve in foreign missions.

1865 - China Inland Mission is founded by Hudson Taylor, but only a handful of their missionaries attempt church planting among Muslims in China.

1868 - MBB Janni Al, the first Indian CMS missionary to Bengali Muslims, challenges expats to go deeper into Islamic context.

1881 - North Africa Mission (Arab World Ministries) is founded in Britain.

1884 - Berlin Conference where European governments divide up Africa, ignoring tribal boundaries, and agree to Belgium's seizure of the Congo causing an estimated ten million deaths between 1885 and 1908.

1891 – Samuel Zwemer travels to Bahrain, inaugurating fourteen years of pioneer missionary work in Arabia.

1895 - The Haystack Prayer meeting launches the Student Volunteer Movement.

1897 - Muhammad Ahmed in Sudan claims to be the Mahdi appearing in the last days to lead the first Islamic Jihad of modern times. Britain defeats his army in 1898, occupying Sudan until 1960.

1904 - Welsh Revival triggers other revivals in India, the USA, Korea, East Africa, and China, but there is little evidence that it led to more missionaries taking up residence among unreached peoples.

1914-1918 - World War I puts Christian missions on hold as Germany, Austria-Hungary, Bulgaria and the Ottoman Empire fight against Great Britain, France, Russia, Italy, Romania, Japan and the United States. The Ottoman Empire's stranglehold on Arabia ends.

1915 - Dissolution of the Ottoman Empire by the West, but missionaries are overwhelmed trying to meet the needs of several million "Christian" refugees.

1917 - Britain takes Palestine from the Ottomans with Arab help. The eventual outcome was the formation of the state of Israel in 1948.

1919 - The Bolshevik Revolution in Russia leads to a Soviet Union; the most destructive anti-Christian tyranny in history, which prevented the preaching of the Gospel not only in Russia but also to the Muslims of Central Asia.

1921-1948 - Incessant fighting in Palestine leaves western Christians becoming increasingly anti-Arab.

1922 - Mussolini seeks to build an Empire in Africa, prohibiting Protestant missionaries in Libya, Eritrea and Somalia. Five hundred thousand Ethiopian Orthodox Christians are massacred by Italian Catholics, which likely did not positively impress the Muslims.

1924-1927- Civil war in Lebanon between Druze and Catholics.

1929 - The Wall Street crash results in worldwide economic depression and widespread poverty until 1936. Depression evaporates funds for foreign missions.

1930s-1960s - Latitudian theology (outside of orthodoxy) denies the need for Muslims to put their reliance on Christ's atoning work on the cross. Evangelistic motive nearly evaporates among the next generation of missionaries within the older denominations. Volunteers from fundamental Bible schools emerge to pick up the dropped torch.

1934 - First Saudi-Yemen war.

1935 - Shi'a-Sunni and Yazidi revolts in Iraq.

1939–1945 - Second World War. Overseas mission once again put on hold as seventy million people perish, mostly civilians, forty million in Europe and thirty million in Asia.

1946 - Iran war with Azerbaijan.

1947 - Partition of British India between Muslims and non-Muslims. One million die and India holds onto Muslim majority Kashmir which leads to recurrent wars in 1947, 1965, 1971, 1984 and continuous violent jihad is Islamic terrorist warfare since 1989 in South Asia, which is home to one third of the Muslim peoples on earth.

1958 - Egypt and Syria merge into United Arab Republic.

1958 - Eisenhower orders U.S. Marines into Lebanon to prevent civil war.

1971 - Pakistani Muslims bomb, pillage and rape fellow Muslims in Bangladesh.

1973 - The largest Arab-Israeli conflict begins as Egyptian and Syrian forces attack Israel.

1976 - Israeli airborne commandos attack Uganda's Entebbe Airport and free 103 hostages held by pro-Palestinian hijackers of Air France plane.

1978 - Communists take over Russian-controlled Afghanistan.

1979 - Shah leaves Iran after year of turmoil. Revolutionary forces under Muslim leader Ayatollah Ruhollah Khomeini take over, expelling all foreign missionaries and jailing or assassinating Iranian church leaders. Iranian militants seize U.S. embassy in Tehran and hold American hostages, forcing the USA and Iran to break relations.

1980-1988 - Iran-Iraq war leaves two million dead.

1983 - Three hundred fifty American and French soldiers plus embassy staff are blown up by Hezbollah in Beirut, Lebanon.

1990 - The first Gulf War with Iraq.

1998 – The second Gulf War with Iraq, destroying Sunni control and sparking continual conflict between Shi'a and Sunni, eventually leading to the rise of ISIS.

2001 – September 11th attacks, planned and instigated by Muslims.

2006 - Civil war between Palestinians.

2011 - Shi'a rebellion crushed in Bahrain.

2011-2014 - Civil war in Egypt.

2016 - Failed coup d'etat against the dictator defeated in Turkey.

2019 - Bagdati, leader of ISIS assassinated.

The point to understand from this partial review of wars between Muslims and by or against Muslims, is that military conflicts and civil uprisings are devastatingly effective in diminishing opportunities for missionaries and MBBs to befriend and disciple lost Muslims!

1

WHY DID THE CHURCH GO TO THE MUSLIMS LAST?

IF PEOPLE THINK ABOUT THE HISTORY OF PROTESTANT MISSION AT ALL (NOT exactly a party topic) the names of William Carey to India, Robert Morrison to China, David Livingstone to southern Africa, Adoniram Judson to Burma (Myanmar), John Paton to the cannibals of the Pacific Islands, or the pioneer Moravians from Europe to the islands of Hawaii and the Caribbean, are most likely to come to mind. Perhaps few, until the last 30 years, would think about mission to Muslims. In short, the followers of Muhammad came to the attention of Great Commission Protestants much too late. Why is this, after so many others had already been commissioned to China, India, or the multitude of pagan tribes across the globe?

To those who yearned for the Great Commission to be fulfilled, the "Moslems" were NOT an urgent task. Didn't they believe in only one God? Therefore, they weren't designated or thought of as heathen who worshiped multiple deities. Not uncommonly, some respected Christian leaders postulated that the ardent followers of Muhammad of Arabia were simply another Christian sect; needful perhaps, but not a priority. The Maronite Roman Catholics, the Orthodox Church, and even Protestant converts who were drawn out of the ancient churches by Western Protestant missionaries, lived in quiet (most of the time) but with seething resentment, having been controlled and culturally "ghettoized" by oppressive Muslim authorities for centuries. They were very much "second class" citizens and seldom people from whom Muslims would accept ideas of God and religion. Most could only content themselves by anticipation that their Muslim neighbors would go to Hell.

In the West, Muslims (if they were thought of at all) were generally regarded as uncouth bandits. Very few Protestant Christians were all that bothered that the Arab invaders had subjected and silenced those "other" Christians who prayed to Mary and other saints. Until that is, European and American entrepreneurs discovered the monetary potential of the Middle East and other Muslim majority lands. Gradually, God's people awoke to the logic that Muslims ALSO needed the Savior. Thus, some began to follow the path to the Middle East and North Africa which had been opened by their governments. Unfortunately, entrepreneurial colonists could easily discern that evangelizing Muslims was bad for business. In no uncertain terms, the missionaries were told that it wasn't the business of the Christians to aggravate the Muslims across the Middle East, North Africa, Asia and wherever else the Europeans needed to influence ruling governments. In any case, Muslims were not the kind of people who would evoke compassion. And besides, Western Protestants to this day find the topic of 13th and 14th century efforts by Roman Catholic armies slaughtering Muslims to win back formerly "Christian lands" (especially Jerusalem) an embarrassing bit of church history that they would just as well ignore or forget entirely.

However, Great Commission minded churches in the West, at the sunrise of the 20th century, bought into the notion that it was "the white man's burden" to also carry Protestant Christianity to Western Asia to restore a knowledge of Christ where the church had been prominent before the Muslim advance. That presupposition, along with the assumption that all peoples needed Western education and culture, bolstered a common motivation that it was God's will to send missionaries to what Protestants assumed were historically "Bible territory." The Protestant church officials in the West were convinced that the Catholics and Orthodox in the Middle East had it wrong as well. Within a few years of the first Protestant missionaries taking up residence there, they reported to the churches back home that the vast majority of the so-called Christians amongst the Muslims were just as lost. They didn't know the Bible and they prayed to saints, which was reportedly the biggest possible stumbling block to seeing any Muslims believe in and become disciples of Jesus.

In reaction to reported "heathen practices and beliefs" among the ancient "Christians," those making decisions back in England, Scotland, Germany, Switzerland, and the United States virtually cancelled further ministry to Muslims. The foremost mandate was to win first the Jews, thus hastening the return of Christ. Then (was the sending church leaders' assumption), the hope was that those regenerated believers, who knew the languages, would shoulder the lions share of the task to win the Muslims to Christ! Surely they would be led and motivated by the Holy Spirit just as the missionaries were. The reasoning seemed logical enough, so the strategy of that day (let the reader beware) caused perhaps 90% of the missionaries to turn away from the Muslims. At most, they produced literature and accepted some Muslim students into their schools. (Though most Muslim parents were extremely reluctant to allow that!) Therefore the missionaries focused on the "ancient Christians," especially when they found the Jews adamantly resistant.

For those reasons and others, Delavan Leonard in 1895 wrote:

Perhaps the chapter "Missions to the Turkish Empire" should be more accurately titled "Mission to the Oriental Churches." Although the missionaries found the Orthodox, Maronites, and Armenians hoping to be protected and educated by the presence of Western Christians, soon the majority of their priests were threatened and threatening, fearing a loss of influence among their flock. Not a few of the Middle Eastern Christians, who became Protestants, were persecuted, a few to death, when they aligned with the churches founded by the Western missionaries. Not a few suffered to a greater degree than they had by the hands of the Muslims.[1]

2

TURKEY

Pre-1860

THE OTTOMAN EMPIRE (REDUCED AFTER WORLD WAR I TO ONE COUNTRY - Turkey) spanned from Hungary to Iran and west toward Morocco, with the capital city being Constantinople (modern day Istanbul). That enormous empire was the first field for American Protestant missionaries who were determined to see Muslims in the Middle East bow the knee to the Savior. It seems they were stunned to realize how "pagan" the ancient eastern Christians had become; even the priests had only fragmentary knowledge of the Scriptures. Tragically, not only did those Christians possess ignorance as to what was inside the cover of the Bible, fewer even possessed a copy. But in any case, it existed in a language they could hardly understand: old Syriac. Adding to that, few were sufficiently literate to read any language.

Thus, the American missionaries were so horrified by what appeared to be paganism among the Christian peoples that, together with the mission leaders in America, they decided to postpone the earlier goal of witness to the Muslims in order to help those who felt they loved the Savior to actually discover him. More disappointment was added when the priests of both the Armenian and Greek churches failed to offer any encouragement to that endeavor (fearing their youth and thinking people would question their authority as they learned what the Bible actually taught). Still, as the missionaries started schools and medical clinics, what some of the Armenians did realize was that they needed help from the Western missionaries if they were going to survive surrounded by hostile Muslims.

Long before the arrival of the Protestant missionaries, various Eastern Christian communities, Greek Orthodox, Armenian Orthodox, Syrian Orthodox, and Maronite Catholics within the Turkish Ottoman Empire, were segregated into *millets* (ghettos) which increasingly undermined their relationships among the Muslim majority. As the Ottoman Empire declined, various Christian ethnic groups, bolstered by contact with European powers, revolted against Ottoman domination. Greece became independent in 1832, but not before fifty thousand Greeks were slaughtered. Some speculate that possibly ten thousand rebellious Orthodox Christians and another ten thousand Maronite Catholics were killed in Lebanon and Damascus by Muslim Turks and Arabs. It is quite possible that these historic events are still a point of serious tension in Turkey: the Turks suspect that the Christian missionaries were the main culprits in stirring up nationalistic independent movements among those who lived in the *millet*, particularly through the mission schools established across the Ottoman Empire.

William Goodell, his wife Abigail, and their children arrived at Constantinople on June 9, 1831. He wrote in his journal about their first sighting of the great city from their ship:

The view of Constantinople was at first indistinct, and presented nothing striking. We began to call into question the correctness of the opinions expressed by writers, of the unrivaled beauty of its situation and of the scenery around. But as we approached the city the prospect became enchanting.[1]

The Goodells had been tasked by the American Board of Commissioners for Foreign Mission (ABCFM) to establish a new mission in Constantinople. After acquiring a house, they set about to make that dream a reality.

However, two months after arriving, a great fire swept through the city, consuming their home and nearly claiming the entire family. About that event, William wrote:

Though cast down, we are not destroyed. We have been afflicted, but not given over unto death. ... My heart sickens and my eyes fill as I think of the wickedness, the sufferings, and the horrors of that day! ... It seemed indeed, like "the great and terrible day of the Lord," when "the heavens, being on fire, shall be dissolved and the elements shall melt with fervent heat, the earth also, and the works that are therein, shall be burnt up." The Lord grant that we may all "find mercy of the Lord in that day," and may our treasure be laid up where the last fire cannot reach.[2]

Question to Ponder

Reflect on William Goodell's response to the fire that claimed his home and very nearly his family. What can we learn from his journal entry about his view of God, possessions and the work they had been called to do?

IN 1832, the Goodells received much needed support in the arrival of two new co-workers: H.G.O. Dwight (who had previously travelled with Eli Smith) and William Gottlieb Schauffler, along with their families. For many years, they all shared the same home: "Never was one family more perfectly united in feeling and service."[3]

William's approach to evangelism was to utilize friendship and warmth to win over Muslims to Christ, but to avoid engaging in a direct worldview clash:

His plan was to exert an influence over those with whom he came in contact, without having the appearance of influencing them at all, and so to avoid exciting opposition. ... He did not feel called upon to make an open assault upon the Greek and Armenian churches. His aim was to cast the leaven into the existing church organizations, leaving it to work by the power of the Divine Spirit. His desire was to see the work of reformation going on within the Greek and Armenian churches... and this was precisely the result that came about in the course of a few years. [4]

Early in his missionary career, Goodell set a precedent for his ministry in that he refused to seek government assistance or defense:

So clear was his conviction of the truth that Christ's kingdom is not of this world, and that it is not to be advanced by worldly authority and power, that he was exceedingly averse to obtaining *firmans* [royal decrees] for carrying on any missionary operations, or seeking official interference and protection from the government.[5]

Rightly or wrongly, many other missionaries during this time took a different approach. In 1841 the ABCFM reported how the mission was enjoying the shield of the U.S. government. Unfortunately, "that over-identification with their home country would have dire consequences for the missionary enterprise throughout the Middle East, when the Muslim countries shed their foreign yokes."[6] For many decades, American, British, and other European missionaries in what became Turkey and throughout the rest of the Ottoman Empire, were largely, almost unconsciously, affected by their own culture's presuppositions. For example, Westerners were deeply influenced by the Enlightenment or elevation of reason which increasingly took precedence over the earlier stance of accepting the teachings of the Bible on face value. As products of their own culture's assumptions, missionaries assumed unlearned people could be coaxed to abandon their backward state when provided with sufficient Western education.

As is true today, we wonder if their emphasis on being practical led to ministry strategies that were considered more doable than church planting among resistant, even pugilistic Muslims. For example, in 1844, the board of the ABCFM chose to work in Lebanon partly because the country was accessible from the coast and had a relatively healthy climate. Most of the pioneers apparently had little awareness of the homogeneous unit principle. In days before much study of anthropology, they would assume the people were homogenous, giving too little attention to the multiple different kinds of loyalties among the Muslims who may have as many "denominations" as does the so-called Christian church around the world.

From 1853 to 1856, Turkey was so dependent on French and British support that the Sultan was forced to grant, grudgingly, not full but partial freedom of religion. Thus in 1856 he issued the famous *Hatt-i Humayoun*, supposedly granting religious liberty throughout the whole of Turkey:

His Imperial Majesty the Sultan having, in his constant solicitude for the welfare of his subjects, issued a Firman, which, while ameliorating their condition, without distinction of religion or race, records his generous intentions towards the Christian population of his Empire.[7]

Agreement which resulted from such pressure from the West was usually sullen and sporadic. This brief period of allowing conversion to any religion backfired in 1856. I suppose the local Christians either knew it would, or their hatred toward the Muslims left no motivation to evangelize or give them the Scriptures.

More missionaries were recruited and Turkish-speaking Muslims began to show more receptivity toward the precepts of Christianity. Some public discourses by the missionaries on religious subjects were well attended and an unprecedented number of Muslims came to visit the homes of the English and American missionaries. Minimal conversions and a few baptisms followed. Missionary George Herrick had an interesting vision of one day, at the call of the *muezzin* (the one who publically calls Muslims to prayer), witnessing Muslims bowing the knee to Jesus while maintaining their Islamic identity. Herrick, like most others, hoped that bringing social lift would set the stage for the effective portraying of the Jesus in the Gospels. However, that optimistic spike lasted only eight years. It was one of the rare times the missionaries thought they might reach Muslims directly; increased sale of Bibles sold openly near the mosques provided ample opportunities for witnessing.

The concept of capitulations, i.e. privileges to exempt outsiders in taxes and keep them under the authority of their country's consuls rather than Ottoman authorities, irked the Ottomans, especially as it was extended to France who claimed the right to protect Roman Catholics; England, the Protestants; and Russia, the Orthodox Christians. Foreign investors in business, skilled at getting around Turkish laws, tended to establish private unassailable, self-ruled "protectorates" which was unethical in the local's eyes. There is reason to believe when missionaries depended too much on their government's protection or allied too closely with western business, they were susceptible to being seen as other than holy men.

As mentioned, few of the earliest missionaries to the Ottoman Empire were prepared to discover that the ancient Eastern Christian churches were considered blasphemists among the Muslims. Eli Smith reported concerning the Roman Catholic and Orthodox Christians:

There are millions of men, sunk in ignorance and sin to a degree that makes the present salvation of any hopeless. Though bearing the same holy name by which you are called, and inhabiting places consecrated by apostle's feet, they are still so degenerate that "the name of God is blasphemed among the Gentiles through them," and Moslems confirmed in the errors of the false prophet.[8]

Lesser known mission agencies, including the German Orient Mission, the Muhammadan Mission in Bulgaria, the French Society, the American Baptists, and the Disciples of Christ had some missionaries in the Ottoman Empire. They also gave priority to converting the Eastern Christians. In several cases priority was given to the evangelization of the Jewish people in the Middle East.

In addition to the other barriers of witness to the Muslims, the missionaries' empathy for the suffering of the Jews, Greeks, Armenians and Assyrians created a wall of enmity between the missionaries and the Muslims. Eli Smith agreed:

To think of exerting much influence upon the Muhammadan mind while the native Christian churches remain as they are is out of the question... the ignorance, idolatry, and scandalous lives of their members preach louder and more effectually against Christianity than the united voices of all Protestant missionaries do in its favor.[9]

What needed to be done for these heathen Christians? The obvious answer was schools and universities, which became the chief strategy for many. Schools, it was assumed, would create conditions for preaching the Message and facilitate acceptance of biblical Christianity. The General Secretary of the ABCFM stated an early general sentiment in defense of starting English medium schools: "It is now the English language, saturated with Christian ideas, gathering up into itself the best thought of all the ages, that is the great agent of Christian civilization throughout the world."[10] This perspective defined being "civilized." The task became, for most missionaries, to deliver Middle Eastern people from their pagan history and cultural practices. Few had a notion of infiltrating Christ within their own culture and community life.

Not many, however, thought winning Muslims through English was adequate. Finally William Gottlieb Schauffler initiated, toward the end of the 1850s, a greater emphasis on Muslims actually reading the Scriptures in their own language. He was charged with transcribing Goodell's Armeno-Turkish into the Arabic characters of Ottoman Turkish but soon felt this was a hopeless task because the Turkish spoken by the Armenians and Greeks was "too coarse and degraded to be...acceptable to Osmanlis," and because "the same terms were frequently employed by the different nationalities in widely different senses."[11] The discussion grew concerning whether the approach to Muslims should involve different methods and language than those used in outreach to Armenians and other Christian minorities. The discussion concerning the issues of contextualization remains a controversy among practitioners and other Christians to this day.

William Goodell wrote in 1859:

Within the last five or six years, several hundred copies of the Holy Scriptures every year have been sold to the Turks. The history of these we never knew; but we now begin to find among the Turks those who really seem to be Bible Christians, spiritually minded, who, with no teacher but the Bible, have become wise unto salvation.[12]

He further noted that some twenty Muslims had been baptized in Constantinople and one particular candidate for baptism was "a nephew of one of the pashas here, who lives with his uncle, and who was educated by him to be one of the four great Mollas [Mullahs] of the empire."[13] In this report, Goodell also highlighted the baptism of Selim Efendi who changed his name to Edward Williams and was "licensed to preach the Gospel."[14] When Selim was summoned to the Sultan to answer to the charge of apostasy, the missionaries helped him escape to Malta. He eventually returned with a certificate stating that he had become a Christian of his own free will. Nevertheless, his baptism caused a stir and he continued to witness to any Muslims who would listen... and lived to tell about it! Most were not so fortunate, as the majority of converts from 1856 – 1864 who didn't revert to Islam were arrested on trumped up charges resulting in imprisonment or sometimes execution. These episodes with Muslims left many missionaries feeling that the best use of their time (and God's resources) was to concentrate more on the indigenous Christian population and hope that they would in turn evangelize Muslims.

1860-1920

Two remarkable events happened in 1862. The first was that the CMS baptized their first Turkish convert. Second, the first volume of a translated version of *The Noble Gospel* by William Schauffler, William Goodell and Selim Efendi was printed in Istanbul. Then in 1866, another fresh translation of the New Testament in Turkish increased interest in the "Injil" among the Muslims. However, severe hostility during this time squelched further efforts at reaching Muslims in Turkey. Christian college buildings were plundered and burned and hundreds of churches and schools were destroyed. Congregations of non-Muslims were scattered, while many national pastors and teachers were either killed or crippled. No permission could be secured to allow them to rebuild their homes or even make necessary repairs on the churches. The members of the congregations were not allowed to attend a church service nor the children continue to schools established by foreigners. Suddenly, even the subsection entitled "Muhammadans" in the ABCFM's annual reports disappeared from the record in 1862. It would seem that the mission gave up its efforts at evangelizing Muslims as the government brought its full weight to bear on the annihilation of the Christian community.

In 1863, Cyrus Hamlin, who had first landed upon Turkish soil in 1839 and established Bebek Seminary in 1940, established yet another institution for higher learning in Constantinople - Robert College. Named after chief financial backer Christopher Robert, it was built for the purpose of bringing quality education to the city. After being open for five years, Hamlin proclaimed: "The college had become very nearly self-supporting, and the experiment had become a great success, far beyond our highest expectations."[15]

It became evident early on that there was a huge need for medical work both for the missionary families and for the people they ministered to. Unsurprising, medical ministry drew off disproportionate amounts of funding and personnel. The establishment of educational and medical facilities led to the growth of multiple walled mission compounds. These developed into Christian communities isolated from the surrounding Muslims. The station at Marsovan (in modern-day Turkey) was described as "a walled American village." Some of the missionary "forts" threatened the Kurds nearby. The

Bible house in Istanbul built in 1872 had five stories housing the offices of the American Bible Society, plus housing for missionaries, a printing factory, and a chapel that sat 250. Mission-built buildings and shops were rented out to cover operating costs. Every building was owned and supervised by a board in New York perpetuating the image of missions as Western-controlled enterprises, suspected of political aims.

From northern Armenia, fifteen converts were baptized, among whom was a 70-year old Vietnamese. Another was a relative of a government official who might have protected him. From this group of fifteen, a certain Ahmed stood firm against solicitations, tempting offers, severe treatment and alarming threats. He was eventually imprisoned for three months, exiled for two more and finally set free to continue proclaiming his faith. Cyrus Hamlin estimated that between 1857 and 1877, "as many as fifty baptisms of Turkish men, women and children may be attributed to the American Mission."[16]

In 1874, members of the Nusairiyeh Alevite sect in southern Anatolia began to convert as a result of the impact of American Reformed Presbyterian mission schools. Alarmed, officials closed the schools, seized the Bible depots, and imprisoned converts from that sect. The government declared that Christian attacks on the true religion of Islam and all proselytizing were forbidden. Bibles could no longer be sold in open markets on the streets, but only in legal bookshops. All propaganda with the purpose of converting Muslims to Christianity was declared illegal. No longer were Muslims at liberty to choose a religion.

Another attempt to pressure the government to reform was made in 1888 when seventy-one missionaries and Protestant teachers petitioned the Turkish government and the foreign ambassadors to suspend official persecution. Eventually, however, many missionaries abandoned the efforts to evangelize Muslims since any movement in that direction seemed blocked as soon as it seemed to bear some fruit.

The ABCFM decided to double-down their efforts in Anatolia and transferred their work in Syria to the Presbyterians when they agreed to become separate agencies. Still, nearly all of the missionaries felt there was no hope of convincing the Muslims of biblical truth so long as the actual "Christianity" the Muslims experienced around them failed to command their respect. Cyrus Hamlin agreed: "The object of our missions to the Oriental churches is... to revive the knowledge and spirit of the Gospel and... by this means enable the Muslims to see the fire of Christianity rekindled upon those Christian altars."[17] We suspect that one of the other reasons why missionaries turned to the nominal Christians was that it was a lot easier to convert Orthodox Christians to become Protestants. Other missionaries thought of Islam as merely a heretical form of Christianity. Therefore, they pre-supposed that when Muslims witnessed the true faith (Protestant) they would be drawn into biblical churches, a notion not greatly different from today's "seeker sensitive" strategy.

Some mission executives in the United States, however, urged for more itinerant evangelism, convinced that the methods of workers like Karl Pfander should be emulated. Perhaps the majority of missionaries, however, felt such methods only created a backlash. Contrary to their assumptions, Pfander, a prolific writer who accurately quoted the Qur'an, Hadith, and other Muslim sources in the original languages, was actually courteous and sensitive in his face-to-face interactions with Muslims. But his book *The Balance of Truth* created fury among Muslim leadership because it sought to prove that Islam's claim to be true revelation from the Creator could not be substantiated by using arguments based on Islamic sources. The Turkish government reacted to the publication of Pfander's book by seizing the mission printing presses, boarding up the Christian bookstore and closing down the Bible society. In response to this, the missionary community once again turned to their Western governments. The bookstore was reopened and the offices were likewise released from the custody of the police, but the backlash to such Christian publications sparked off a literature war between both sides.

William Goodell described the backlash as such:

The Rev. Dr. Pfander, of the Church Missionary Society, a very worthy and excellent man, came and opened his batteries against Islamism. We earnestly advised him not to publish those books; we entreated him not to do it; we solemnly protested against his doing it. But this good brother having what the great Dr. Edwards attempted to prove nobody can have, viz., *a self-determining power of the will*, went on and did it; and the effect has been to bring all our missionary and Bible operations into great danger, --the very thing of which we had repeatedly warned him.[18]

Though Pfander appealed to reason, he was either unaware of or ignored the influence of developments of biblical criticism and latitudinarian* theology in Western theological institutions. Muslim scholars were quick to use these arguments by "Christians" to undermine what the missionaries were teaching.

Christian apologetics spawned a huge collection of reactions by the Muslims of anti-Christian polemics in the Ottoman Empire and beyond, particularly in Egypt and India. This led to a new trend of Christian-Muslim dialogue including the works of a greatly influential spokesman for Islam, Muhammed Abduh, (1849-1905) who had been the presiding leader of Al-Azhar University in Cairo. He attempted to prove that Christianity was anti-scientific and irrational while demonstrating that the Qur'an was scientific and rational. Abduh's disciple, Rashid Rida (1865-1935), was even more confrontational, demonstrating a violent hatred of Christianity even to the rare level of attacking the person of Isa Al Masih himself; a tact rarely done by Muslim apologists. "With the death of Dr. Pfander in London in 1865, the death of the most faithful Muslim convert, Selim Efendi, and the closing of the Church Missionary Society work in 1877, missionaries returned to concentrating on the nominal Christians."[19]

Questions to Ponder

Do you think it wise that Karl Pfander openly sought to provoke Muslim scholars? Would this be advisable today? Why or why not?

IN HIS 1872 book *A History of Missions*, Secretary Rufus Anderson came to regard strengthening the existing Turkish churches as a substitute for the failure to evangelize Muslims. Anderson wrote: "Experience has also developed the great law here, as well as elsewhere, that the main work of winning races to Christianity must be performed by men of the same race."[20] Anderson was persuaded that a Muslim would listen more patiently to a Christian Turk (renegade though he may be) than he will to an Armenian, or even an American. Whatever theories or strategies were discussed, however, the missionaries held the course, focusing mainly on educational and medical work plus some church planting among the Christian minorities. This went on for another forty-five years.

Heavy emphasis was also continually put upon the production of apologetic and polemic responses to Muslim objections to Christianity. William Muir (1819–1905), a Christian scholar in India, focused on the authenticity of the Bible and William St. Clair Tisdall (d.1928) in Iran looked at the ancient sources for the Qur'an, concluding that the final book was cobbled together by human hands and not divine. Tisdall's book, *The Sources of Islam* (1901) seeks to trace material in the Qur'an and Hadith to pre-Islamic Arabian pagan, Jewish, and Christian heretical and apocryphal sources as well as contorted bits from the Bible. Because Muhammad would have heard "Bible stories" orally when visiting misinformed Christians and Jews as a caravan trader, one can understand why the stories were likely often passed on inaccurately.

Some took the less polemical route. In an area of Istanbul, missionaries re-opened a coffeehouse reading room in 1886 which was frequented by Armenians, Greeks, Assyrians, Jews and even some Turks. It was the one place in the city where there could be Bible teaching among a few Muslim men who would never enter a church. However, we are not aware of any record of Muslims converting to Christ through that coffeehouse ministry.

The Lutheran Orient Mission Society

During the historic Edinburgh conference in 1910, Lutheran mission leader L.O. Fossum decided their church's mission agency would evangelize the Kurds without using the Eastern churches as an intermediary. As latecomers to the region, they had the advantage of learning from the failures of those who preceded them. Fossum felt that the Kurds might be open to Christ because he saw them as warm-hearted, quick to make friends, known for loyalty and friendship, and even somewhat democratic, to which teachings of Christ might be appealing. He also believed that the social conditions in Kurdistan (Eastern Turkey today) gave women more status and freedom than the Arab or Turkish Muslims did. Finally, he hoped that family solidarity and loyalty might lessen persecution of a convert to Christ.

Fossum was an excellent linguist, producing a Kurdish grammar and lexicon and translating the four Gospels, Luther's small catechism, and a hymnbook into Kurdish. Henry Mueller joined the Fossoms, but the Lutherans were only allowed to work there for five years, from 1911 to 1916, since as Germans they were forced to depart during World War I. Though they returned after the war, Fossum died near Van in 1920 at the age of 41. Yet, reportedly, during that period they birthed a Kurdish congregation and established an orphanage and medical dispensary.

Political Strife

In 1914, the Young Turks dissolved the Caliphate and abrogated earlier agreements with Western governments. The Ottoman Empire was thus dissolved and replaced by Turkey, which was immediately plunged into World War I on the side of the Germans. Supposing the Armenians of being allies with the British and French, by the end of that war, the Armenian population, once over two million persons, was virtually eliminated. (Except in Istanbul where a small Armenian Christian community survives to this day.) Try to imagine the emotions and feelings of helplessness the missionaries felt living in the midst of the slaughter. A lesser, but real discouragement was seeing the church and school buildings they had raised funds for being destroyed. The Christians who didn't flee could not obtain permission to rebuild their meeting places.

Seeing the Eastern Christians as the enemy, Muslim hostility led to the depopulation of the Christian community in all but a few remote regions. According to former missionary among the Kurds Bob Blincoe, the missionaries as a whole, had no "Plan B." They had invested almost exclusively in the historic churches and now they were left with a scarcity of Christians alive remaining in the juvenile country of Turkey. Those Christians who did remain bore an understandable attitude of apathy toward the missionaries' concern that Muslims would suffer in Hell. Having few to disciple, the last of the missionaries still there who were evangelistic had their hopes completely dashed of ever seeing the Christians being witnessing bridges to the Muslim majority.

Joseph Greene, writing in 1916, said:

We had hoped that through the revival of spiritual religion in the Oriental churches and through the living testimony of 60,000 native Protestants, the Moslems of Turkey might get a new and more correct apprehension of Christianity...[we hoped that] through the genuine sympathy and rejoicing of

Americans at the time of the revolution of the Young Turks in 1908...the Americans living in Turkey might have been recognized as the true friends of the Turkish people.[21]

While not maligning Greene's sincerity, it would have admittedly been difficult for the Turks to appreciate that the primary goal of the missionaries would not be the recognition of Americans as true friends of the Turkish people, but the conversion of Muslims to the Christian faith as taught in the Bible.

1920-1978

1922 marks what Ron Coody calls "the Turkish Mission Blackout." After Ataturk established the Republic of Turkey in 1922 there was no missionary presence, no MBB Turkish church and strict suppression of any Christian witness until the entrance of modern missionaries in the 1960s."[22] In 1961, Roger Malstead and Dale Rhoton, two of the original members of what would become Operation Mobilization (OM), took up residence as tourists in Ankara, Turkey. They birthed and coordinated short-term teams into Turkey whose goal was to place at least one Bible correspondence course invitation into the mailbox of every home in all major cities. The course traced God's plan of salvation from Adam and Eve through the Old Testament Patriarchs and Prophets to Jesus Christ. OM missionaries lost count of how many thousands of correspondence invitations were posted in the mail both from inside and outside the country over the years.

This Bible Correspondence Course effectively drew out interested Turks across the country and resulted in the first modern Turkish MBBs. The remnant of Evangelical Armenians and Assyrian believers still part of local churches, particularly in Istanbul, became the first places that the new MBBs found fellowship.[23]

A Greek-American missionary Tom Cosmades and his wife joined TEAM (The Evangelical Alliance Mission), doubling the workers with Muslims in Turkey to four! Cosmades gave himself to translating the entire New Testament in modern Turkish. A few notable courageous Assyrian brothers, e.g. Kenan Araz and Behnan Konutgan, were faithful in those early years to witness to Turks as staff of the Bible Society. A remnant of evangelical Armenians and Assyrian believers in Istanbul, Ankara and Izmir even received the few Turkish inquirers when brought by a known trusted Western Christian worker. In a May 1962 report, missionary Dennis Clark spoke of Orhanbey, a Muslim who converted at a Billy Graham rally who returned to Turkey as an evangelist. He wanted to get involved in the literature work.

Largely because of cultural and language barriers, Greek congregations worshipped in Greek, Armenians in Armenian, and Assyrians in Arab and Syriac. By the 1980s, Turkish and Kurdish house groups of Muslim-background believers would gradually emerge. It was helpful that some of the first Turkish pastors were converted in Germany and elsewhere, and then courageously returned to Turkey. Thirty-five years later, adding Bible translation and many other books, films, and information on the Internet, many more Turks have become pastors. Presently at least forty different mission agencies have placed reportedly nearly a thousand long-term (intent) church planters into residence in Turkey. It is estimated that perhaps five thousand Muslim Turks are gathering in Christian fellowships (mostly in the Western half of the country). Still, five-thousand among eighty million is not even 1% of the total population.

3

PERSIA (IRAN)

PERHAPS THERE IS NO PLACE ON EARTH MORE ENCOURAGING FOR THOSE WHO have been laboring to see Muslims fully surrender to the Lord Jesus Christ than what God has done in Persia (Iran) since the 1979 Islamic Revolution. This book's accounts, however, predate that breakthrough. Let us relive what were the seemingly hopeless efforts of God's servants on behalf of the Muslims in Iran BEFORE the Lord of the Harvest engineered an unprecedented response beyond what anyone could have expected or even hoped for.

Try to imagine the years when missionaries were taking up residence among peoples in Persia whose experience of Westerners were Russians and British dividing up their country for their own colonial interests. Those in authority in Persia were already suspicious and tended to be hostile because their country had been continuously threatened and occupied by several foreign powers over the centuries: Alexander the Great and ongoing wars between the Persians and the Romans had weakened both those powers, thereby opening the door for the invasion of the Muslim Arab Sunni hordes in about 635. The Persians didn't become Shi'as until the 1500s when the Safavid dynasty made Shi'a Islam the official state religion and aggressively proselytized the Sunnis.

Iran's current southern and eastern boundaries were determined by the British during the Anglo-Persian War (1856-57). Such was the context Protestant mission agencies faced when they eventually began to dispatch missionaries to Persia in the 1870s, while Russia and England were rattling sabres. The British wanted to safeguard their exclusive route to India. The Russians were expanding their southern border, as well as seeking access to strategic oceanic waterways through the Black Sea, the Persian Gulf, and to the Pacific Ocean. Then in 1908, a British company struck oil in Persia, the first big petroleum find in the Middle East. This event set off a wave of exploration, extraction and exploitation, and new greed from the Western nations that would change the region's and the world's history.

Is it any wonder then, that the peoples of Persia were suspicious of the missionaries' true purpose? It is not so difficult today to imagine how frightening and threatening it must have been for the early pioneers in the northeast of Persia to be looking over their shoulders continuously wondering when (not if) they were going to be attacked by hostile anti-Christian Kurds or Persians who perceived Western Christians as the enemy. Under those historical circumstances, it is easier to imagine why, as so often is the case, the first missionaries from Scotland and the United States swerved away from their original intention (Muslims) to evangelize the ancient Christians in Persia: the Armenians, and Assyrians. Perhaps that's why the persecuted Nestorian Christians were more open to friendship with Westerners.

1700–1850

Early Happenings

Neder Shah, in 1740, commanded that the Bible and Qur'an be translated into Persian. Jews were instructed to translate the Old Testament, Roman Catholics were given the Gospels, and the Armenians were assigned the remainder of the New Testament. However, it is not clear if anything more than one manuscript was produced particularly for the Shah. In any case there was no printing press available to multiply copies.

Two German pioneers, C.F.W. Hoecher and Johannes Rueffer from the United Brethren Mission (Moravians), arrived in Persia in 1747 with the intention of going to Yazd to bring the Gospel to the Zoroastrian despite being warned by the British Council not to proceed to Persia. At the border city of Makhan, the governor, who had been blinded by the Shah, asked them to pray for his healing, but sadly there is no record of success. On route to

Isfahan, the Moravians were attacked by a band of Kurdish robbers losing everything they possessed, even the clothes off their backs! Hungry and cold, the Germans made it to Yazd where the British agent told them that it would be madness to try and do missionary work in chaotic Persia. Yet in faith, they set out and again were robbed of everything they possessed. With great difficulty they reached the Persian Gulf where the Dutch East India Company enabled them to leave Persia. They eventually arrived in Egypt. Rueffer died there, and Hoecker returned to England in 1750. Their total time in Persia was one year.

We learn nothing more of efforts among the Muslims in Persia until Henry Martyn, over 60 years later in 1811, established a base in Shiraz en route from India to his home to England. Martyn, determined to upgrade his translation of the Persian New Testament, acquired a language assistant (Murz Saiid Ali). By February of 1812, the New Testament and Psalms were completed and later published by the Russian Bible Society in 1815. Not satisfied with producing a translation, Martyn, though naturally shy, took every opportunity to dialogue with a few curious Persian scholars. Van Gorder wrote:

Martyn was well received among the Shiraz intelligentsia as "Mullah Martyn" and was often found debating half the night with them about the fundamental truths of Christianity. Not a few gathered at Martyn's residence for long conversations in hopes of being able to convert the gracious and courteous foreigner to Islam.[1]

Campbell says of Martyn: "He was a mystery to the common people; a threat and offense to the Christian Orthodox priests, yet met with classic Persian hospitality and courtesy."[2]

In increasingly poor health, Martyn left Persia in 1812, but not before he attempted to present his New Testament translation to Shah Salih Muhammad Rahim. Rejected by the prime minister, Martyn gave his translation to the British ambassador in Tabriz, Sir Gore Ouseley, who did get it into the hands of the Shah. The Shah then reportedly agreed to read it. Martyn rode on horseback, though ill, over Persia's border in July but died three months later in Turkey, failing to reach his home in England.

Another hero of the faith was Joseph Wolff, the son of the Jewish rabbi in Germany who joined the Church Missionary Society. He traveled widely, including three years to several Persian cities, utilizing his six languages

(Russian, Italian, French, German, English and Syriac) to preach the Gospel to Jews. On November 5, 1823, Wolff travelled from Baghdad to Bushire, Persia. He spent three weeks there meeting Armenian Christians and, surprisingly, founded a small school for them, launched through the good offices of a rich business man by the name of Constantine. After three weeks, Wolff left on horseback. Though he detested that form of travel, he tolerated it for the joy of confronting a new audience at each resting place. On his way to Shiraz in Southern Persia, he was constantly stopping in small villages, reportedly never failing to preach the Message of God's love in Christ.

In Shiraz, Wolff found particular encouragement in the way Henry Martyn's legacy and memory lingered. Martyn had left a reputation as a humble man of good morals who lived near to God, and a man who was persuasive in dialogue, which was a characteristic that appealed to Wolff. He was told in Shiraz that he was now Martyn's successor, and at that point he felt that he had discerned that his calling should include Muslims. He could not restrain himself from writing in his journal one evening, "Martyn! Oh my Martyn! Thou hast kindled a light in Persia which will never go out!"[3] He eventually left Shiraz and moved to the capital city, Tehran. Upon arrival, he was immediately invited to conduct a service in English for the British Charge d'Affaires, Henry Willcok and his retinue according to the rites and ceremonies of the Church of England.

In Tehran in 1830 he had long serious discussions with the local Muslim mullahs as he attempted to balance his two callings: Jews and Muslims. He was told later that the mullah's view of him was "a man who rivets the attention to everything he says, for he speaks with such force, as none of the most eloquent of our nation could do; and in spite of his foreign pronunciation and his foreign manners, he rivets us because sincerity speaks out of him."[4]

Wolff, desiring to improve his Persian (his seventh language), engaged Mirza Ibrahim, who was one of the city's leading scholars, and a friendship was born. Ibrahim expressed a desire to visit England with Wolff and once the trip came about, Ibrahim was appointed to the staff of Haileybury College as Professor of Persian and Arabic. He remained in England from 1826 until 1847.

Wolff left Tehran for Tabriz. His first Sunday there, he preached at the British Embassy at ten in the morning, the Italian Embassy at noon, then until two o'clock, he preached German and French sermons and finished the day speaking to an Arabic-speaking congregation!

In Tabriz, Wolff was introduced to Prince Abbas Mirza, the Governor of Azerbaijan. He at once raised with the Prince the question of establishing a school in Tabriz similar to those in Mesopotamia, assuring him that if he would give it his backing, "your Royal Highness will become by such an act the Sun of Persia."[5] Wolff was learning the gentle art of flattery without which it was difficult in Persia to get authorities on one's side. The Prince in fact did grant Wolff a plot of ground and a building for the envisioned school; however, since no one followed it up, the school never materialized. Not unlike other pioneers, Wolff was oblivious to the difficulty of finding financial supporters and staff to establish a school in unknown areas of Persia when no workers in the country committed to his envisioned projects. Soon after, Wolff left Persia and journeyed into Russia, never to return.

Sustained Missionary Presence

In 1817, five years before Wolff arrived, the Edinburgh Missionary Society sent out William Glen. He updated Martyn's New Testament and completed the Old Testament in Persian. He personally supervised the printing in Scotland and escorted the Bibles back to Persia. Glen's greatest joy was the baptism of Mirza Muhammad Ali, the son of a judge, who in turn was the son of the Shah's Prime Minister. The conversion of a Persian Muslim of such high ranking caused a great stir. The Orthodox Bishop of the Nestorian church blocked the missionaries from baptizing him for fear the Muslims in reaction might destroy his church building. Not one to give up easily, Glen got permission from the Ministry of Religion in St. Petersburg, Russia, to hold the baptismal service. It was performed in Persian, Turkish and English, with Mirza taking the name of Alexander Kazem Beg. He was pressured later to leave Persia and eventually became a lecturer of Arabic in a Russian university.

In 1822 the Edinburgh Missionary Society, who up until that time did not have a strong missionary presence in Persia, welcomed new workers from the Basel Society. They soon transferred their work to Germans, Dittrach and Zeremba, who were joined by Karl Pfander (available after leaving Norris in Baghdad) and Friedrich Haas. Haas opened a school in Tabriz for twenty (probably Nestorian) children and distributed Christian literature to the Jews, but was totally rejected by the Muslims. Meanwhile Pfander published a number of tracts in Persian, his most famous being Mizan al-Haqq (Balance of Truth), which was translated into Armenian, Arabic, Persian, Urdu, and Turkish between the years of 1831-1843. The Basel missionaries also opened a mission station in Tabriz in 1833. Yet "none of these efforts were known to have resulted in the establishment of any Protestant, Persian-medium churches,"[6] although according to VanderWerff, "a number of mullahs and Muslim laymen became secret believers."[7] Pfander eventually moved on from Persia in 1840.

In 1833 Justin and Mary Perkins, both under thirty years old, were sent out by the ABCFM (American Board of Commissioners for Foreign Mission), arriving in Tabriz two years later. They worked under British protection until 1839 when the Russians took over their region (the British did not regain control until 1851). However, as will be repeated *ad nauseam*, Justin and Mary were ordered by their mission leaders (and to be fair, they also felt led) to help the Nestorian Christians gain a saving knowledge of the Bible and the Lord Jesus Christ. His instructions from the American Board were clear:

Your main object will be to enable the Nestorian Church through the grace of God to exert a commanding influence in the spiritual regeneration of Asia. With respect to the Muhammedans, and the adherents of the Papal church, you will do them good as you have opportunity, nor is it probable that you can make much impression upon Mussulman, until they see more of the fruits of the Gospel among its professed believers among them. Concentrated effort is effective effort.[8]

Once more, missionaries turned their backs to the Muslim majority. To their credit, the Perkins did adopt the dress of the locals and referred to Assyria as "our nation." They devoted themselves to reducing modern Syriac to writing and translated the New Testament by 1846. Soon after arriving, Justin travelled to Urmiah with Friedrich Haas to meet the Nestorian Bishop. He decided then to establish his base of operations in Urmiah, near the Russian and Turkish borders, despite being surrounded by hostile Kurds.

Question to Ponder

Justin and Mary Perkins sought to establish commonality with Assyrian nationals by adopting their style of dress and referring to Assyria as "our nation." Do you think that all missionaries should have this mindset, regardless of where God calls them, or did the Perkins go too far in their efforts to relate?

THE PERKINS WERE JOINED in 1835 by Dr. Ashael Grant and several other missionary families. During Justin and Mary's thirty-six years in country, they founded and led one of the most sustained mission efforts in Persian history. The goal of the ministry, as explained by Grant, was to "help restore the decaying [Nestorian] church."[9] However, Muslims were not entirely neglected. Their mission established a school for Muslim children and a medical practice with Dr. Grant, which was appreciated by a few Muslims.

Questions to Ponder

Do you agree with the express purpose of Perkins and Grant to focus most of their efforts on restoring the Nestorian church? Was this a wise use of their time and resources in your opinion? Explain your answer.

IN 1835, James Merrick of the American Presbyterians finally instigated a "Mission to the Muhammadans," teaming up with members of the Basel Mission in Tehran and Isfahan. He preached publically in the streets and distributed Christian books critical of Islam. Because of this outspoken criticism, his public ministry invited not a few death threats. This led Merrick to back off, explaining to his overseers: "I am at length convinced that public preaching to the Persians is at present, not only inexpedient but impracticable."[10] Merrick visited Isfahan in April of 1837 for ten days. In a letter back to America, he wrote: "In Tehran the prospect for missionary labour was but fain starlight. Here in Isfahan, it is a clouded midnight."[11] While there, he received a proposal from the Armenian archbishop to assist them in the founding and support of a school, but they could not agree upon the principles on which it should be conducted. Merrick eventually set up a permanent base in Tabriz, near the Afghan border, and was joined there by William Glen. While there, Merrick distributed his own Gospel tracts but saw little evidence of receptivity. The Presbyterian Mission reported: "Mr. Merrick believes that a public renunciation of Muhammadanism would be followed by a violent death even in Shiraz"[12] (where the Muslims appeared to be most open). Perhaps out of frustration, Merrick's "Mission to the Muhammadans" was discontinued.

Other missionaries from the United States included Albert and Mrs. Holladay, William and Mrs. Stocking (1836) Willard Jones (1839) and Austin Wright and Edward Breath (1840) who joined the Presbyterians in Urmiah. David Stoddard constructed the first grammar in modern Syriac and their printing press, managed by Edward Breath, published 110,000 volumes of the Bible and Christian tracts. Dr. Grant's wife Judith attempted to establish a girl's Bible school with the help of four Nestorian women, but she was called home to Heaven only four months into the project.

In 1843, Fidelia Fiske, the niece of pioneer Pliny Fiske, took over a school for forty girls (a revolutionary innovation at the time) in Urumiah (Urmia). Presumably to increase attendance and focus, Fiske developed it into a boarding school in 1844. Her services as a nurse for the region, including her willingness to risk traveling in the countryside among the mountain tribes, gradually won her respect and helped set an example that contributed to a slow improvement of the life of women in Persia. She remained in Urumiah for fifteen years, until ill health forced her back to America in 1858. Richter wrote of her: "Few missionaries in Persia have had the joy of leading so many souls to the Savior."[13]

In the early 1840s, Perkins wrote: "Some of the native clergy, who had been a considerable time under the influence of the mission, are becoming themselves very able and faithful preachers of the Gospel. Often have I heard them address their (Nestorian) people, with solemnity and power."[14] Perkins and Grant increasingly utilized local Nestorians while staying in a background supportive role. One of these young men, Benjamin Badal, became a traveling evangelist and Bible salesman, eventually selling over 30,000 Bibles and New Testaments.

Dr. Grant died of typhus in 1844. Historian Julius Richter wrote about him: "His utter devotion to his Savior, and his tactfulness, won him the confidence even of men who did not trust one another."[15] Perkins remained, right through the American Civil War, succeeding in translating the Bible and a Nestorian hymnbook into the modern spoken Syriac. Perkins went Home to meet the Lord of the Harvest in 1869. The final sentence of his memoirs aptly summarizes his missiological zeal: "How soon would the light of the moon be as the light of the sun – the light of the sun be seven-fold – and all the ends of the earth behold the salvation of our God."[16]

1850–1900

Key Figures

The Presbyterian Mission, after an agreeable split off from the ABCFM, was able to send more medical and educational missionaries. By 1855, the church of converts for the Nestorian church in Urumiah claimed 158 members. In 1862, an indigenous presbytery of several churches was organized. Dr. Benjamin Labaree joined the Presbyterians in Urumiah in 1860, where he helped develop the modern Syriac language, revising Perkin's Syriac translation of the Bible. Labaree had the joy of seeing both his adult son and daughter join them in the Presbyterian Mission. His son Benjamin was, in fact, the first recorded Protestant missionary martyr in Iran; murdered in March 1904. Labaree's second son took up the work in Urumiah the following year when his father Benjamin's illness led to his death on March 9, 1906.

In 1869 the CMS dispatched Robert Bruce to minister in India, but he stopped in the Armenian town of Julfa, Persia and remained there for two years to work on yet another revision of Henry Martyn's New Testament. When the famine came in 1870, Bruce ministered among seven thousand victims, supported by Pastor Haas of the Basel Society. In 1871, just as Bruce was preparing to leave for India, nine Muslims in Isfahan (with whom he had many conversations) asked for baptism! Baptism of a group of Muslims was then almost unknown and unbelievable among the missionaries.

When the Anglican CMS in Iran became a reality, Robert Bruce requested permanent assignment to Persia, which was granted. During the famine of 1871-72, Bruce was able acquire £16,000 for relief work from the saints in

England, Germany and the British churchmen in India. He thus won a foothold even among the most fanatical Muslims of Iran's population. But only the Armenians took advantage of the orphans' home he founded.

Unsurprisingly, the work of evangelism among Muslims was slow and arduous. Bruce's famous response, (still used today by pioneer missionaries among Muslims), to the British sending church's inquiry "Are you reaping yet or still sowing?" was: "I am not reaping the harvest; I can scarcely claim to be sowing the seed; I am hardly ploughing the soil, but I am gathering out the stones." He went on to write: "That too is necessary missionary service; let it be supported by loving sympathy and fervent prayer."[17]

Question to Ponder

Reflect on Robert Bruce's response to the CMS when asked if he was reaping or sowing. How does his theology, as revealed in his answer, impact your own missiology?

IN 1879, the CMS at last responded to Robert Bruce's incessant appeals. They sent out a medical missionary Rev. Dr. E.F. Hornie. The agency kept their station at Julfa equipped and staffed for ten years, enabling the small group of workers to establish a medical mission which included a hospital, dispensary, and a small printing press. Robert Bruce retired in 1893 after twenty-four years of "clearing rocks," though the Lord did not allow him to leave without also sowing. Mirza Ibrahim, a convert under the ministry of Bruce, was faced with severe backlash because of his public renouncement of Islam. His wife left him, taking both children, and he lost all his property. Undeterred, he travelled to local villages preaching the Gospel and was promptly arrested and thrown into a filthy prison. "Accounts of his arrest tell of captors beginning to choke him until he would renounce Christ. His response was 'Jesus is true. Choke me if you will.'"[18] The same year as Bruce's retirement, Mirza Ibrahim died in prison.

James Bassett, also sent by the American Presbyterians, arrived at Tehran in 1871. He had the distinction of being the first protestant missionary in that city after William Glen died. Bassett focused on what he called "preparatory work among Muslims" which he hoped might open the way for their future acceptance of Christ's message. He argued that Muslims had

no intellectual and religious preparation which might incline them to accept the distinctive, but puzzling doctrines of the Bible. Whatever of Christian faith had reached them earlier, had come in the distorted and perverted form presented in the Koran, which was intended by Satan to prejudice their minds against the Christian statement of God's message and provision.[19]

Bassett argued that, in history, every people who have been brought under the power of the Gospel had "a long period of preparation before any great reformation has been effected."[20] Yet he did organize a church in Tehran in 1876 with twelve Persian-speaking charter members including one Muslim convert named Husain.

In 1878, Bassett ventured to Khorasan where he found many willing to buy a New Testament and/or his Christian books. During that time, he was secretly translating the Gospel of Matthew into a local tribal language. Of that venture he said:

The Persian tongue is known by all classes of the people, but there is the possibility that the Persian governors will forbid the use of the Persian language for the Bible, owing to the fact that it is not the tongue of the non-Muhammadan races. Its use might be considered evidence of an attempt to proselyte the Muhammadans to the Christian faith.[21]

Eventually however, he was overruled by his colleagues, who determined to make Farsi the medium of missionary work in teaching and especially in preaching.

Despite resistance, proclamation of "a Savior Who delivers any who call upon Him from fear of Judgment Day" found greater response among the Muslims of Iran than among the Arabs or Turks. Bassett found, to his surprise, isolated communities in Khorasan, as well as citizens of Tehran, willing to listen to the claims of Christ. Encouraged, he determined to translate into Farsi, a Persian hymnbook, a primer and the Westminster Shorter Catechism. By 1883, two congregations were birthed with fifty members including four converts from

Islam and three from Judaism. The Evangelical Church (i.e "Presbyterian") by 1900 had an average attendance of over one hundred, including perhaps a dozen Muslim-background believers.

Dr. Joseph Cochran, also an American Presbyterian, was appointed in 1878 to take over as head physician at the Westminster Hospital in Urmiah, the first and only hospital built by the Presbyterians during the next seventeen years. Astonishingly, Cochran was only twenty-three years old at the time! Dr. John Wishard, the director of the American Presbyterian Hospital in Tehran, also reveals that Cochran had been born in Persia, thus "he knew the language perfectly, and was counted by the sheikh his friend."[22]

Not only was Dr. Cochran's extensive practice in itself much appreciated, it also increased respect for Christianity among the Muslim Kurds and Persians, which resulted in the Nestorian and Armenian Christians being less subjected to oppression and violence.

One of the best examples of this occurred in 1880, when the Kurdish sheikh, Obeid Allah, surrounded Urmiah, threatening to destroy the city. In the midst of general panic and despair, Cochran, the missionary at that time, a youth of twenty-five, stepped in, succeeding to induce the sheikh to march away from Urmiah. He convinced him of the many benefits which the Kurds had derived from his medical mission. Cochran also "reproduced" by training Assyrian doctors and other locals to be medical assistants. At significant risk of attacks by bandits, he organized medical clinics carried out in their mountainous regions. The Mission asked Cochran to transfer from Persia after seventeen years, when he was forty years old, in order to help organize and conduct numerous other medical mission endeavors on other fields. Submitting, he did so until the Lord called him Home, ten years later, in 1905 at the age of fifty. What might have happened if he had stayed in Iran focused on the Muslims whose respect and friendships he had obtained?

Esselstyn

Lewis Esselstyn and his wife Mary arrived in Persia to join the Presbyterians in Tehran in 1887. Over the next thirty years he would travel to countless villages to make friends and speak to them about his best friend and Savior Jesus Christ. In one town, Semnan, an Imam whom he befriended, invited Esselstyn to preach a sermon in the mosque! One wonders if that might have been the first known such incident in history when a Christian missionary was invited to speak in a mosque?

He wrote about this after a second such encounter with a mullah:

Early in the morning I had sent greetings and enquiries to Haji Mullah Ali (the chief mujtahid in the city) whose friendship I had gained on previous visits. Soon a servant came from the Haji with salams and enquiries. Later, we received another messenger inviting us to the Haji's house Tuesday afternoon. Mr. Jordan accompanied me. The Haji met me very cordially and before all the Sayyids and mullahs who were there, he took both my hands in both of his, and kissed me on both cheeks and gave me the seat of honor. We exchanged all the Persian courtesies and then tea and fruit were brought in abundance. Then I read First Corinthians 13 and John 3:16 followed by a talk on God's love and His crowning love in Christ Jesus all of which Haji Mullah Ali and all present listened kindly and without controversy. About sunset we took our leave.[23]

Not all his days in Persia were so encouraging. On one journey to the city of Meshed, Esselstyn was attacked by an angry mob and would have been killed if not for a brave Muslim gentleman who pulled him away from the hostile crowd.

Intending to be a book seller, he returned to Meshed with many mules laden with Bibles and Bible portions in the Persian language. Most of the time, he was able to soften Muslim hardness with his sense of humor and a friendly manner. When people were genuinely interested in the books, he gave them copies of the Psalms, the Gospel of Matthew, or, if they so desired, the entire New Testament. Not a few received the Injils with great reverence as a holy book. Esselstyn made countless trips to other towns of Khorasan with his books, and was long remembered as the foreigner with the long red beard who spoke Persian very well. In one instance, he was handing out books when some angry mullahs approached and demanded that those who had taken books throw them away, for they contained inaccurate teaching. Esselstyn then turned to those who had taken the books challenging them:

My friends, you decide who is right: your mullas or me. They have dyed their beards red with henna because it is said that their prophet Muhammad had a red beard and they want to be like him. But I did not need to dye my beard, for God made it red. And if your mullas should take off their big turbans from their heads, you would see that they have shaved all the hair off their heads. They say that Muhammad used to shave his head, and they want to be like him. But I did not need to shave my head, for see what God has done for me![24]

Lewis then removed his hat and showed the audience his bald head. The audience would smile while the mullahs walked away not a little confused. His mission agency reported that although Esselstyn had other frightening situations during his ministry in Meshed, courage, wit and a sense of humor allowed him to remain there bearing light.

1900-1978

Another example of Esselstyn's bold approach was seen at Semnan in 1900. Calling privately upon Haji Mullah Ali, a chief mujtahid whom he had earlier befriended, he spent three hours explaining the path of salvation and Christ as the crowning expression of God's love. Esselstyn reported:

I sent word to Haji Mullah Ali that I wanted a secret interview with him. Accordingly, I was at his house about 7 a.m. on Friday. He received me with his usual kindness and I had 3 solid hours with him. At the beginning, with the doors shut, and Haji and I alone I said to him "Haji, I have come to you to repeat my plea of nine years ago, i.e. I believe salvation is with us and not with you. I am saved, and you are not. I beg you to forsake your religion and come to mine. You have been kind to me and I love you and I want you to accept Christ's Gospel and forsake all else." Tears filled the old man's eyes and ran down his cheeks and he replied "What more have you to say. Say on." Requesting a Bible, he confessed, "You have the way of salvation, be faithful."[25]

Another time Esselstyn was invited to attend prayers at the mosque, and following worship, requested to speak to the 1,000 men assembled. His message on the Prodigal Son and repentance was so well received that again he gained the Haji's praise.

Lewis and Mary were alone for four years without teammates in Persia, yet he carried on quietly selling books and persuasively sharing the Gospel, gaining respectful audiences and welcoming a constant stream of visitors to his home. In 1905, Esselstyn, alongside his colleagues, Samuel Jordan and Joseph Potter, had the privilege of baptizing Rajab Ali, a former Muslim who changed his name to Nozad, which means "newborn." Nozad became a senior elder in the

Teheran Presbyterian Church and more significantly was also a fervent evangelist for almost forty years, up until the time he went home to be with his Lord in 1944.

In 1906, Mary Esselstyn returned to the United States with their two sons and a daughter in order to continue their education; Lewis Esselstyn was then alone for ten years in Iran without his family! Adding to the loneliness, he also had no co-workers until 1915 when he was briefly joined in Meshed by Dr. and Mrs. Joseph Cook, who came to investigate whether the people would welcome the work of a medical doctor. Upon seeing how well received they were, Dr. Rolla Hoffman moved to Meshed in 1916 and opened a clinic. Esselstyn worked alongside Hoffman and together they ministered to hundreds of patients. When helping the sick, Esselstyn would often tell them about the Great Physician Isa Al Masih, offering literature to those who were literate. Imagine their joy when they saw their faithful Lord of the Harvest birth the very first all-MBB fellowship in Iran, and that, in Meshed, one of Iran's most fanatical cities.

Questions to Ponder

Make three lists. On one of those lists, write down some of the practices mentioned above that you feel were right for the missionaries to do *at that time* but may not be appropriate today. Secondly, what you might want to emulate in this present era. And thirdly, note what you disagree with and would avoid doing altogether.

Do you think it wise that Lewis Esselstyn stayed in Iran for ten years apart from his family? Would this be advisable for workers today if it meant more opportunities and open doors for the Gospel?

BY 1910 THERE were scores of MBBs as well as Persian nobles who were quietly sending their children to Protestant schools. At that time one-third of all children in their schools were Muslims. Work among Muslims continued to be blessed with greater fruit in Iran than in other Islamic majority countries. Only in North India and Indonesia were Muslims more responsive. Christy Wilson Sr., William Miller (see below), and a few more like-minded missionaries who kept focused on the Persian-speaking Muslims developed a simple presentation: our need of a mediator, our need of an exemplary example, our need of divinely-provided power to follow his example, and finally, how these three needs are met in Jesus the Messiah.

Question to Ponder

Does making comparisons with Christianity create a need for the Muslim (out of honor) to defend Islam, whether he believes it deeply or not?

PERIODICALLY, Iran faced terrible famine and many people fell ill with typhus. The two missionaries both became seriously ill themselves. Dr. Hoffman, after a long break, recovered and could continue his work as a doctor, but Esselstyn died there in Meshed from Typhus in 1918, three years after Hoffman arrived. The stone placed on his grave was engraved with the words, "Greater love has no man than this that a man lay down his life for his friends."

William Miller

Another mission hero of the 20th century was William Miller, who sailed across the Atlantic to Istanbul in 1920 with Dwight Donaldson and Christy Wilson Sr. All three were denied entry into Turkey because of a plague, so the ship took them to a Black Sea port in Romania. From there they had to cross the mountains of the Caucasus in Russia by train and then take a ship across the Caspian Sea to Persia. Miller will not soon forget seeing so many shacks full of destitute Armenian refugees from Turkey's holocaust: "Never before had I witnessed such human misery."[26]

The Presbyterian Board of Missions had assigned Miller to Meshed, Hoffman's station near the Afghan border. In 1898, Samuel Jordan and his wife were responsible for the school; 150 students, half of whom were Muslims. Miller wrote: "While learning the beautiful Persian language, I tried to evangelize in English as much as I could to accomplish the task for which I had come to Persia: to make the Good News of Christ known to as many as possible."[27] Miller found some of the best opportunities to be with older male students whom he would invite to discussions outside their school hours, presupposing that "friendly conversation is one of the best ways to lead Muslims to the Savior." Although none of his students became Christians, "one able young man told me frankly that he knew that our religion was true."[28] However, the burden and shame that a conversion would bring on their family was too much for these young men to contemplate. Years later, after Miller had been transferred to Tehran, several asked other missionaries to baptize them.

Six months after arriving at Tehran, Miller wrote to a friend:

The impression I have gotten since coming to Tehran is that in this capital city at least, Islam is fast losing its hold...a friend told me the other day that among the educated young Persians anyone who said prayers or kept the other religious observances of Islam was made fun of and called old-fashioned. A man of some standing who applied for Christian baptism recently said that it was his conviction that among the mullas and religious leaders there was not one in a hundred who in his heart believed that Islam was true, but everybody was afraid to express his doubts...the majority of the 500 students in our mission school are Moslems in name at least, but most of them are deeply interested in their Bible study. They believe that the Bible is true, and as this conviction deepens most of them come also to believe that Islam and the Koran are false.

Miller further wrote in his autobiography:

As it was difficult in the time of Jesus for Jews to confess Him openly as Messiah and Lord, so it is difficult for Muslims and others to do so today. But the messengers of Christ in their desire to draw many to Him have no right to make the way any easier than He did. He called men and women to take up the cross and confess Him before others and follow Him, "the Crucified One." We can do no less.[29]

Miller soon left Tehran and returned to Meshed because Rola Hoffman and the Donaldsons requested he join them. He took the 560-mile journey in the back of a horse-drawn wagon, yet he had hardly arrived when he started receiving letters from a man in neighboring Nishapur, Mirza Gholam Ali, who expressed a desire to become a Christian. Miller and his assistant Mirza Muhammad Ghasem, the only baptized convert in Meshed at that time, travelled to Nishapur to meet Ali and another man, Haji Hassan. Both men asked Miller to baptize them. Miller wrote: "How thrilled I was; here was another Cornelius being guided by God to salvation."[30] On October 3, 1920, less than one year after arriving in Persia, Miller performed his first baptism of Muslim converts and a tiny church was birthed in Nishapur. Several weeks later, Mirza Gholam Ali's entire family and several other people were baptized. Donaldson baptized fourteen on Christmas day and a follow-up medical team led by Rolla Hoffman led to several more people professing faith in Christ and being baptized. Thus "an all-convert church was ushered into existence"[31] and by 1940 this congregation had grown to ninety.

Question to Ponder

Why do you suppose the vast majority of missionaries focused on Muslims are NOT led to such prepared people?

EARLY IN 1921, Miller determined to go to all the towns in Khurasan to seek and find people whom God had prepared. In regard to the many baptisms he participated in, Miller wrote:

Was I justified in giving baptism so quickly to people who would have no pastoral care after baptism? I believed that the Holy Spirit might use baptism to strengthen their faith and hold them to Christ when they would be alone. As far as I knew, no missionary and probably no Christian would be able to visit these believers again. So, since Jesus said to baptize those who believed, I did what I thought was right... I hope I will meet these people in Heaven.[32]

Questions to Ponder

What would you wait for before baptizing a Muslim if there were no local believers there to do it? How public do you think such a baptism should be? Do you agree that at least a few local believers should witness it? Would not a lake, sea or river be preferred over doing it in a bathroom (which is considered "unclean")?

WHILE IN A HOSPITAL in the United States for medical care in 1923, Miller discovered that his bills were being paid by Mrs. Robert Haines, a faithful supporter of his during his first stint in Persia. Mrs. Haines had a daughter, Isabelle, who had become a widow five years prior and had three children. While recovering from his illness in Mrs. Haine's cottage, Isabelle looked after him and Miller took a liking to her.

As I got to know Mrs. Haine's lovely daughter better, I learned she had always wanted to be a missionary. And it gradually became evident that she was interested in Persia and would not be averse to serving the Lord there herself as a missionary... it seemed too good to be true that she loved me and was ready to go to Persia with me. It was indeed asking a great deal of her to request that she give up her home in Germantown, take her children out of school, and go to a strange land. But she believed that this was God's will, and with great courage and faith she agreed to go with me.[33]

Upon arriving in Persia in 1925, Isabelle remarked:

We reached Tehran at a season of Noruz (New Year) when the many Persian acquaintances of the missionaries received callers. Varieties of oriental dainties and tea are served, with much Persian conversation. It was a chance for which I was glad to make calls with missionary women and to meet many Persian women in their own homes.[34]

Miller wrote to friends regarding an Easter service held in Meshed in 1926, in his seventh year on the field: "It was the largest meeting of Christian converts from Islam ever held in Meshed. Every one of the 27 men now in good standing in the church was present, and the 19 women met separately."[35] Four years later, in December of 1930, Miller preached a series of sermons in Tehran at an evangelistic event organized by Harry Schuler:

I preached in the first of the public meetings. There was a large congregation in spite of the bad weather, many of those present being Muslims who had never been in a church before. The attendance was very good all during the week. Each night at the close of my sermon I said, "If any of you want to be saved from sin, will you kindly come forward at the close of the meeting and sit in the front seats, that I may explain how one can be saved." Every night, from 30-50 men and some women would come forward.[36]

Elsewhere he wrote:

It looked as though a minor "mass movement" toward Christianity was beginning. However, when the police became concerned about the numbers who gathered, many stopped coming. The police were nervous about anything that looked like political propaganda. Sad to say, after a time the movement came to an end, but not before a number had been baptized.[37]

Miller felt responsible, not only for Meshed, but also for the whole province of Khurasan which was as large an area as France; his challenge: to evangelize the one million Muslims residing in that province. To do this, he adopted the policy of visiting the half-dozen larger towns as often as possible for the purpose of establishing groups of believers in each. He had hoped that from these centers the Gospel would spread to the hundreds of surrounding villages. Since the women were unable to follow Christ without the approval of their husbands or fathers, the work was entirely among men. One of the newly baptized men from Nishapoor, Ali Akbar, went into discipleship training with Miller. They visited towns together north of Meshed. In Kuchan, where no missionary had visited for ten years, they found a house in which to live and began to sell Scriptures in the streets. But the mullahs rose up against them, attacking Ali and beating him shamefully. Still he refused to deny his faith in Christ Jesus. Obeying Jesus' admonition, they shook the dust off their feet and moved on to Bujnord, a three day journey farther north. There they found one of Miller's first disciples, Haji Hassahn, whom he had baptized in 1920.

By 1933, much had been written in America about the missionaries having the wrong motives, the wrong methods and being unfit for the task. Miller responded:

We have great sympathy with much of what is said about us, for we know our faults better than any of our critics do... but we are convinced after years of close contact with the attractive people of this land that only Jesus Christ can meet their deepest needs... therefore, our one purpose is to bring Christ to them. The church in Iran is still too small and weak to make Christ known to all the people of this country so if better missionaries are sent we will turn the work over to them, but if others are not sent, we will continue to do the best we can to accomplish the task for which God sent us.[38]

In 1936, he wrote this in a letter to a friend:

In January I was urged to become the Pastor of a church in Tehran, as no Iranian pastor was available. From that time, I have been engaged in church as well as evangelistic work. I have had the joy of receiving sixty members into the church, so that our flock now numbers about 360. I baptized fifteen adults and sixteen infants on Palm Sunday, and another group of converts will receive baptism soon. For three weeks this summer we had a Bible School in which about 200 young people and children were enrolled for serious study.[39]

Questions to Ponder

I suspect this church in Tehran was overwhelmingly made up of converts from the Assyrian and Armenian communities. Would you think it better for them to have three different fellowships, including one especially for those coming out of Islam?

Given his skills with Muslims and the open doors, should Miller have refused the call to be pastor of that mixed church?

MILLER MADE A VISIT TO QUM, the fanatical Muslim center, in 1944 and on the second visit baptized a man he had met on the first visit. "As far as I know," he wrote, "this was the first time a convert from Islam had been baptised in Qum."[40] He mobilized prayer for Iran having 1,200 people on his prayer-letter mailing list. While on furlough in 1945, he wrote: "I tried to help the people in America realize the great opportunity we had in the Muslim land of Iran, and the urgent need for new missionaries, since the number of missionaries had become very small, but I had no success in finding recruits."[41]

Miller worked with newly arrived missionaries in Kermanshah, southwest Iran, but there was still a tendency to get more occupied with mainly the

Assyrian Orthodox Christians. Then he took one to the Kurdish area where no missionary had visited for many years, where Dr. Sa'eed Kurdistani was born in 1863 and converted.[42] They were able to gather several men who had believed in Christ from other surrounding cities and have a Communion service together: "Probably the first Persian Communion ever celebrated in that town."[43]

Although the missionaries in the 1950s found greater freedom for Christians to speak of the Good News, Miller's appeal to the mission to send fifty more missionaries to Iran was ignored, even though most of the veterans were retiring. After Christmas 1957, Miller took a workshop at the Urbana conference for three thousand students who were seeking God's will for their lives. Sadly, he concluded that serving Christ in Muslim lands was not one of the students' considerations; few responded to the call. Then when the Southern Presbyterian Church and the Presbyterian Church USA merged, Miller was very disappointed that it did not result in a stronger missionary thrust by his denomination that had pioneered the Middle East.

Miller's pilgrimage in Persia ended after forty-three years on December 12, 1962. He wrote to his supporters:

The visible results of Christian effort in Iran are small. Nevertheless, I never regretted coming to Iran in the service of Christ. Rather, I rejoice that I was given the privilege of spending my life in this land where the harvest is so great, and the laborers are so few, and the difficulties so many. If I had my life to live over again, I think I would return to Iran and try to be a better missionary – or maybe to Afghanistan.[44]

Miller spent an additional twenty years preaching and challenging people in America to the need of the Muslims to know the Savior, including teaming up with North Africa Mission's candidate school when Livingstone was the North American Director.

Other Reports from Persia

Norman Sharp arrived at the shores of Iran in 1924 as an Anglican missionary for the CMS. He remained in Persia for the next forty-three years and William Miller would later write about him, "he was one of my dearest friends."[45] Sharp was a longstanding professor at the University of Shiraz, as well as a prolific church planter, founding "churches in Yazd (1928), Shiraz

(1938), Qalat (1944) and Bushehr (1944). He incorporated decorative tile work with biblical quotations in Persian and designed the stained glass windows with glass reused from old Qajar houses."[46] It is unknown, however, if he had any evangelistic impact on the Muslim population of Persia.

Work continued in Persia throughout the middle years of the 1900s. While reports are sparse, there is evidence of continued perseverance by various agencies and missionaries. International Missions Inc. (now Christar), for example, began work in Iran in January of 1955 to create and produce a Gospel broadcast in the Persian language, although their work centered around the Faraman Orphanage. Several other agencies were at work in Persia in the latter half of the 20th century, including the Assemblies of God, Bible and Medical Missionary Fellowship, the Christoffel Blindenmission im Orient, the Elim Missionary Society, International Christian Fellowship, the Navigators, Operation Mobilization, the Southern Baptists, World Vision, and the Worldwide Evangelization Crusade (WEC).

In May 1962, missionary Dennis Clark reported that while in Tehran, he met a Muslim convert named Dibad, who was very interested to assist in the distribution of Christian literature. In a letter dated June 1964, Richard Corley of Christar wrote to Edwin Frizen at IFMA headquarters, reporting that their Emmaus Bible School correspondence course, especially geared toward Muslims, had over 2,600 students enrolled. We read in another report about a different correspondence course claiming that within one year, it had "close to 6,000 enrollees who were studying in 150 cities, towns and villages." According to this report at the time of writing, over one hundred had made professions of faith in Christ and some were even baptized.

In 1967 the Far Eastern Gospel Crusade sought to justify their working in Iran because of the high interest among candidates to work in the Muslim world. While the exact number of converts from Muslim backgrounds is unknown, we have reason to believe that many were discovering Jesus as more than a prophet throughout Persia. In 1967, WEC reported that they had five missionaries in Iran, mostly involved in the training of Muslim-background believers. We also read in a 1977 prayer bulletin that there was a young church in Iran comprised mainly of converts from Islam.

End-of-Chapter Reflections

From 1956 until 1960, the father of Sam Yeghnazar (an Armenian Christian associated with Elam Ministries) led one of the first house church meetings for Muslims in Tehran. Father and sons, working with established churches, traversed the countryside with a small team of volunteers giving out Scriptures in hundreds of towns. Imagine Armenians who had suffered under Muslims reaching out to their tormentors! Building or utilizing church buildings then, and even less since the 1979 revolution, went from impractical to impossible. The answer was house churches. One positive characteristic of the house church movement evidenced in many different regions of Iran today is that it is a movement that is no longer entirely an urban affair, unlike the past. Possibly because of satellite TV and the Internet, there are now countless house churches, even in unheard of small towns and villages.

Haik Hovsepian Mehr and his younger brother Edward, both Armenians, became Christians in Yeghnazar's home in January 1994. Much later, Haik, when he was the Bishop of the Assemblies of God churches, was assassinated for campaigning for the release of Mehdi Dibaj, an MBB who also had attended Sam's father's house church. Mehdi joined my OM university team in Europe in 1966 but despite the danger went back to his Shi'te people. After nine years in prison, he was stabbed to death on the streets of Tehran after being released from prison because Bishop Hovsepian instigated international pressure on the government in the 1990s. That led to Hovsepian's assassination soon after! Another Christian leader who attended those initial house church gatherings was Tateos Michaelian. Another outstanding Armenian who cared for the Muslim majority, he eventually became the moderator of the Presbyterian churches of Iran. After he translated sixty Christian books into Persian, he too was assassinated.

In those house meetings of the 1950-60s much prayer was made for all of Iran. Today, reasonably verified estimates think there may be over 500,000 Muslim-background believers meeting regularly in house churches throughout the country. Some skeptics wonder if that number includes those only investigating the claims of Christ on the Internet. Note - this explosive growth of followers of Isa Al Masih happened in the 35 years after the missionaries were expelled, and many Assyrian and Armenian church buildings were closed due to the fierce opposition launched by the 1979 revolution. Yet the house church movement continues. What events did God use to accelerate this movement to Christ?

Iran was at war with Saddam Hussain's Iraq by the summer of 1988. When the Iran–Iraq conflict finally ended, 300,000 Iranians had died and another 500,000 were seriously wounded, most of those being teenagers. "What did our children die for?" thinking people asked. Disillusionment spread like wild fire when tens of thousands more teenagers were executed, accused of communist ideology. Next they faced a huge depression of Iran's economy. Saddam's planes had bombed the oil-producing areas so by the mid-80s paper and soap were scarce, while breadwinners had to take on two jobs just to survive.

By the early 1990s there was bitter disillusionment amongst Iranians over the brutal political violence after Ayatollah Khomeini set up his "government of God." In 2005 Mahmoud Ahmadinejad, "a man of the people" determined to take Iran back to the true teachings of Ayatollah Khomeini, while vowing to destroy Israel. His extremism created such disillusionment that it became easier for Iranian Muslims to renounce Islam and follow the Prince of Peace.

In God's mercy and providence, Muslims' brutal treatment of fellow Muslims turned thousands of thinking people to doubt that Islam was indeed the way to truth and life. Might that be a cause for Syria, Iraq, Libya, Afghanistan, and Pakistan to turn to the Savior.

4

MESOPOTAMIA (IRAQ, SYRIA, LEBANON, AND JORDAN)

ANYONE WHO QUESTIONS WHY ARMENIAN, COPTIC, NESTORIAN, AND ASSYRIAN Christians living in Mesopotamia did not take up the challenge to make disciples among Muslims should recall the indescribable atrocities by the Ottoman Turks and Kurds of those Christians in the 1890s and again in 1915. As if that was not sufficiently horrifying, a famine of biblical dimensions struck the Middle East in the 1830s: "An estimated 200,000 people perished in Istanbul alone and several times that number in the provinces from Egypt to Syria,"[1] writes Michael Oren, historian and lecturer at Harvard and Yale. Although American President Woodrow Wilson tried to intervene, the missionaries who didn't die attempting to rescue the Greek, Arab and Armenian Christians were banished by the Ottoman government that more or less controlled the lands from the Balkans of Europe to the borders of Persia, and all the way west to Morocco.

Missionary activity resumed in 1916 after the conclusion of World War I, but mainly as educational institutions, including the American University in Cairo in 1919 and the Syrian Protestant College, which became the American University in Beirut a year later. A.U.B. was the first university in all the Middle East to admit women, but its aim to develop democracy in the region had a greater effect at masterminding nationalistic coups in several Arab countries. Furthermore, while the American missionaries were challenging church members back home to invest in more mission schools and church buildings in the Arab countries, many in the West became more interested in investing their money into oil wells.

By the 1940s, the Middle East was in almost unremitting turmoil. Britain and France went back on their promises to grant independence to the peoples liberated from the Turks, for fear of the German advances into the region. President Truman backed down on his pledges to respect Syrian independence when the French refused to remove their garrisons from Syria: their U.N. granted mandate. When protests broke out in Damascus and Aleppo, the French responded with artillery fire and warplanes leaving more than four hundred Syrians dead. Is it any wonder that western missionaries found doors closing to their witness?

Yet despite the closed doors, God always maintained beacons of light in these lands that have been left in the dark. Little known to the warring powers in both the 19th and 20th centuries, Christ's faithful, under-the-radar ambassadors were continuing to infiltrate Mesopotamia, committed to fulfilling The Commission given by their Lord nearly 2,000 years earlier.

1812–1860

Anthony Norris Groves was the first Protestant missionary to the Muslims in Mesopotamia. He and his team lasted only four years in Baghdad, but it was a heroic effort with no preparation or guidance beyond Groves having some elementary dentistry skills and an extraordinary confidence in the Lord and His Word. The significance of Groves will not primarily be found in what he personally accomplished among the Muslims, Armenians and Assyrians of Baghdad and Aleppo (which we might judge as relatively little), but more for the impact of his total abandonment to Christ's commission: his story is worthy of our reflection.

Anthony Groves was not the first evangelical missionary to the Muslim world. When Groves was only eleven years old, Henry Martyn arrived at Calcutta in 1806. Groves was twenty when the Anglican Church Missionary Society (CMS) set up its printing press on the island of Malta, and when he was twenty-seven the Basel Mission of Switzerland sent their earliest pioneers to the Caucasus in Russia. It was in Armenia where Karl Gottlieb Pfander of the Basel Mission began work on his magnum opus, *Mizan ul-Haqq* (The Balance of Truth). By this time the American Presbyterians were already set up in Beirut but had nearly given up on their original goal of direct evangelism to Muslims.

Thus when Groves, his wife Lydia, and their two sons Henry and Frank set off to Iraq in 1829, those who preceded them were only nibbling the edges of Islamic populations. Their goal was to establish the first Protestant mission effort among Arabic-speaking Muslims and they planned to do this in the very heart of Islam: Baghdad. The Groves family was not appointed by a mission board and had no salary or pledged support, nor was Anthony ordained by a church denomination. He did not have a team of experienced colleagues to advise in matters of language and culture. What he did have however, were the promises of God and a heart taught to love everyone he met.

Groves' first team member was a deaf printer named John Kitto, who served as a tutor to Groves' two sons who were both under the age of ten when they set out for the Muslim world. A ship captain provided the small party safe passage from England to St. Petersburg, Russia, free of charge. Once there, they took on the extra burden of escorting a Mrs. Taylor, the wife of British Consul Major Robert Taylor, and her entourage to Baghdad. This naïve band of travelers, which also included Lydia Groves' younger sister, were advised to turn back by a local physician in Russia, yet they set off to cross the Caucasus mountains on two large horse-drawn carriages loaded with bags of biscuits, coffee cakes, lemons and six large boxes of Bibles and individual portions of Scripture, presumably literary Arabic. The cost of their overland trek was paid by new Protestant friends they met in St. Petersburg.

Near Volgograd, they visited a Moravian settlement of 1,200 people. Russian government pressure, influenced by the Orthodox Church, had stifled the Moravian's earlier evangelistic zeal. Groves was disappointed that the settlement, once a thriving mission station, had become a simple colony of craftsmen.

In Astrakhan, Russia, they discovered Dr. William Glen from the Edinburgh Mission Society, who is considered by some to be the first Protestant missionary to establish an ongoing evangelistic outreach to Muslims in Russia. Hard at work translating the Bible into Persian, Glen provided them with accommodation but did not socialize until dinnertime so he could continue his work on the Bible translation! His Persian New Testament was used for many years as a revision of Henry Martyn's earlier translation.

The Groves party next faced the bandit-filled regions of the Caucasus Mountains. For thirteen days and nights they had no opportunity to change their clothes. The wagons proved to be real bone shakers and the ladies in particular suffered bumps and bruises all the way to Shushi near the Georgia border. There they were received by five Swiss and German Lutheran missionaries who had trained at the Basel Mission Institute. The Lutherans had opened a school and were translating Christian books and the Scriptures into Armenian, presumably not attempting to witness to the local Muslims. Reaching Teflis, Georgia, Groves found a German pastor seeking to teach the Bible to the Nestorian Chaldean Christians whose priests had evidently left them in total ignorance of it. Even though they still had no example of proclamation to Muslims, meeting other missionaries in those early days encouraged Anthony, who began to feel less odd in the presence of other pioneers; they were thus fortified to press on.

They prayed that one of the German missionaries of the Basel mission would join their team to minister to the Arab and Persian Muslims. To their amazement and delight, the Basel missionaries felt the same burden and offered them Karl Pfander! Having completed the first draft of *Mizan ul-Haqq*, Pfander wished to study Persian and Arabic for two years in a location where those languages were spoken. Since he already understood Turkish, Groves considered him a great provision for the team. At the age of twenty-seven, Pfander was a good-natured German eight years younger than Groves who had decided to be a missionary when he was sixteen years old. He was accepted at the newly established Evangelical Institute in Basel, Switzerland where his studies included Arabic and the Qur'an. After arriving in Russia, he astonishingly also learned Armenian, a bit of Persian, and a Tatar dialect of Turkish. Pfander came out of the pietistic, Bible-adhering wing of the Lutheran State Church with its strong tradition of disciplined Christian living. Even more importantly, he had outstanding evangelistic gifting. When Groves met Pfander, Karl was already a widower, his wife having died in Shushi a year after their marriage.

The next stage of their journey took them on horseback through the mountains of Georgia and Armenia to Tabriz (Iran) where their horses were twice stolen from their encampment before they finally crossed into Persian territory. Their single lady teammate, a missionary named Charlotte Taylor, left them in Tabriz to marry an official of the East India company. This event increased Groves' presupposition that single missionary ladies going out to the East would have their call crumble as soon as they met one of the British diplomatic or commercial post bachelors. Ms. Taylor apparently assuaged her guilt or their criticism by donating her missionary funds to the rest of the team.

It was a nightmare period of torrential rain, frightful roads, more robbers, and fierce dogs. Daggers were brandished at the slightest provocation, which was attributed to a recent burning of Kurdish villages by the Persian authorities. During this time, a Shi'ite Muslim carrying dead bodies for burial in a holy place, joined their traveling party. Learning of the animosity between Shi'a and Sunnis served as an unforgettable introduction to the racial and religious complexities of the East.

They were warned by the British army to turn back, but Pfander and Groves kept the party going forward in firm reliance on the Lord. Reaching Suleimaniya (Northern Iraq today) Groves gave a New Testament and other books to some Nestorian Christians who only had the Scriptures in a language they could not comprehend. Pfander, while witnessing, was threatened with death by a dagger-wielding Kurd who ordered him not say another word lest he, a Muslim, become an infidel.

Finally, ten years before David Livingstone sailed to Africa, Groves and his weary band of travelers arrived at the gates of Baghdad after riding horses or camels more than 2,000 miles from Russia across deserts and the mountains of the Caucasus. In Baghdad they were astounded to meet Joseph Wolff, a CMS worker who had spent a month there preaching and circulating hundreds of Bibles among those of his calling: the Jews.

Pfander was convinced that the entire Islamic world had reached a turning point in its history and was ripe for conversion to Christ. He believed, like many of his day among Bible believers, that Islam was a divine scourge sent for a period of time to chastise the apostate churches of the East. As the Eastern Christians returned to the true faith they would see Islam collapse as a result of vigorous preaching of the Gospel and the testimonies of Muslims transformed by it. The disintegration of the Ottoman Empire, the progress of Western technology, the extension of "superior European moral, social and political systems," the birth of mission vision in the Protestant churches, the recent translations of the Scriptures; all these remarkable signs of change heralded the imminent conversion of the Islamic world in Pfander's mind. Groves, on the other hand, influenced by J.N. Darby, had an early dispensational view that the world would only get worse until the return of Christ to the earth. He hoped they could help at least a few Muslims escape the Judgment.

The presuppositions among the more educated of the day were more optimistic. Church leaders assumed that religious and political leaders in Muslim countries would adopt Western innovations or face extinction. Therefore, they urged missionary effort to focus on Western education, presuming it would lead to the conversion of thinking persons who would usher their own people into a new age of universal Christian civilization. That would explain the excitement of the Presbyterians who at great cost established Roberts College in Istanbul and the American Universities in Beirut and Cairo.

But a day of reaping seemed far away then to Grove's dilapidated party of pioneers. They found they were the object of rumor and suspicion from the moment they arrived. They hoped for a welcome by the Eastern Christian Nestorians and Armenians in Baghdad, but Roman Catholics had already poisoned the minds of the residents to believe that Protestants were of the Devil.

Once in Baghdad, Mrs. Taylor was reunited with her husband. Delighted to see his wife in good health after such an arduous journey, Major Robert Taylor offered a house adjacent to his own for the use of the missionary team as well as a teacher who could help them learn Arabic. Joseph Wolff testified that Major Taylor was an accomplished Arabic and Persian scholar. Fortunately, Norris realized they must learn the heart language spoken by the actual residents, as opposed to the literary dialects. Groves, like the Basel missionaries, was convinced that Christ's calling was to lay aside everything of this world's greatness to descend to the level of those ignored and left in physical and spiritual poverty. So he insisted his party live in houses outside the "Western quarter," similar to the locals.

Aspiring to that goal was one thing, but actually adjusting to the level of living surrounded by the ignorant, superstitious people God was sending them to was a daunting task. Still, they persevered. The men on his team decided to learn the Arabic spoken by the majority of the population while Lydia Groves set about learning Armenian in order to teach the Gospel to the "Christian" women and children. They were frustrated, however, that few language helpers were available who had the necessary patience to teach a foreigner.

Groves' vision had been to make Baghdad a base for outreach to the surrounding region, including the mountains of Kurdistan and Persia. Although between the years 750 and 1258 Baghdad had been the political capital of the house of Islam, after the sacking by the Mongols in 1258, Muslim leadership had shifted to Damascus. Thus, for over 200 years Baghdad had languished in neglect while subject to the Turkish rule of the Ottoman Empire. The fact that the Roman Catholic, Jesuits and Franciscan missionaries publicly opposed the Nestorian Church reinforced the conviction among the Muslim majority (ignoring their own Sunni-Shi'a divide) that Christianity was a confusing, inferior religion. Suddenly, the Muslims were hearing yet another very different message from European "Christians" as Groves and his team were preaching a simple biblical story which was different from what all the other "Christians" taught! It didn't help that the Roman Catholic Bishop was loudly proclaiming that the Protestants were even worse than Muhammadans or Jews! The Jesuits weren't doing so well themselves. They were resented by the Eastern Christians as unbelieving infidels and suspected of being spies in the pay of a Western nation with expansionist ambitions. So, Groves moved their team far away from both the Catholic missionaries and the British government officials. He gave Kitto, his deaf teammate, a project to compile a handbook describing the differences between the various religions, both for inquirers and for future Christian missionaries they prayed would join them.

Pulled in two directions, they concluded their mandate was to both speak directly with Muslims about Christ and to strive to awaken the apostate Eastern churches to discover a redemptive personal knowledge of Christ. Along with those who came to the Middle East after them, their hope was that the nominal Christians would be converted, then proclaim biblical truth to the Muslims. The local converts from Islam would have many opportunities, it was reasoned, to witness every time they were asked why they didn't keep Islamic customs. But even then Groves realized that the animosity between the Muslims and "Christians" was so severe that few Christians, even if they were converted, would be sufficiently motivated to reach out in compassion to Muslims. It hardly helped that the Muslims were afraid to read Christian books, having been warned that doing so would lead them into becoming infidels!

Groves decided to open a dental clinic to which he aspired to add a department for eye diseases, hoping that doing so would win the trust and respect of the people so he could introduce them to the Savior. Neighbors increasingly came to their house for treatment and some stayed to talk with Pfander about spiritual concerns, as the clinic afforded an excuse for Muslims to meet with the missionaries unsuspected. Groves, though a dentist, courageously operated on a number of cataracts, helping several people who had been blind for many years regain their sight. With the combination of his limited medical knowledge and Pfander's evangelistic skills, the two men proved to be invaluable teammates. Groves wrote: "I cannot sufficiently thank God for sending my dear brother Pfander with me, for had it not been for him, I could not have attempted anything, so that all that has been done, must rather be considered his than mine..."[2]

After only two months, they decided to start a school which they hoped would also help them become more acceptable in the community. The Armenians were responsive; the Catholics less so. In any case, how could the so-called Christians around them read the Scriptures in their own language unless they were taught to read? Grove's dream was to see some of the boys and girls they taught in turn eventually translate Scripture into Muslim languages. However, their tactic to establishing schools for nominal Christians took them from the Arab quarter into the Armenian neighborhoods where there was a great demand to learn English. English was rumored to be the door to commercial and political uplift because of British influence in the East. Some of the team hoped they could make disciples in the English language, but in the end they decided to teach the children to read the colloquial Arabic of the region which was understood by almost everyone. The next idea was to extend the school to admit children from Muslim homes, hiring an Arabic-speaking schoolmaster. However, it took a long time to find a Muslim teacher who would consent to its pupils reading the Christian scriptures. There were some encouraging moments. The Armenian schoolmaster longed for a form of prayer that was spontaneous, not memorized and the Muslim imam who taught them Arabic started reading the New Testament with another imam.

Initially, we might frown on these early Europeans for continuing to wear Western clothes unless we realize that by custom and Ottoman Empire law, the different religious groups were required to identify themselves with distinctive clothing. To break this taboo, it was thought, might do more harm than good.

Pfander focused on looking for opportunities to discuss the Gospel openly with Islamic scholars in Baghdad. Doing so was radical because for generations the harassed Christians of the Eastern churches had maintained an uneasy truce with their Muslim masters, preferring a measure of peace to attempting to engage Muslims in debate; much less attempt to convert them to Christianity. The Muslims in Baghdad had never met anyone like Pfander. He continually refined his arguments, seeking fresh illustrations and evidence that would prove Christ's claims. Yet because neither the Orthodox nor the Roman Catholics' paltry efforts had yielded any notable results, Pfander had few examples to follow or build on. He did achieve his goal to learn Arabic, however, then proceeded to stay at home, upgrading his ability in Persian. This caused Groves to feel he'd lost his chief co-worker, no longer at his side in the daily ministry.

After months of no news from Europe, three packets of mail arrived announcing that a new group of would-be missionaries was on its way to the Baghdad team. One of those coming was John Parnell, and another was Edward Cronin, who determined not to waver from his call even though his wife died only weeks before their planned departure from England. Accompanying them was Cronin's elderly mother, his infant daughter, Minnie, and his sister Nancy who was engaged to Parnell. A late addition was Dr. Frank Newman whose fiancée refused to accompany him. The last member of the party was an Irish schoolmaster named Hamilton, who was a friend of Parnell. Groves was thrilled and repented of his unbelief. These reinforcements opted for a route through France, sailing on the Mediterranean as far as Antioch. From there they travelled over land to Aleppo where they took a boat down the Euphrates to Baghdad.

Discouragements

Dr. Frank Newman immediately set up a dispensary but was perplexed by the difficulty of conveying an inward faith to people accustomed to an outward display of piety. He was further discouraged by the lack of receptivity among the Muslims and the refusal of his fiancée to come out and marry him in Aleppo. In his desperation, he decided to identify with the people by smoking a long Turkish pipe and wearing an Assyrian gown and heel-less slippers, though he found it difficult to keep the slippers on his feet. Reflecting the medical knowledge of the day, when Newman came down with a fever he directed his co-worker to put leeches on his temples and bleed his right arm; this did not have a positive effect.

Hamilton, who was ill much of the time, felt himself incapable of learning the language and decided shortly after arriving to return home. John and Nancy Parnell escorted Hamilton to the ship, but heavily pregnant, Nancy fell off her donkey and died on the road between Baghdad and Aleppo a few days later.

In the midst of all this, Karl Pfander felt led to move on and travelled east to Tabriz and Isfahan, leaving the Groves team bereft of someone with a command of the heart language or even the trade languages. The weather did not ease the burden of the missionaries. For six weeks of the summer, the temperatures in Baghdad reached 118F (48C) in the shade. Then, infested with fleas, the city was devastated by a plague which killed 65% of the population. To the missionaries' deep disappointment, these tragic happenings did not open the people to listen to their message: fatalism reigned. Fifteen thousand who survived the plague died from the flooding Tigris River which collapsed two thirds of the houses. There wasn't even sufficient clean water available for washing the bodies of the thousands of dead Muslims.

As if that wasn't sufficient suffering and tragedy, civil war broke out, trapping them between three rival sheikhs wanting to rule over Baghdad. In the midst of all this, they reported that Mary Groves' spirit was amazing: "I never in England enjoyed that sweet sense of my Lord's loving care that I have enjoyed in Baghdad."[3] Mary maintained her peace even when her baby was deathly ill, after which she died herself from the plague. Tragically, all the wives died. The team's household became exclusively male, except for little daughter Minnie and the servant Harnie, who was a rescued orphan. How could they now minister to Muslim women?

Still they didn't quit. Groves' team followed the "new" ministry principle made widely known by George Muller (living by faith without a salary). Critics of that conviction somewhat mockingly wrote that it was rather obvious that anyone with means, observing his team's poverty, would feel obligated to cover their expenses. So why, Groves asked God, since they were dutifully living by faith, did they have no news or provision from England for more than once a year? Why didn't the Lord speak to those who had been supplying their needs? Why had the Lord allowed their provision to not be met?

Finally in 1832, though they were attacked in Antap (Gaziantep), Turkey after giving a Turk a New Testament, Dr. John McNeill arrived with the third group of workers. McNeil found Groves, one of his sons, and Kitto emaciated and depressed.

Departure and Hindrances

In a letter from William Goodell of the ABCFM (American Board of Commissioners for Foreign Mission was the first American mission agency in the Middle East), Groves was informed that next door in the region which became the country of Syria, not a single Muslim had bowed the knee to Christ. Other reports from workers in Syria indicated that scarcely anyone knew of an individual Muslim who had received the Message. Groves reflected that there seemed little reason to hope for progress of Gospel acceptance in the foreseeable future. Wherever the blasphemous influence of Muhammad reigned ironbound against the truth, these struggling pioneers were very susceptible to the challenge from Arthur Cotton, a Colonel in the British Army, to move their base to India where the East India Company in 1813 was finally allowing unrestricted missionary work in the areas under its control. Groves decided to visit India to see for himself. He witnessed both millions without access to the Gospel and hundreds who professed Christ sorely in need of teaching if they were to persevere. Thus, India took over his life and his team and the English Plymouth Brethren effort among Muslims in Iraq ceased.

Question to Ponder

Norris Groves moved his team to India when he witnessed many confessing Christ as Lord and Savior, but also lacking sound instruction and teaching. In your opinion, was this a wise or foolish decision? Defend your answer biblically.

BUT GOD HAD NOT DESERTED the Arab Muslims. The arrival of the American Presbyterian mission brought some hope regarding Syria. Initially, visitors from the various creeds came to converse with the missionaries on religious questions. Several schools were established in and around Beirut; even a hundred girls entered their schools, something hitherto unheard of in Syria. Such was the bright springtime of the American mission.

Very soon, however, bitter enmity, especially on the part of the Roman church, was displayed against the Protestants. In 1824, not quite twelve months after Americans had settled in Beirut, the Roman Catholics induced the sultan to issue a Firman (royal mandate) forbidding the distribution of the Bible in Turkey and beyond in the Ottoman Empire. The Maronite Patriarch hoped to gain influence over the Greek Orthodox bishop to help drive away the Protestants. He laid on the Americans the following curse:

We allow no one to receive the Americans; by the word of Almighty God, no one shall dare to visit them to do them any service or render them help, to remain in these regions. This we forbid most strictly. Everyone must avoid meeting them. Whoever dares in his obstinacy to transgress this command, will all at once and without fail fall under the great curse of the Church from which I alone can absolve him.[4]

Not only did such defamation divert the attention of the missionaries from ministry to Muslims, it led to the death of Assad Shidiak, a Maronite who was tortured for assisting the missionaries. He died in October 1839 after three years in prison; the first known martyr of the Protestant mission in Syria.

Another huge hindrance to Protestant mission was the warring disturbances which continued from 1820 to 1840 across the Ottoman Turkish Empire. Beirut became a target city to slaughter Christians suspected of involvement in the Greek's war for independence. Because of the danger for twelve years, from 1828-1840, the missionaries had to abandon their work and seek refuge in Malta. Their war zone included fighting between Turkey and Egypt. Ministry was halted when the Egyptian Army conquered and occupied Palestine and Syria as far as Aleppo. In 1831, Ibrahim Pasha of Egypt renounced his loyalty to the Ottoman Empire and overran Syria, capturing Damascus. He imported thousands of Egyptian villagers to populate the plains of Southern Syria, rebuilt Jaffa and settled it with veteran Egyptian soldiers aiming to turn it into his regional capital. In the process, the Egyptian ruler crushed the Maronite and Druze rebellions. The missionaries had to again abandon their work to seek refuge; this time in Cyprus. By 1840, however, Ibrahim Pasha had to surrender the area back to the Ottomans.

In 1842 and 1845, Syria was once more disturbed by internal strife, in which the Maronite Catholics attempted to annihilate the Druze, who were about one third of the population. This action was most likely portrayed as yet another example of "Christians" attacking Muslims. In spite of the fighting all around them, the American missionaries continued the distribution of evangelical tracts and books from Aleppo in the north to Nazareth in the south. However, it was quickly realized that the Arabic books they possessed were defective and badly printed. Thus, to ensure their publications would be well received by the Arabs, they determined to upgrade to the best standard of Arabic handwriting. Dr. Eli Smith, an excellent Arabic scholar, collected about a thousand particularly beautiful characters out of the most perfect Arabic manuscripts; these he had cast by a clever type-founder who worked under his guidance. This preparatory labor was tedious and expensive, but the results were that the productions of the Beirut Mission Press became esteemed as honoring the Arabic language; much appreciated by the literate community.

Further Endeavors

The Mission of the American Board of Commissioners for Foreign Missions (ABCFM), which was the largest Protestant agency at work in Turkey for the first decades of Protestant mission in the Middle East, continued to play an important role also in Syria alongside the younger Presbyterian reinforcements. Their work began in October of 1823 with the arrival in Beirut of the Reverends William Goodell and Isaac Bird, who were joined by Eli Smith in 1827; four years before Dr. Goodell was transferred to Constantinople. When further reinforcements arrived in 1838 and 1840, the Beirut ministry became more effective. In "Greater Syria," at that time, the Christians constituted about one-fifth of the population. The majority were concentrated in the larger cities of Beirut, Tripoli, Damascus, and Aleppo.

Addison, writing a history of mission to the Middle East in 1941, accepted, without question, the majority opinion that directly approaching the Muslims was next to impossible[5], so why not minister to the tens of thousands of

Christians whose spiritual needs were evident? To reach those people, the most obvious methods were the use of literature and the establishment of schools. Thus literary and educational ministry among Christian background people was their concentration almost from the beginning. Few could conceive of a way to make disciples among the Muslims!

The first purely Arab Protestant Church formed in Beirut in 1848 consisted of twenty-seven members, mainly Greek Orthodox background Christians who defected to the evangelicals; perhaps enticed by the Protestant schools? In many cities and larger towns in "Syria," requests for teachers, schools, Bibles and assistance in forming churches sent the missionaries fanning out across the region. Four of the most prominent Scottish clergyman, among them Andrew Bonar and Robert Murray McCheyne, a Scottish preacher of renown (despite the fact that he died at age thirty after only seven years of ministry), were sent to make enquiries in Syria with a view to championing the establishment of Protestant churches. Hence, the Free Church of Scotland was birthed in the Middle East in 1853 by launching fifteen village schools. However, thirty years later, the Ottoman government struck what it hoped would be a death blow to the schools of the Protestant mission by forbidding, under pain of punishment, the attendance of Muslim children. The Druze schools evaporated as the first victims. An attempt later by the CMS failed to resurrect them.

With Safed in the north of Galilee as a center of operations, an American single missionary, Miss Ford, began work among the Druze Muslim sect in Palestine. Reportedly, she found some open doors for her work after which she requested the Presbyterian Mission to take over. That happily led to two small Protestant congregations being birthed, in Kharabeh and Khasfin.

In 1843, the Irish Presbyterians, conjointly with the Free Church of Scotland, sent a deputation consisting of Dr. Wilson (the eminent Scottish missionary from Bombay) and Dr. Graham of Ireland to Syria with the intent that they would make preparations for a joint mission of those churches. A few workers arrived in Damascus, but the work was abandoned until later taken over by the United Presbyterians from America.

In 1854 Dr. Bowen Thompson, a man of wealth, with his wife's assistance, was active in evangelistic work in Antioch, reportedly with some encouraging response. He recruited his brother-in-law, Mentor Mott, to open a new effort in southern Syria. Reverend S. Lyde, an English independent missionary, began an evangelistic work, starting from Bahamrat among the Shiite Nusairiyeh sect in Northern Syria. Because of his work, several of the Nusairiyeh were later baptized and then employed as teachers. However, the Turkish authorities soon closed some forty mission schools and forcefully drafted the converts into the Turkish army. This successfully removed them from the influence of the mission and successfully halted the work of the Christians among the Nusairiyeh Shiites.

1860–1915

Other Missionary Societies

The year 1860 opened a new chapter in the history of Protestant endeavor in Greater Mesopotamia. By then, the appeal of mission work in the Near East was much stronger among the Congregational and Presbyterian churches in America than it was in England, Scotland and Germany. That changed, however, with the arrival of two German agencies. One of these societies was the Kaiserwerth Deaconesses' Home which received 130 girls into an orphanage called Zoar and inaugurated an advanced school for the older daughters of more well-to-do Syrian families. In 1861, the Prussian Order of St. John founded a Protestant hospital in Beirut and John Arnold founded an Anglican society intending to evangelize Muslims. Calling it "The Moslem Missionary Society," it had a significant presence in Syria within a few years.

Also at that time the British Syrian Mission was founded by Elizabeth Bowen-Thompson whose husband Dr. Bowen-Thompson died in the Crimean war. Subsequently, she used their family wealth to open schools for girls. A network of these schools spread across Greater Syria, so that by 1902 there were fifty-six schools with a total of 4,262 pupils sitting under Christian teachers! The personnel of that mission consisted of one medical doctor, one English lady missionary, and 128 Syrian female teachers. Twenty-five Bible women were employed to read the Scriptures to women and children in the villages imparting an elementary knowledge of Gospel truth. The response varied:

In 1870 one of them writes: "I am happy to say that…in nearly every place I go, they receive the word with gladness… Concerning my work among the Moslems, they used to be very bigoted… but they seem to be now more open.

Some of the Bible women were able to visit even in the harems of the wealthy Moslem effendis and speak to the women about Jesus Christ; in some cases, to teach them to read, using the Gospels and Psalms as textbooks. One Moslem lady of a high family frequently called her servants also to hear the reading. It was almost impossible for them to confess openly their desire to become Christians, but it is clear that some were secret believers."[6]

In Beirut, that British mission maintained an institute for training native female teachers and Bible women, but it was not ministry to Muslims.

Antioch, Syria was occupied by various societies; first in 1855 by the American Board, then by the United Presbyterian Church of Scotland, which, with Aleppo as its starting point, carried on missionary work among the Jews. That was taken over in 1895 by the Presbyterian Church of England. Thus, in the course of the twenty-five years after 1860, every village of a significant size in the whole of Syria, from Latakia in the north and south into Galilee, had ministry by Protestant missions. However, disappointingly, very few congregations of believers were left behind.

In 1861, several missionaries became concerned about providing a Christian institution of higher education in the international port of Beirut to meet the needs of Protestants, but open to anyone who could qualify. Presbyterian Daniel Bliss decided to launch what became the American University of Beirut, registered in the State of New York. Under Bliss, who acted as the College's first president (1866-1902), it aimed to be educationally evangelical (if not evangelistic). Initially, all students attended morning and evening prayers, daily Bible lectures, and Sunday services. Later, under the presidency of his son Howard Bliss and Bayard Dodge, the college moved toward religious neutrality.

One report from 1870 noted that Islam had not been forgotten:

The Bible has gained ground and the Koran has lost some of its controlling influence in the land. Some Muhammadans are among the attendants of our preaching and these would doubtless be more numerous, but for the risk to property and life. Not without results, have the children of the Muslim Druze been taught in our schools during all these years, and many conversations been held with adults of that sect.[7]

Direct Muslim work was still essentially blocked however. When the Nusairiyeh, a Muslim sect, began to convert as result of American Reformed Church and Presbyterian Mission schools, Turkey closed their schools in Beirut and Damascus. The Syrian Mission also frequently found its school and church doors sealed, construction delayed and/or applications pigeonholed.

From 1890-1900, various attempts to reach the Bedouin Arabs of Northern Arabia were frustrated. Yet, there was some fruit. Two Muslim converts, Jedaan Owad (baptized February of 1889) and Kamil Aietany (baptized January of 1890) received training in Lebanon and returned to proclaim Christ among the Arab tribes near Homs and Hamath. Kamil became a full-fledged apostle to the Muslims. He accompanied Cantine and Zwemer, exploring Oman and other Gulf regions, then pioneered in Basra, Iraq before his pre-mature death.

Dr. Henry Jessup was the most noted exception for taking advantage of the opportunities to reach Muslims. He decided to be a foreign worker to the Muslims in 1852 when he was challenging his church to pray that new missionaries would be sent abroad! Convicted himself by his challenge he, alongside his friend, Lorenzo Lyons, offered themselves to the American Board of Commissioners for Foreign Missions (ABCFM), which was the first Protestant American mission agency to send Americans overseas.

Henry's brother, Samuel Jessup, also volunteered to serve in Syria though he considered doing so an act of self-immolation! Henry attended medical lectures, learned first-aid from his cousin, Dr. Mulford, for two months and then picked up what he could about dentistry between outings of tract distribution in Pennsylvania. Samuel gave up his business to study theology before sailing nine years after Henry to Beirut.

Leaving his severely ill fiancée behind in December 1855, Henry, with Rev. and Mrs. Daniel Bliss (founder of the American University of Beirut) set sail for Smyrna, Turkey with five other new missionaries of the ABCFM and a cargo of rum. Eventually arriving in Beirut (then a city of Syria), Henry was sobered visiting the grave of Pliny Fisk, who lived only six years on the field until 1825. Fisk had nearly completed an Arabic/English dictionary when he died at the age of thirty-three. A greater jewel was Asaad es Shedak, a Catholic

Maronite, the first known convert to Christ in Syria, who was tortured and starved to death in 1829 in the Catholic Bishop's prison.

Henry Jessup reported that in the Sidon district (South Lebanon) there were 250 Muslim students in the Christian school. During his fifty-five years in Syria, Henry personally baptized thirty Muslim converts and was acquainted with nearly fifty! In his later years, he baptized two per year. No one else had comparable fruit among Muslims. Sadly, many of those believers decided to flee from the Middle East to the West for their own safety. Those who didn't leave faced all types of persecution and struggled with much temptation to revert to Islam or to simply be mainly secret believers.[8]

Since public preaching was not permitted in Syria, the missionaries who were not involved in schools or medical work continued to focus on literature evangelism. In spite of the Ottoman government's opposition, which limited what could be taught in their schools and the censorship of literature, the mission press continued to be a disseminator of Christian truth. Because Arabic was the language of both the Muslims and the Christians, many felt that evangelistic literature should be the main emphasis of ministry. The missionaries produced fifty editions of the Smith-Van Dyck Arabic Bible by 1910, a weekly Arabic paper Neshrah (The Herald), a popular four-volume New Testament commentary, as well as many educational and devotional materials.

In 1898, Presbyterian Mission Agency Secretary Brown mildly rebuked the missionaries for clinging to literary and education centers, urging for more itinerant evangelism using Samuel Jessup as an example. But his brother, Henry Jessup, disagreed:

...the real evangelistic work of the future is to be done by native evangelists and these can only be fitted for their work by large and systematic Bible study...teaching the Bible IS evangelistic work. Translating, editing, and training theological students are only different forms of evangelistic work... let us not pit "institutional work verses evangelistic work," but "the institutional work is for the sake of the evangelistic work."[9]

Nevertheless, Secretary Brown had a point. In fact, far too few nationals became evangelists to Muslims despite their training, probably because most missionaries were not often setting an example, i.e. modeling how to introduce Christ to Muslims.

Still, a few westerners didn't lose sight of the Muslim majority. Mary P. Eddy was the first woman doctor to gain an Ottoman Empire diploma in medicine. Her itinerate camp work and clinic may have "reached" as many Muslims as any other single effort. However, the ministries focused directly toward Muslims were few and far weaker than those focused on Eastern Christians. How long did it take before the missionaries lost hope that the developing Syrian Evangelical Church would be utilized by God for the evangelization of Muslims?

Perhaps the most serious defect in the Syria-based missions was the failure to attract and train local men for the Christian ministry, especially those few who were gifted and desired to evangelize Muslims. While the loss of talent through emigration explains this in part, it is clear that the missionaries failed to motivate and prepare the new believers regarding their responsibility to participate in God's rescue operation among Muslims. No wonder why there were so few Muslims embracing the Redeemer. The great temptation even for Bible-loving Christians was that Western sciences and new technical skills afforded a new opportunity for personal advancement to a minority people long under subjection. It is not difficult to understand why students turned their backs on ministry and pursued these alluring marketable trades. Although ninety-five Middle Eastern Christians had taken theological classes by 1908, only fourteen had been ordained for full-time ministry, and those would focus on pastoring other Christians.

Though the missionaries all hoped "a full-time native ministry" would develop, some confessed later that they failed to give that goal the priority and the quality training necessary. The allurement of the ministry could not compete with the professions advertised at the Syrian Protestant College (AUB) in Beirut. Furthermore, theological education probably seemed far removed from what was needed to enable even the most keen evangelical students to make disciples among Muslims. The continued occupation of church pulpits by foreign missionaries, while qualified nationals turned to medical or business education, may indicate an unwillingness by some missionaries to pass the baton. Whatever the causes, the scarcity of locals going full time in ministry severely handicapped the Syrian churches and led to the work among Muslims by Arabs to be almost negligible (as is still true, if less the case, today in the Middle East).

Emigration drained off nearly one half of the evangelical church membership from Tripoli and Beirut, Lebanon. Thus after nearly a hundred years, by 1910, even the more nominal-heretical groups of Muslims, i.e. the Druzes, Metaw-ileh and Nusairiyeh (Alawites), remained largely untouched and the orthodox Sunni and Shi'a even less confronted with the claims of Christ. The reader will understand that the missionaries then had not realized the points empha-sized in Henry Riggs' 1938 report[10] that: A) Middle East people make the most important decisions corporately, not individually, and B) even "open" Muslims needed to be personally acquainted with significant, respected (most hopefully) members of their own clan who had decided to follow Christ Jesus as Lord and Savior before they could take His claims seriously. In an honor-shame society, to be the first Muslim in their clan to "become a Christian" was and continues to be unthinkable.

In 1856, the number of American missionaries had reached its peak: thirty! By 1870, that number had dropped to only eighteen adults. Later that year, the missionaries in Greater Syria transferred from the American Board (ABCFM) to the Board of Missions of the recently reunited (after the Civil War) Pres-byterian Church in the United States.

Questions to Ponder

Do you agree with the premise outlined by the Riggs' Report (Appendix 1)? If so, what are the implications for ministry among Arab Muslims today?

OTHER REASONS for Little Sowing and Few Conversions

It is important to realize that the Presbyterian missionaries launched ministry in Syria and Lebanon at a very inauspicious time in history. The Greeks were fighting the Ottoman Empire for independence which became so bloody the missionaries were forced to retreat from Beirut to Malta. This was followed by bloody civil wars between the Maronite Catholics and the Druze sect of Islam. When were Muslims going to be in a mood to sit down with the missionaries and discuss the claims of Christ? Understandably, literature became the main strategy with the moving of the printing press from Malta to Beirut in 1834. Once there, seven million pages of tracts and books were printed and a system of colportage spreading them from Aleppo to Jerusalem was developed, with intermittent success. Literature production came to be seen by some as a sly way of shirking direct evangelistic responsibility. Missionaries challenging those from the Eastern churches to witness to Muslims were countered with the question, "Are you asking us to do what you missionaries will not attempt?"

Other reasons for little sowing and reaping were also prevalent at this time. First, neither the Ottoman government, nor succeeding Turkish and Syrian governments, permitted open work among Muslims. Religious freedom was only theoretical and an inquirer (or convert) knew that life was forevermore precarious. Even so, one Muslim sheikh admitted the existence of secret believers: "Many Christians will rise from Moslem graves in Syria."[11] Secondly, while transfer from one religious community to another is always difficult, actual provision for re-registering one's religious community iden-tity (after conversion) was nearly impossible, as it is in most Muslim majority countries today. Third, the competitive spirit of "Christian groups" in Syria-Lebanon made them jealous of growth in another, e.g. Maronites would attempt to block any widespread Muslim movement to Protestantism. Fourth, evangelical churches constituted of former Roman Catholics or Orthodox were very reluctant to receive and assimilate a convert from Islam due to assumption they were spies and/or fear of their church building being dese-crated by Islamic reaction. Finally, missions had vested interests; namely, they did not want to jeopardize huge monetary investment in buildings, medical facilities, or the printing presses by the hostility which would arise if Muslims deserted their religion in appreciable numbers. Thus by 1914, although thirty-nine Protestant churches nurtured about three thousand members, extremely few were from a Muslim background.

A moment of encouragement happened at the pivotal Edinburgh Conference in 1910, at the peak of the movement to see all peoples have access to the claims of Christ through a new host of missionaries. A new agency, the Amer-ican Lutherans, declared:

Direct evangelistic work among Moslems is more than ever possible today, whether by means of visiting, conversation, production and careful distribu-tion of Christian literature, and Bibles, medical ministries, or schools for

Muslim boys and even girls. It is certain that the time has come for a wisely planned and carefully conducted and intensely earnest forward move in work among Moslems in Syria and Palestine, and the attention of all the Societies already working in these fields should be directed toward immediately making a forward move.[12]

Such declarations by a few visionaries, usually while in a conference, tended to be in sharp contrast to the feeling most had once on the ground, surrounded by wary and often hostile Muslims.

Hope among new missionaries for a breakthrough dissipated as Turkey sided with Germany in World War I. The British missionaries were forced to leave Syria and the American missionaries were overwhelmed with refugee relief work among the Armenians and Greeks who were being slaughtered in Turkey and beyond. During the war, evangelism among Muslims seemed to be even more impossible to most missionaries, as well as to their agency leaders back home. Education, medical work, and refugee relief became the "we do what we can" alternative.

The Presbyterians in Syria took the lead for the Near East. Protestants (as did Roman Catholics) built a full system of education reaching from village school to college. Syrian Protestants soon became leaders in many fields including journalism, medicine, and even politics. The Protestants eventually had one hundred elementary schools, plus advanced secondary schools for girls and boys at five locations, with the American University in Beirut at the top of the pyramid. Up to 1910, this meant that missionaries were able to wield some influence on about 8,000 students. Since only one-quarter of the students were Protestant, many Orthodox and Roman Catholic students became somewhat acquainted with biblical theology. Although Turkish government regulations prohibited Muslims from attending these schools, about one hundred managed to do so.

Questions to Ponder

Is it disobedient to Scripture for a Muslim, who has entered the Kingdom of God through reliance on Christ's redeeming death on the Cross, to remain officially a Muslim? Can an obedient believer who obeys Isa Al

Masih in accordance with the New Testament be seen as a Muslim in his/her community?

1915–1978

DISCOURAGEMENT IN IRAQ

What is known today as Iraq had its modern borders demarcated in 1920 by the League of Nations when the Ottoman Empire was divided by the Treaty of Sèvres. A monarchy was established in 1921 and the Kingdom of Iraq gained independence from Britain in 1932. In 1958, the monarchy was overthrown and the Republic of Iraq was created. Then from 1968 until 2003, Iraq was controlled by the Arab Socialist Ba'ath Party of Saddam Hussain.

A boundary was drawn roughly halfway across "Greater Syria" from east to west, creating the Palestine, which was assigned to Great Britain then further subdivided into Palestine, in the west, and Transjordan - an entirely new country - to the east of the River Jordan. The northern part, divided as Syria and Lebanon, was assigned to France while the British drew arbitrary lines to create Iraq's borders. Thus, the Arabs submitted to the French and English as their new governors at the end of World War I as the Ottoman Empire, their previous ruler, was reduced to merely the country of Turkey by the Allies. In 1920, the British reneged on their promise of independence, deciding rather to establish "mandates" in Palestine, Jordan, and Iraq, under their control, while the French did likewise in Syria and Lebanon. For the time being, the Arabs submitted to new "Christian" masters to replace the Turks, their fellow Muslims.

Most of the missionaries, understandably, liked the arrangement. They assumed control by the West would enhance freedom to proclaim the Good News. It wasn't long, however, before the missionaries realized that the Western overlords (Britain and France) plus the local Christian people were a great embarrassment. Their hope that "Christianity" would demonstrate its superiority to Islam quickly faded. The mission agency executives continued to direct the missionaries to give priority to making true disciples among the Christian Catholic and Orthodox population; the logic unremitted being that those Christians redeemed and motivated by Christ's commands would be led by the Holy Spirit to become missionaries themselves to those Muslims who spoke Arabic, a language the Christians understood, if not preferred. However, having been westernized by Western education, most of the new generation of Christian-background believers decided French and English, not Arabic, would be most helpful for their futures. Thus the gap between Christians and Muslims widened.

However, the newer missionaries were stunned by the vicious opposition of the priests of the ancient churches and the Roman Catholics in reaction to the missionaries' efforts to help them become "biblical Christians." The Oriental clergy became known to the pioneer American missionaries in Syria/Lebanon as "the enemy." Facing repudiation then from both the Christians and the Muslims, understandably, well-meaning missionaries lowered their aims, settling for providing Western education and medical services when their evangelistic efforts, both among Eastern Christians and the Muslims, appeared to remain an exercise in futility.

Furthermore, the small number of Eastern Christians who became biblical disciples and the small number of converted Druze, saw little future in studying theology to become ordained ministers. Finally, they had opportunity through higher education to attain lucrative employment! So even though the Protestant church leaders and the missionaries established the Near East School of Theology in 1932, the mostly Armenian and Assyrian students that attended on financial scholarships from churches in the West were not highly motivated for church.

Question to Ponder

Given that new believers from any background need a solid grounding in the Scriptures and a sufficient number of them be able to teach biblical truth, how do you suggest MBBs can obtain that goal?

ROGER CUMBERLAND

Roger Cumberland, born in Los Angeles, California in 1894, became a Presbyterian missionary who wanted to go to Afghanistan. The American Presbyterians had no work there at the time, so he accepted an assignment to Duhuk, Iraq in 1923. After meeting Dr. Van Ess in Basra, he took a train for twenty-four hours on to Baghdad. Although intending to work among the Kurdish Muslims, he was befriended by Robi Pera Mirza, the leader of 5,000 Assyrians who had fled from the Turks. Still he and a few others made several attempts to make friends in the villages of "Kurdistan." The only people who responded were the Yezidi Zoroastrian tribe and some Chaldean Catholics. Nevertheless, encouraged by Samuel Zwemer, he continued to study Kurdish with the hope that a door would open among the Muslim Kurds. A leader among the Yezidi, Ismail Beg, asked Cumberland to temporarily adopt his daughter so she could be the first girl to be educated.

After he married Harriet Gunn, a missionary kid from the Philippines, Cumberland, in an effort to win Kurdish hearts, bought a thousand acres of land, which was an amazing step of faith since the whole world was in the financial depression of 1929. Cumberland's vision was that he would assist the hungry by his demonstrating how to raise vegetables on it. Dr. Potter, secretary of the United Mission to Mesopotamia, received a letter from Roger written from Beirut in May of 1938.

The promises of God are to those who endure and I like to live by them. I do not think there's much danger to me personally and less to my family, but even if there were, that would be no reason for leaving. Ever since the world began, people have been called cowards if they did not risk everything for tribe and nation. These days how many thousands are daily in danger as a simple matter of duty without any heroics about it. The church might make more progress if we had the same attitude.[13]

IN AN UNPUBLISHED ARTICLE CUMBERLAND WROTE:

I don't resent being under suspicion; the right to suspect may have been bought and paid for in installments over 1,000 years of conflict with foreign governments and commercial firms who do what they can to prosper here. Is it not much more right and necessary that some represent the Christian faith and take the initiative in opening the way of understanding and friendship? Although often the situation seems hopeless full of problems that all the goodwill in the world can hardly balance against the seemingly never ending hostility and continued conflict between Christians and Muslims. Yet even if it appears hopeless, I continue to throw my weight into the effort, being confident of ultimate success.[14]

On June 12, 1938, Cumberland was ambushed in his home and killed.

The United Mission in Iraq

In 1923, the United Mission of Mesopotamia (later renamed the United Mission in Iraq) was established by the American Protestant Mission. A distinguishing feature of this new mission was that it was the first which sought the inclusion of other Protestant agencies as a joint-venture partnership in the region. Participating branches were the Church of the Elders in the United States and the United Reformed Church, which merged with the Evangelical Synod of North America in 1934 and created the Evangelical and Reformed Church (reformed then in 1957 becoming the United Church of Christ). Members of the mission arrived in Mesopotamia in the fall of 1925 and immediately opened schools for both girls and boys while establishing mission stations in Baghdad, Mosul, Kirkuk, Buhok, Bashiqa and Hillah, all of which eventually closed except for the station in Baghdad.

In addition to converting a few Christians to Protestantism, one of their main achievements was the establishment of a high school for girls. The American School for Girls in Baghdad, started as a primary school and a nursery, but later became exclusively an institution for intermediate and secondary education covering both literature and the sciences. Because of the high level of education it provided and the success its students achieved in the final exams, the school expanded to include three hundred and twenty students by the time it was placed under Iraqi government jurisdiction in 1972.[15]

Reports from the British Syrian Mission

As mentioned previously, the British Syrian Mission was founded in 1860 by Elizabeth Bowen-Thompson. The mission reported in the beginning of the 1900s:

Medical work was begun first of all in Tyre, when that station was re-opened in 1923, with two Danish members of the Mission, Miss Paludan and Miss Olsen. It was obvious that this medical work offered valuable contacts. Some patients who needed daily treatments were given opportunities to hear the

Gospel day after day. The Biblewomen taught the women and children in small groups or individually. Some were visited in their homes and there again were open doors to speak of the One who died for our sins. Often it was apparent that some had come to the clinic from distant villages, and this gave our workers the chance to get an entrance into such places, following up the contacts made in the clinic. Damascus became a strong center of evangelism, both in the city, where in the 1930s we had a team of four national women evangelists as well as Miss Harrison and Miss Strong, and also in the districts around. Evangelistic trips were made as far south as Jebel-ed-Druze and Hauran, sometimes breaking new ground and at other times, following up earlier made contacts.[16]

In 1952, the British Syrian Mission had twenty members spread over the Mesopotamian region. The following are various reports sent from the missionaries as to what was happening among Muslims in their respective areas[17]:

JANUARY 1952

Theodora Raad (Tyre): A drunkard lived in Tyre – "an evil man." His daughter heard the message of Jesus and wished that her father would believe too.

That evening her father sought the Lord and also listened to some encouraging testimonies given by believers who met with us. The man went home and his wife saw the change in him; even people in the shops remarked that the man was changed. The fight is not over against the power of the enemy, yet our Lord is victorious.

M. Carter: A young Palestinian girl named Vera was sick and died. Her teacher, who was a Christian, had faithfully maintained a public witness to the class of children, which was evident in Vera's last words, as recounted by her mother: "I am going to be with the Lord Jesus ahead of you, but I shall be looking out for you to come." Then, in the presence of the mourners, "one of our number was then able to say what a blessed thing it is that we Christians can know that we are going to be with the Lord."

P.M. Ballantyne (Tyre):

There are two Moslem girls for whom we praise the Lord and for whom we ask your prayer. One is "Y," who was able to take nursing training in a mission hospital in Palestine, but has now been married into a very bigoted Moslem family. Amidst very difficult surroundings, she is daily seeking to stand up for Christ and, although persecuted, she is persevering to win her husband. The other one is "A," who is showing a bright Christian witness in a post of special responsibility in another Mission school.

JULY 1953

W.N. Enderby (Damascus):

A missionary's life is not necessarily preaching the Gospel to large crowds of people, who are eagerly listening to every word. Sometimes we long for such opportunities – that would seem a grander, perhaps even easier way. But rather, it means seizing every little opportunity that comes in one's daily contact with ordinary men and women, boys and girls, doing ordinary tasks, perhaps teaching secular school subjects, yet always on the alert for an open door into someone's heart to point them to Christ.

P.W. Stammers (Damascus): Talking about a shoemaker called "B" who made a profession of faith but many doubted his sincerity:

About eight months ago he witnessed openly in baptism. His wife also loves the Lord, and now they have a home into which it is a benediction to go. "A"... found Christ a few months ago while in hospital; he walks in most evenings from a nearby village to attend the different meetings. Last week we visited him in his home, where indeed all things have been made new; his wife told us that before his conversion, he hardly ever entered the house without beating her, and none of his nine children ever dared come near him. Now love and peace reign because the Lord of Peace has entered heart and home. "G"... a young Palestinian, who sits up near the front, has recently accepted Christ as his Savior, and is seeking to bring in others.

OCTOBER 1953

Grace Weston (Beirut):

Praise God for the Moslem girl in my class who converted on Founder's Day this year, and for the little group of praying Christians in the class who have now become her friends... after a year here I know that we need to pray most of all that Christ Himself may so live in our hearts by faith that we may be enabled to live out His life here before those who do not know His name.

Questions to Ponder

What do you think about "starting" with women and girls? Do you know of evidence that witness can increase in a clan if the first believers are female? Does it depend on which Muslim culture? Do you know of examples where conversions have multiplied via women?

JANUARY 1954

Martha Becker:

It was last summer that Muhammad, a student of our Boys' School in Beirut, one of God's chosen ones out of Islam, had been visiting the villages of his ancestors. He had never been there before, and as he confessed Jesus Christ as his personal Savior, he was driven away.

Question to Ponder

How would you have coached this boy to hopefully get a better result?

APRIL 1954

Lily Iliff:

Sister Martha Becker and Miss Dora Raad, who are specifically set apart for evangelistic work in Tyre and district, have almost unlimited opportunities for preaching the Gospel of our Lord Jesus Christ in the homes, and too in the refugee camps. The chief impression one got of Tyre was that the harvest was plentiful in the schools, camps, homes, villages, but the laborers are so few; a handful of workers trying to buy up every opportunity and sadly in need of reinforcements.

Question to Ponder

Might Lily be mistaking hospitality and politeness for genuine openness and interest?

THE INTERNATIONAL CHRISTIAN Broadcasters

The ICB was created in the mid-1900s by a group of five missionaries (from five different continents) dedicated to the ministry of radio among the unreached. Originally known as the World Conference of Missionary Radio, the name was changed in 1964 to International Christian Broadcasters.

Membership in ICB was open to regional and national radio and television organizations or commissions; Christian broadcasters, recording studios, program producers, and auxiliary organizations; or any person interested in radio and television as a medium of proclaiming the Gospel.[18]

Though the focus of ICB was primarily non-Muslim, they did have a presence in the world of Islam. For example, in 1969 (when the Livingstones moved there), 81 missions were operating in Beirut, Lebanon and a television station was opened in Amman, Jordan. Also from that same year, we read the following in a letter from Sudan Interior Mission General Director RJ Davis, written to Abe Thiessen, Director of the International Christian Broadcasters: "I verily believe from all I see and hear that God is doing something now in the Muslim world and that this is the day to get the job done."[19] ICB also oversaw a Bible correspondence course which had, in 1969, 144,882 Muslims enrolled and 28,797 Muslims who had completed one or more courses.

Questions to Ponder

Indeed, the 1960s saw many Muslims contact radio ministry offices and through them (and through tract distribution) enroll in correspondence courses. Where did it go from that point? Why don't we find house churches of MBBs in North Africa and the Arab Middle East as much as they exist in Turkey and Iran?

IN FEBRUARY OF 1974, the International Christian Broadcasters hosted a "Media Ministries to Muslims" conference in Marseilles, France. The stated purpose of the conference was "to analyze the Muslim culture in its religious, social, and psychological aspects, considering the areas of receptivity through the media of literature, broadcasting, and films."[20] From the detailed records of that conference, we find many fascinating items of note, including the fact that ICB had broadcasts targeting Jordan, Syria and Iraq. Lebanon received the most attention. During a panel discussion, one missionary, Bible Society Director Lucien Accad, argued that greater involvement of the existing Christian churches was essential for missionaries to see lasting fruit in a region.

Questions to Ponder

Do you agree with Accad's opinion about joining existing churches? Why or why not?

IN A LATER Q&A session, Suhail Zarifa commented on the production of Christian literature by converted Arab Muslims, e.g. Mazhar Mallouhi. Adly Fam rejoiced that over the last few years in Beirut a small congregation of seven people had grown to nearly 180, and William Dunn, Dennis Hilgendorf and John Stelling all reported that they were working on the development of a specific medium that would more effectively communicate the Gospel to Muslims in Beirut. The results of their endeavor, both physical and spiritual, are unknown.

Question to Ponder

If you were to write scripts or videos for satellite TV today (in the efforts of Muslim evangelism), what would they be? Be descriptive.

IN ANOTHER PANEL DISCUSSION, Sam Schlorff shared that missionaries were currently training new converts in North Africa. We don't know for sure the religious background of these new converts (the title of the conference would lead one to assume they were former Muslims), but from 1961 missionaries on the ground among the Muslims of North Africa were attempting to visit those contacted through radio ministries of North Africa Mission and Gospel Missionary Union.

Due to competing radio ministries and financial hardship, 1978 was the final year of ICB's existence.

Question to Ponder

We read in the report that "due to competing radio ministries and financial hardship," 1978 was the final year of ICB's existence. What are we to learn from this?

A Final Note of Encouragement

IN A PRAYER UPDATE to their friends and supporters dated December 1958, Nazarene missionaries Don and Elva Reed wrote from Beirut:

Pray for the new work in Sin-el-fil that God may establish the people in faith. In our regular preaching service there, we are having an average of 40-45 adults. Several have been converted and we hope to organize a church there in the near future. Three men prayed for salvation in the little village of Munseph last night.[21]

They also write about Hani, a Muslim boy blinded since birth: "But, his blindness was a means to lead him to the light, for in the school for the blind he was taught about Jesus Christ and came to known him as Savior. Christmas has real meaning for him."[22]

5

THE ARAB PENINSULA

Pioneer mission, proclaiming where Christ is not adhered to, has always been a ministry of suffering, too often disappointing; slow, up-hill work. However, China was not so dark, nor India so neglected, nor Japan so convinced their ways were far superior to any foreign customs, as much as were the Muslims in Arabia in 1800. However, since this present volume focuses on the Arab world, in addition to Turkey and Persia, let's remind ourselves of their pre-Reformation background.

Arabia's major population areas had been penetrated by Christians as early as the year 300, about the same time that the Church was birthed in Armenia by Gregory the Lamplighter. However, in 303 AD, the Emperor Diocletian had issued edicts ordering the destruction of church meeting places and the burning of the Scriptures. He also mandated that punishments be levied against Christians in places of honor, as well as slaves who converted from acceptable Roman religions to solely obeying Christ. Church leaders were to be imprisoned and offered release only if they would sacrifice to the Emperor. Those who refused these commands were subjected to horrific torture (to what degree this took place among Arab Christians on the far edge of the empire is not evident).

Nevertheless, by 353 AD, church buildings existed in Yemen and by the year 400, Christian tribes lived east of Jordan. The Arabian kingdom of Ghassan, an ally of Rome, became somewhat "Christianized" by the year 600 and in east Arabia, Qatar reportedly had congregations presided over by a bishop, likely initiated by missionaries from the churches of Abyssinia. Thus the Christian faith was nominally represented in some form on the Arabian Peninsula when Muhammad arrived on the scene. The southern region was influenced by African churches and Eastern Arabia by the Nestorian Christianity of the Persian Empire. There is also a record of Christians at Najran, Yemen, being persecuted by Jewish rulers in 520 AD. Sadly, not all were willing to endure persecution. The regional Syrian church was granted state recognition on the condition that the Christians would abstain from proselytizing. Their submission to Rome over Christ tragically birthed a tradition which later influenced Christian agreement to abstain from evangelizing Muslims after the followers of Muhammad raided and took control of the regions surrounding Arabia.

What Muhammad learned from Catholic monks was hardly good news. They mumbled prayers addressed to dead Christians and taught that the epitome of spirituality was to refrain from sex while engaging in painful self-affliction. No wonder that by the time of his death in 632, many of the Arab tribes, including those with a Christian veneer, had been persuaded to become Muhammad's disciples. At the dawn of the 8th century, it could already be said that Muslims were dramatically stalling the growth of Christianity and in the process, eradicating all existing churches. We can understand how the iconoclast Muslims would be horrified as they witnessed Christians praying to "Mary the mother of God," as well as petitioning saints for special favors.

Although by 825 there was still a bishop in Yemen and at least one Arab tribe from Syria that had moved to Byzantine territory in order to remain Christians in 982, Caliph Omar II's restrictive policies for the Christian (*dhimmi*) led to countless people of Christian tradition bowing the knee to Islam, choosing to trod along the broad road (Matthew 7:13). After the capitulation of the tribes in Arabia, there exists almost no record of Christians in the Gulf seeking to make biblical disciples among the Muslims. The "evangelism" that was taking place involved Muslims pressuring Christians to convert to Islam.

The Roman Catholic Crusaders' rampage through greater Syria eventually halted in 1291 without noticeable influence on the more primitive inhabitants of the Arab Gulf. Meanwhile, the industrial revolution re-motivated European "Christian" states to find another way to take up residence among

Muslims! French merchants in the Gulf were granted trading rights from the Ottoman government which allowed them to establish a network of consuls, outposts and even colonies in the Arab-speaking regions. The English followed their example in 1580 and the Dutch in 1612. But the idea of sending missionaries to Arabia for the express purpose of winning Muslims to Christ would not come for nearly 300 more years!

Even as the year 1800 dawned on the world's stage, disciple-making among the Arab Muslims was hardly thinkable due to the overwhelming influence of Abd al-Wahab and the Salafi movement across the Arabian Peninsula. In 1818, Muhammad Ali of Egypt invaded and for some years broke the power of the Wahhabi Empire, but that didn't open a door for Christ's ambassadors. In 1820, however, the British signed a business treaty with Arab sheikhs in the Gulf. That led to the British competing with the Ottomans for influence in much of the region. The Arab Peninsula consisted of several tribal regions that today are separate countries. By the time the missionaries arrived, the Ottoman Turkish Empire, to different degrees, still could and did make residence by foreigners problematic. There were local daunting challenges; for example, Yemen was not very accessible due to the high mountains. Few had contact with the British beyond their tiny outpost in Aden. The heart of the Wahhabi region, including Qassim and the Najd (Riyadh) were beyond the control of either the Ottomans or the British, totally inaccessible to Western missionaries.

Nevertheless, British awareness of their growing incursion most likely provoked the newly awakened Great Commission advocates in Britain and the United States to assume that God was opening the Arabian Peninsula for His messengers. Still, Protestant Christian mission to Islam was a relatively recent endeavor, but not because the earlier missionaries didn't see a need for Muslims to follow Christ as Lord and Savior. Rather, it was because the leadership of the mission societies were fully convinced that until the Eastern Christians had a more accurate understanding of the faith, the Catholic and Orthodox presented the greatest stumbling block to Muslims by committing "shirk" by praying to Mary and the "saints" as mediators to Allah. For the Protestants, the consensus was nearly unanimous that it was necessary to see the Christians in the Arab, Turkish, and Persian regions know and live out the Scriptures before anything could be done for the Muslims. It was an almost universally accepted presupposition that the missionaries' primary goal should be to make biblically-literate disciples among the Catholic and Orthodox living in Muslim-majority regions. It was presumed that once they would live under the Lordship of Christ, the Eastern Christians would, in turn, make disciples among their Muslim neighbors; an unfortunate presupposition.

Samuel Zwemer and the Arabian Mission

Survey of the Early Days

The Student Volunteer Movement for foreign missions (SVM) birthed many initiatives from Britain, Germany and the United States. Serious Christian university students were electrified by the slogan "The evangelization of the world in this generation." In 1900, John Mott declared it God's purpose to give all people an adequate opportunity to know Jesus Christ as their Savior and become His genuine disciples: "Such a goal involves a massive distribution of agency-sponsored missionaries who will make the knowledge of the Gospel accessible to all men everywhere."[1]

Unfortunately, as critics point out, the conviction to reach the world for Christ was somewhat polluted by the West's sense of "manifest destiny." It was popularly assumed not only did the peoples of the world need Christianity in order to experience all that God intended, they also needed the education, culture, and values of the "Christian" West. Without the protection of Western governments, missionary lives were not safe, nor were they able to stay residentially in the place of their calling. It was widely assumed by the missionary community that without Western government protection of the lives of both the missionaries and the converts from Islam, there would be no lasting results.

Admittedly, the development of superior armaments, accelerated means of communication and transportation in the Middle East and beyond, plus a more productive and efficient system of education, gave Europeans the edge. Gaining control over the means of production enabled them to dominate the economic and political systems in their expanding colonies in Africa, the Middle East, and Asia. Such was the historical context in which the modern Protestant missionary movement was birthed. Both the Catholic and Protestant missionaries utilized the influence of their governments, who in turn utilized the goodwill the missionaries produced among the colonized peoples. However, this "cooperation" of western governments and the missionaries severely backfired on the missionary cause when oil was discovered in the Arab Peninsula. The oil companies mostly brought in uneducated, insensitive, parochial, women-chasing, whiskey-drinking laborers to ensure oil was produced and transported back to the West. When the Arabian American oil company Aramco was negotiating for land, they were given the choice of being able to either have liquor or churches, but not both. They chose liquor, knowing the hard living habits of the American driller. Officially, they got neither.

The message and impact of biblical proclamation upon Arab Gulf society by mission hospitals and schools was thereby compromised by the invasion of pagan "Christians" from the West. Once the oil was flowing and the money was filling the Arab sheikhs' pockets, missionary-provided education and medicine were no longer worth the risk of the missionaries converting Muslims. Until the collapse of the Ottoman Empire in 1919, missionaries were banned from the western half of Arabia and Northern Yemen, but not from the Gulf or the south of Yemen where Zwemer and Faulkner ventured. Wherever they did have control however, the Ottomans did all they could to limit Western missionaries' presence and influence, including jailing Muslims who decided to adhere to Christ.

In 1882, British Major General F.T. Haig, after making extensive journeys around the coasts of Arabia, sketched plans for a mission in southern Arabia. He published a plea for Protestants to dare to evangelize Arab Muslims:

There is no difficulty about preaching the Gospel in Arabia if men can be found to face the consequences. The real difficulty would be the protection of the converts. Most probably they would be exposed to violence and death. The infant church might be a martyr church at first like that of Uganda, but that would not prevent the spread of the truth in its ultimate triumph.[2]

Backed by the strong but almost unprecedented encouragement of Professor Lansing, Samuel Zwemer and James Cantine, two recent seminary graduates in the United States, founded the Arabian Mission in 1888. Though they lacked money and official Reformed Church backing, they persevered to raise the needed funds themselves. Since it was countercultural in the American denominations to solicit for one's personal financial support, Zwemer visited churches west of the Mississippi River to raise support for Cantine, and Cantine did the same for Zwemer in the churches east of the Mississippi River.

After noting that these pioneers raised their launching funds, the administration of the Arabian Mission was transferred to the Board of Foreign Missions of the Reformed Church. Cantine sailed for the Persian Gulf in 1889 and Zwemer joined him there in 1890. The two neophytes visited American missionaries of the first Protestant mission agency from the United States, the ABCFM (American Board of Commissioners for Foreign Mission) in Egypt. Next, they met with the Keith Falconer's mission, of the Church of Scotland, in Aden (Yemen) seeking to discern where God was leading them to open a new work on the Arabian Peninsula. They eventually decided to initially base in Basra, Iraq, then known as Mesopotamia or Greater Syria, to work their way into the Arab Peninsula. The Church Missionary Society (CMS), the evangelical wing of the Church of England, was working in Mosul in the north of Iraq, but there was no Protestant Christian witness south of there in the Gulf in 1889.

Not one to settle down, Zwemer soon moved to Bahrain. About that small country, he commented: "All Arabs are hospitable to strangers, but on the whole Arabs (of the) Arabian Coast...have to suspect a Christian who comes with the book (the Bible), but they received me with less prejudice than I had expected."[3] Zwemer immediately set about to procure property, renting a little house with an upper room where he could receive visitors. Located up against a mosque, it had sixteen small windows but no window panes and a leaky roof. Still, it served as his home and dispensary for two years. Subsequently, Zwemer rented a small shop between the tinsmith's and the grocer, setting up a box for a table and a bench to sit with visitors who came to chat and drink coffee, receive minor medical treatment, and occasionally discuss their respective religions. From that little shop, Zwemer practiced his minimal dentistry skills which were considered an improvement over the blacksmiths' technique of extracting teeth!

For the first few years Zwemer divided his time between Bahrain and Basra. In 1895, Miss Amy Wilkes arrived from Australia with the Anglican Church Missionary Society. When she married Zwemer, the CMS demanded Zwemer refund her travel cost to the field. Thus in true Oriental fashion, Zwemer "bought his wife" from her former people! Soon, he and Amy were joined by

Dr. and Mrs. Thoms, who quickly shouldered much of the medical practice proving to be invaluable co-workers. During this time Mrs. Zwemer would make house calls, doing what she could for children and their mothers while Samuel based at home to receive visitors and watch over their two daughters Katharina and Bessie. Multi-tasking, he received Arab friends who stopped by to talk. After putting the children to bed, he would hang a white sheet in the largest upper room utilizing the "magic lantern" (an early type of image projection employing light filtering through pictures on glass slides), illustrating stories from the Old Testament or about the earthly visit of Isa Al Masih.

Having Christian missionaries in residence tended to be an embarrassment for the staunch Muslim sheikhs, but eventually good will and sacrificial service gave the rulers reason enough to sell the mission land for schools and medical facilities. Eventually, the missionaries resided not in the Muslim-owned houses, but in the institutional buildings they had built by funds from America. It seems at least some Arabs were favorably impressed that these foreigners would build something not only for themselves, but for the benefit of the local people. It was also not unnoticed that the missionaries were willing to live in the stifling heat for five years at a time before returning home to visit their own families. The fact that very few missionaries were expelled is testimony that, friendly or not, influential Muslims were grateful for education and medical help.

Of course, the Gulf Arabs didn't realize that furloughs were no time of rest for Samuel Zwemer. He was either recruiting or raising money from sixty "friends of Arabia," for the hospitals as well as for buildings that would serve as a combination church and school. Because the Muslims had a special building for worship, as did the Christians back home, most missionaries assumed that house churches would not be an acceptable option.

In 1904, a minister of the Reformed Church in America reported about a chapel being used by a group of Christian worshipers:

The present [chapel] does not pretend to hold the congregations which are beginning to assemble. People are willing to stand outside looking in at doorways and windows for awhile; but you cannot expect that to keep up. A chapel room double the size of the present one is wanted.[4]

It is not clear how many of those chapel attendees were from Muslim background. The Mission house eventually became too small to be a healthcare facility. Although $6,000 was promised from America, Zwemer's appeal for land was refused by the sheikh due to objections from local residents. However, Zwemer reported, not long after, the sheikh had a vision of Jesus commanding him to be generous with his property! Thus negotiations were reopened and the ruler himself sold them the land.

In the first years, at daily chapel meetings in the hospital, both the ordained and the doctors would read Scripture, talk about its meaning and even follow hymn-singing with prayer. Before an operation, a doctor would tell something about his faith and say a prayer out loud in Arabic. Afterwards a missionary pastor would visit patients in their homes to speak about Jesus, being sure to end with prayer for his hosts. Especially remembered for this was Dr. Paul Harrison, who served there thirty-one years, from 1917–1948.

One Arab woman who came to the hospital feared that she would not live after medical treatment by the "infidels." After she was well, she told the nurse that the doctor was hated by everyone because he was a Christian and everyone thought he had come to make them Christians. However, after seeing first-hand how the hospital operated and the treatment she received, she declared she trusted them with her life.

The first decade of the 20th century saw Mrs. Emma H. Worrall join Dr. Worrall in the Mission in Basra. Miss Elizabeth G. De Pree arrived and married James Cantine and Miss Fanny Lutton was another intrepid pioneer.

Dorothy Firman, who arrived in 1909 and later married John Van Ess, was influenced as a child by a visit to her home by Cyrus Hamlin, co-founder of Robert College in Constantinople. Years later, Dorothy was sitting in chapel at Carleton College in Northfield, Minnesota, where she taught English literature. Samuel Zwemer was speaking for the Student Volunteer Movement. Presenting a graphic description of the Arabian Peninsula, he made an appeal for a young woman teacher to go to Basra to open a school for Arab girls. Not long afterwards, Dorothy arrived in the Arab Gulf accompanied by three other new missionaries: Dr. Christine Iverson and Edwin and Eleanor Calverley. Eleanor was a doctor who later founded a medical work for women in Kuwait and Edwin was a pastor who became an outstanding Arabic and Islamic scholar, eventually becoming the director of the Kennedy School of Missions in Hartford, Connecticut, the first such American institution focused on making disciples among Muslim peoples.

James Cantine gave the new missionaries Arabic lessons every day on the ship. It is worth noting that to get to Bahrain, the ship went to Italy, Pakistan, Oman, and then up the Persian Gulf to Bahrain. By the time they came to the end of the journey, they had all learned to read Arabic, as well as recite the Lord's Prayer and venture a few halting sentences. In Bahrain, Dorothy met John Van Ess, but marriage was not permitted until a person passed their Arabic exams! Although the powers of darkness, sensing an invasion, smote the invaders in body soul and mind with sickness, temptations and doubts, steadily the Arabian Mission team grew. The Christian Reformed Church was fascinated by the example and spectacle of her sons and daughters attempting the impossible. They prayed and gave generously, although perhaps unfortunately, mostly for buildings.

In the 1930s, Jerome Beaty of the American Magazine wrote a series of articles on the most important Americans abroad. Among his ten top names of statesmen, businessmen, journalists, etc. were three missionaries: Dr. Ida Scudder, Dr. Paul Harrison, and Dr. John Van Ess of the Reformed Church in America. When Van Ess was later asked how many converts he had made, his simple response was: "Only Allah knows."[5] John and Dorothy Van Ess were characteristic of the men and women who went to the Arabian Peninsula: courageous, adventurous, politically astute and academically sharp, with keenly developed social awareness and unbounded physical energy. John Van Ess, soon after the founding of the Arabian mission wrote: "Deep in the heart of each member of the Arabian mission has always been a sense of imperativeness to the point of slavery, and yet with it, a sense of emancipation that comes with the consciousness of being held by an irresistible and ultimately triumphant idea."[6]

For sheer effrontery, their vision was unsurpassed in the Arabian Peninsula. After all, this was the birthplace of Islam, the greatest adversary of Christ and His message. The Muslim was imprisoned behind a simple but unyielding creed and surrounded physically by trackless deserts that historically were dreaded for their invincibility. The path to the Arab Muslim's mind and heart was also guarded by an appallingly difficult language.

The Arabian Mission was known particularly for its medical work in the Emirates and Oman, although John Van Ess and his wife were primarily educators. In 1912, he started a school for boys in Basra, which immediately attracted the sons of the local sheikhs. In the same year his wife opened a school for girls. Van Ess' school in Basra reached its height of influence in the late 1920s and early 1930s, when the majority of its students were Muslim. By the end of the 1930s however, as nationalistic and anti-British feelings intensified in Iraq, influential Muslims no longer sent their sons to be educated there, preferring to send them to the government schools. After that, the mission school attracted mainly the children of the most poor.

Every individual missionary to the Gulf was a pioneer depending largely upon their personal (given or acquired) ability to obtain a hearing. The physicians and trained nurses found the widest openings through their professions. House-to-house visiting was a new thing for the Gulf Arabs to experience, but most of the missionaries made attempts, though it was at that time counter-cultural to visit without an invitation. Sometimes when visits were made admittance was refused. On one occasion, Mrs. Cantine called at the house of the Sultan's brother in Muscat. He sent down word that he was very sorry indeed, but his women were so ignorant that they were utterly unable to converse with anyone. Mrs. Cantine learned afterwards that the Sultan rebuked him because at the Sultan's own house, she had been cordially received and invited to keep visiting. Once the barrier was removed by this precedent, not only the immediate family, but the whole neighborhood would gather to entertain the new and interesting guests, thus providing the missionaries opportunity to speak to greater numbers, even if doing so was less personal. Increasingly when someone was too ill to leave their bed, Mrs. Cantine would be invited into their home. Whenever and wherever the occasion arose, prayer would accompany a visit:

One young woman seemed impressed with the difference between Mrs. Cantine's prayers and her own: "You Christians ask much better things from God than we do. You ask Him to help you to lead better lives and to keep you from sin and you seem to be much more in earnest than the Moslems are. You live according to the teachings of your book and they are all so good." This girl and her mother were frequent visitors at the mission house and they attended the Sunday services regularly. They read the Bible and the mother said that she knew that the religion of Christ was the true religion.[7]

Often the women listened to the reading of the Bible as if they expected to hear something evil and were quite surprised when everything they heard sounded so positive.

Many efforts were made to smaller towns and villages where the medicine chest would be in constant use. Usually occasions would arise in which the women could be told of the Great Physician. In six months during one year, Mrs. Cantine made 107 visits not counting her medically-related visits. Often, opportunity for Bible reading was freely given. At one house where she visited regularly twice a week, the women of the family seemed deeply attracted to the Christian faith. On returning after a furlough, the lady missionaries would first of all call on all their old friends, as culturally a visit was compulsory after so long an absence.

Questions to Ponder

What can you imagine were the pros and cons of the missionaries buying or building their own houses or shops for literature and hospitality? What would you do if you resided in Bahrain today? Why?

What are the implications of the local Muslims today having their own government social help now, as opposed to Zwemer's time?

If Amy Zwemer and the other pioneers, to become deeper in their Muslim community, gave birth among the Muslim people they sought to win, why do a large percentage of today's missionaries return to their home country to give birth? Pros and cons?

Country Snapshots: Kuwait

THE ARABIAN MISSION first put missionaries into Kuwait in 1900 and again in 1903. However, when a Bible shop was opened soon after their arrival, there was immediate opposition from Sheikh Mubarek, the ruler of Kuwait. "He refused at that time to give permission for such establishment or any kind of missionary activities in his country, asking them to close their shop and leave the Sheikdom immediately."[8] The missionaries appealed for help from the British Agent in Kuwait, in a letter written by Samuel Zwemer:

I wish to inform you that we (the missionaries) have been in Kuwait for about six months with the permission of Sheikh Mubarek. We had offered to come to Kuwait before, and the Sheikh was fully informed about our work. The day before yesterday he ordered me to leave the country. I do not yet know the reason for this decision. We await your help.[9]

However, when Sheikh Mubarek's daughter was healed with "missionary medicine" in 1910, all hostility ceased.

When Dr. and Mrs. Edwin E. Calverley were appointed to Kuwait, it was seriously questioned whether the time had come for a woman to work in that country. Up to that point in history, there is no record of such an action taking place. Yet, at the end of the first year, it was reported with much thankfulness that there had been no greater unpleasantness met with in the Kuwait station than in any other. The Calverley's reached Kuwait in December of 1912 and opened a dispensary on the first day of January. Clinics were held daily and the numbers grew steadily until there were twenty patients a day. At first the cases were of a discouraging chronic type difficult to cure, but as confidence increased, more mendable cases were brought – eye operations were especially popular. When Mrs. Calverley was away for any reason and only the male assistant was available, the numbers fell at once because the Muslim women would utilize only a female doctor. Thus whenever she returned home to the USA for furlough, medical work for women in Kuwait had to be suspended. On her return, the Muslim women gained sufficient confidence to be willing to undergo operations, a most encouraging sign of acceptance and trust.

The Calverleys also succeeded in opening a mission school. However, within three months of opening, strong Islamic opposition arose, resulting in the withdrawal of most of the pupils from the school. Al-Tameemi observes that there were several reasons for the opposition, including the fact that "Mr. Calverley usually took the boys to the Sunday services" and "he taught them the Christian faith and gave each one a copy of the Bible in Arabic to give to his parents."[10]

In 1913, permission was given to the Arabian Mission by the sheikh in Kuwait to build a hospital.

In 1913 the corner-stone was laid for the Men's Hospital, and in 1914 the hospital was ready for use. Before that time medical services were provided by Drs. Binitt, Harrison and Mylrea in a native house. Thus this establishment was a step forward in the evolution of the Mission's humanitarian services in that region.[11]

Seven years later, a Women's Hospital was also opened, much to the delight of Arab women when they realized that in this separate hospital they could unveil without fear of being seen by men. A second women's hospital was constructed and opened for business in 1939.

In 1967 the Mission decided to give up its work in Kuwait because of the local development in the area and because of the argument between its staff there, especially Dr. R. Scudder and Dr. Fell. Each of them saw the problem of dealing with the people in a different way.[12]

Country Snapshots: Bahrain

Because of Bahrain's location and it being a British Protectorate, the missionaries found Bahrain to be relatively easier, especially after Samuel Zwemer moved there in 1899. A mission station was first established, followed by the opening of a school and hospital.

"The missionaries' basic work at Bahrain was the medical service. It was developed when Dr. and Mrs. Thoms came from Basrah in September 1900."[13] The Thoms moved into the Zwemer's house, no doubt due to the gratitude Zwemer felt at finally having a qualified doctor on his team. Gibrail, a colporteur presumably of Christian background, was hired to work at the hospital. He learned to dress ulcers while Zwemer treated fever patients and put water into infected eyes. Dr. Thoms dealt with the more severe illnesses. After treatment, they would often take the patient to lie in the mosque next door where he could recuperate. The medical work in Bahrain led to the establishment of the Mason Memorial Hospital, which soon became the crown jewel of the Mission and greatly bolstered the reputation of missionary doctors throughout the Arabian Peninsula.

The Arabian Mission's educational service at Bahrain began at the same time as its medical service. The first western style school was founded there by the

Mission in 1892 and opened by Amy Zwemer. This school was not only the first one in Bahrain, but also in the whole Gulf region.[14]

Both girls and boys attended the school and the primary motivation was to learn English, although arithmetic, geography, history and evangelism were all part of the curriculum. In 1974, Ahmad Ibrahim, one of the first students in the school, recalled:

The daily study usually started with Christian prayers and reading from the Bible. In fact we argued with the teachers about our religion. We had studied the Islamic religion from the earliest age at home. We had a solid grounding, and they could not affect us by their religion, and I am still a Moslem.[15]

Due to this overt effort to convert the children, many parents protested the work done by the school and local mullahs got involved, attempting to persuade the youngsters not to attend their classes.

By the second decade of the 1900s, several Islamic educational schools had been built nearby to "counteract" the missionaries' work. Undeterred, the mission pressed on and by 1932 the boys school reported an enrollment of 151. Mr. Hakken, one of the teachers, gave this interesting report:

Some boys had been there since 1924, when the school was opened on its present basis. It is interesting to note that the longer the boys stay in school the less they resent Christian teachings. It is the new boys that have the most objections and feel most confident in Islam.[16]

Sadly, the Arabian Mission was forced to close the boys' school in 1936 due to lack of finances. The school was reopened in the late 1950s and, as of 1977, still existed.

Thus after three quarters of a century, the Mission's educational service [in Bahrain] has yet to achieve its fundamental aim, but no doubt it has served the people of the area and has helped them educationally at a time when they had nothing modern of their own in this field.[17]

Questions to Ponder

If you had been on one of the teams of the Arabian Mission as described above, with the perspective you have now, what would you have advised the team to do or to desist doing?

Are we now advantaged or disadvantaged when the civil authorities no longer need or want help for the poor or disadvantaged? Does that mean ex-pats should only go where invited, which is the policy of some agencies?

Country Snapshots: Qatar

WHILE AN ESTABLISHED missionary presence in Qatar is a relatively recent phenomenon, the area "was toured many times by the missionaries of the Arabian Mission before permission was given to them to act there."[18] When that permission finally was granted, Rev. G. Van Peursem and Dr. W.H. Storm undertook a medical-evangelistic tour of Qatar in 1945. After assisting the sheikh with his high blood pressure, they were given permission to build a hospital, which was completed in 1947. "The medical service in this area however, did not long survive. In 1952 the Mission had to give up its activity because of problems of staffing and the hospital was handed back to the local government."[19] Thus, Al-Tameemi sadly concludes that "the Mission lost forever the chance to work in Qatar."[20]

Questions to Ponder

How has ministry to Muslims in the Arab Gulf developed since the days of the Arabian Mission?

What do we think we understand better now?

REFLECTION ON QATAR

The observant reader may have noticed that Qatar was a rather brief section. Has the fruit been minimal all the way through until today or is there any reason to rejoice?

Expats have been worshipping there, mostly undisturbed, for many years in schools, homes, or rented halls. Finally, after decades of gathering in borrowed spaces, Qatar's growing Christian community celebrated - albeit quietly - the opening of the country's first church building. Construction of buildings for other Christian traditions, Anglican, Coptic and the Greek Orthodox communities, as well as an interdenominational center where eleven Indian churches converge under a single roof, exist now.

Nevertheless, the presence of an official space for Christians, however unassuming, does not sit well with many Doha residents, although other Muslims reason that accepting a Christian presence is an important step toward respect and tolerance. The more official Christian clergy have promised not to proselytize among Muslims due to the laws against conversion. Still, churches are increasingly seen as one way to attract more needed skilled foreign workers. It is hoped by Christians that Doha allowing open churches will lead to other Arab communities doing likewise. Doha's Catholic community now comprises 90% of the city's 150,000 growing Christian expatriate population. In what manner might that be a positive or negative? As has happened in Egypt and even occasionally in Libya, Jordan and Lebanon, the visibility of a church building means a few intrepid spiritually hungry Muslims are likely to make some inquiries concerning the Christian Faith. Hopefully some of such persons will discover the Savior and become part of His family.

Country Snapshots: Saudi Arabia

In August of 1913, Jenny De Mayer, an intrepid Russian Red Cross missionary, set out for Jeddah, Arabia. Much of her ministry was in hospitals caring for sick, often times among elderly men and women. Yet, she had several episodes worth noting: "One evening when the pilgrims were returning from Mecca, on coming home, I noticed in a lane a dying woman, lying on the ground, alone. I hurried on and went to the chief medical inspector of Jeddah who lived in the same block as I."[21] She called on the doctor and informed him that this woman needed to be taken to the hospital. He answered courteously, but swerved off at once, changing the topic to other work begin done among the pilgrims on Hajj. Then he said with an unpleasant sniff: "If you would only once repeat the Shahada (*There is no God but Allah, and Muhammad is the prophet of Allah*), I would take you to Mecca where you would find a wonderful field of work amongst women there!" De Mayer wrote:

I was struck to the heart and cried out: "Never shall I repeat the Shahada! I am a Christian!" His evil smile gave place to rage and scorn: "Is that so? Well, then I am henceforth your enemy and you need not reckon on any help from me! Let that woman die wherever she lies!"[22]

He then spat at her feet.

In July 1914 she had an encounter on a ship with Sheikh Abdullah, the future King of Arabia, who offered to teach her the correct pronunciation of her Arabic. She recounts:

He evidently knew who I was, for he never asked me why I was traveling to Jiddah. We spoke partly in French and partly in Persian. My lack of Arabic filled me with grief! Here was the future ruler of Arabia who, next to the Khalifah, is the foremost man of Islam, but I was not able to proclaim to him, in the proper way, the Truth for which I was known to stand! And how was it that the Lord had chosen no one else to reach the Sharif's ear and declare His message, than me?[23]

She eventually read him some of her tracts:

He took the tracts from my hands, turned to the sheikhs and read the titles to them in Arabic. Then he turned to me and said, "Let us find an interpreter and talk about these matters!" I asked the ship's doctor to come and interpret as he knew Arabic as well as French. He came and we started at once to discuss the Person of the Lord, regarding Jesus as the divine Son of God. To our displeasure, the Doctor treated his questions and my answers like a joke, making fun of what was a serious matter to Sheikh Abdullah as well as to me.[24]

After that, they decided to communicate without the doctor. Although nothing seemingly significant immediately resulted, De Mayer took heart that she "had put into the hands of the future Ruler of the Muhammadans literature which exalted our Lord Jesus Christ, and had freely and joyfully witnessed to Him, even though it had been with stammering lips in a mixture of languages."[25] Eventually, Jenny returned to her native Russia and was arrested for "religious causes, which our [Russian] government insisted on calling 'contra-revolutionist' ones."[26] She was eventually released and continued to faithfully serve her Lord until He called her Home. Jenny's memoirs were published in 1942.

In 1917, Paul Harrison received the first invitation to go to Riyadh and attend to the needs of the Royal family and their friends. Although the Harrisons were lured by their vision to expand their mission into Yemen, they realized that they, plus the Dykstras, Vanes, Van Peursems and Pennings, were very close to the end of their overseas ministries – who was going to replace them at the existing stations?

Harrison wondered if it was a temptation for missionaries to become preoccupied with the difficulties of the work where they were and therefore be tempted to see a new place as possibly more fruitful. He himself was tempted to move to Doha, Qatar. In contrast, Dalenberg, who served in the Arabian mission from 1921 to 1961, observed that her predecessors saw themselves as

Christ's soldiers in a foreign land sacrificing themselves for His service; an advanced arm of a campaign that would eventually succeed. Like soldiers entering the battle, any of us could be taken at any moment. We were prepared to sacrifice our careers, our well-being, our health, and even our lives.[27]

But there was no spiritual campaign that would cause Islam to crumble, especially with so few missionaries focused on the redemption of Muslims. There were even fewer in the next generations due to missionaries being affected by theological "latitudinarians." Sadly, proclamation, i.e. calling Muslims to repentance and faith in Christ's atonement, devolved mostly into a mandate to simply "live the Christian life," ministering to their physical and educational needs as sufficient missionary accomplishment.

Until after World War II, the few missionaries who were hoping to reproduce disciple-making disciples from a Muslim background understood that Arab nationals faced far greater opposition than the missionaries who were protected by Western governments. Of course, the Arab Christians understood the dangers as well, and therefore assumed that they should simply pastor their own people and let "sleeping dogs" (the Muslims) sleep on.

Nonetheless, if the early missionaries to the Arab Gulf were anything, they were innovative and eager to try everything. In 1908 they purchased a diesel-driven boat which lasted for ten years. Then in 1920, they purchased a British-built war surplus forty-foot launch, but only one person in the mission knew how to pilot it.

Until its dissolution, the Ottoman government controlling the Arab populations forbade direct evangelism of Muslims by foreign nationals. They didn't need to formalize that ban toward the empire's citizens who were Roman Catholic or Orthodox because they knew harsh Muslim reaction would be sufficient detriment to the proselytization of Muslims.

Duke Potter, the secretary of the board of foreign missions of the Reformed Church at the funeral of James Cantine in 1940, remarked:

It is easy to turn aside in a country like Arabia or Iraq, to work with the ancient Christian groups when one finds the Muhammadan will not listen to the Gospel. So, the alternative was to build up a church or school among the non-Muslim elements of the region. But Dr. Cantine insisted in both the Arabian mission and the United Mission in Iraq that however meagre the tangible results are, our great object is to minister to the followers of the Prophet.[28]

In Saudi Arabia itself, the only missionary activity was occasional sojourns invited by the royal families to provide medical services. John Van Ess pled for residency, but the Saudis feared their presence would contaminate "holy soil." The emphasis on starting schools, as missionaries were doing in the Levant and Egypt, was accepted by the first generation of missionaries as long as proclamation was included. But except for chapel in the hospitals, medical clinics, and schools regulated by Muslim governments, "mission" after World War I became essentially "good deeds to the Gulf peoples."

Country Snapshots: United Arab Emirates

The UAE was earlier under British protectorate called the Trucial States, a federation of seven sheikdoms. Once the domain of pirates, the area was subdued by the British in 1820 and existed as a protectorate from 1892 until the 1960s. Most of the Trucial States, which consisted of Abu Dhabi, Dubai,

Sharjah, Ras al-Khaimah, Umm al-Qaiwain, Ajman and Fujairah, would become the United Arab Emirates in 1971.

The first American missionary effort in the United Arab Emirates was instigated by a colporteur named Isa who arrived in Dubai in 1896. An official representative of the Arabian Mission, Isa was a peddler who sold Bibles and other books on his journey throughout the Arab Peninsula as he made his way toward Oman. "It is recorded that he did visit a large village called Thabbee (Abu Dhabi) and while he did not make much of an impact, the terrain was mapped out for others to follow."[29] Historian Andrew Thompson observes that Samuel Zwemer made his first trip to the UAE (known at that time as the Trucial Coast) in 1900. Zwemer "travelled extensively in the Trucial States and crossed the desert over to Buraimi where he preached the Gospel for the first time. The ruling sheikh allegedly asked for a reading of the Gospel and even purchased a large Arabic Bible."[30] On a later visit to Abu Dhabi, Zwemer reported the sale of two dozen Bibles.

In 1901, Arabian Mission member James Moerdyk relocated to Sharjah and established a treatment clinic, though he had no medical qualifications! He was keen to distribute Christian literature and Bibles to his patients despite their hesitancy to accept these gifts. Moerdyk remained in Sharjah for two months, which was up to that point, the longest any missionary had remained in the UAE. Unfortunately, his desire to proselytize in the open led to a public boycott of his services and materials. Missions scholar Fatma al-Sayegh also suspects that during his time in Sharjah, "Moerdyk had been falsifying accounts in order to impress his prayer supporters back in the United States."[31]

Some fully qualified doctors arrived over the next few years, including Stanley Mylrea in 1908, who encountered a less-than-charitable reception at Sharjah and did not remain there long. Coinciding with his departure was the "Hyacinth affair," which was "provoked by the British insisting they search every ship that entered Dubai in the belief there was arms trafficking taking place."[32] This led to a violent clash, resulting in the deaths of four Britons and nine Arabs: "the subsequent bitterness meant that any goodwill toward Westerners had evaporated and the door [to missionaries in Sharjah] was firmly closed."[33]

Not until after World War I were missionaries once again allowed access to the region. In 1918, Dr. Paul Harrison was invited to Abu Dhabi by the sheikh himself, who was desperate to receive medical care for his uncle. This marks the first time in recorded history that a medical missionary received an official invitation to the Emirates. "Harrison and his party were assured of a warm welcome. Their visit ushered in a new era for the missionaries and promised to melt any mistrust that had developed."[34]

In 1939, Dr. Sarah Hosman resigned from her post in Oman due to a theological divide between herself and the Arabian Mission; she subsequently joined the Independent Board for Presbyterian Foreign Missions. After leaving Oman, she travelled throughout the Emirates before settling down in Saham in 1941 where she opened up a mobile clinic. She was joined in 1945 by a Miss Edna Barter and they worked tirelessly together praying that God would grant them a breakthrough in the Trucial Coast.

That breakthrough came in 1951:

The Sheikh of Ajman's wife was very ill. Sarah Hosman happened to be in Sharjah at the time and she treated her; the Sheikh's wife recovered. Her husband understandably was very keen to have Sarah Hosman stay in his territory and offered her a place in one of the palaces in Sharjah. She consented to do so but was only willing to open a hospital if written permission were given to share the Gospel with her patients.[35]

Permission was granted and that same year the Sarah Hosman Hospital opened its doors. It was the first hospital of any kind established in the UAE.

Medical needs continued to dominate missions effort throughout the 20th century. In 1960, Sheikh Zayed commissioned the Oasis Hospital to be built in Al-Ain. In November of that year, the hospital was ready to receive patients and under the leadership of Drs. Pat and Marian Kennedy. A maternity hospital was also built in Fujairah and run by a Christian medical team.

In 1966, a young American family felt God was speaking to them through the words of Isaiah 40:3. It read, "A voice is calling, clear the way for the Lord in the wilderness; make smooth in the desert a highway for our God." Thus it was that Carl and Barbara Sherbeck found themselves in the Arabian desert working first at the Oasis Hospital in Al-Ain and then moving to Abu Dhabi in 1972.[36]

Carl's desire was to build a church, and by late 1972 a congregation comprised mostly of American families based at the Crestwave Oil Company was quickly running out of room. Boldly, Carl sought an audience with Sheikh Zayed:

He made a request for a grant of land upon which to build housing. The Sheikh asked Carl if he wanted land for a church. He answered, "No, not at this time, but you need to know that wherever we live people will come to pray with us." The Sheikh replied: "You can build a house on the land we will give you and use it as a church, but it is not allowed to look like a church."[37]

The church was completed and occupied in 1975 and eventually openly known as the International Church in Abu Dhabi.

Country Snapshots: Oman

Muscat was the third important station of the Arabian Mission, and was considered the most important one in this field. A boys' school was begun there by Rev. Peter Zwemer in 1896. It was indeed the outcome of his individual effort. About eighteen boys were handed over to his care in the beginning. This school was named, "The Freed Slave School." The missionaries gave this name to the school because it was established basically for the slaves' children, to care for them, educate them and convert them. Most of these children were orphans.[38]

Girls were taught by Mrs. Cantine and the curriculum included Arabic, English, Bible, sewing and lace-making. Several of the eventual graduates of these schools were sent to mission stations in Bahrain and Basrah.

The medical service there started shortly after the opening of the Muscat station. The area was rife with many diseases, and its needs exceeded the Mission's capacity; nevertheless the medical staff did their best to help the suffering people despite their own limited numbers and facilities.[39]

The women in Muscat would come into the dispensary during the day, at various times, as it provided a break in their monotonous lives to hear and see something new. Ruth, an Indian Christian nurse, was faithful in giving Gospel talks, but only to the Hindu women who said, "We are not afraid that the doctor will turn us into Christians, but we are afraid of Nurse Ruth, because she is one of us and she knows how to make us believe in her Christianity."[40]

Dr. Harrison, who opened the station at Kuwait, pioneered again as one of the only two doctors for some years in Muscat, Oman.

Of the policy of the Arabian Mission and of his own experience in carrying it out, Dr. Harrison wrote vividly in his book *The Arab at Home*:

Unaffected friendship is ninety per cent of missionary method...as we are able. We learned not to enter a place until we are invited. So the method of procedure has been to work out from a base hospital, school, or evangelistic station on the coast. In accomplishing our mission, the most powerful instrument is the example of Christian family life lived in full view of the people. Add one's professional skill with unfailing human sympathy and personal interest, then the missionary becomes almost irresistible. We can present and explain Christ's teachings to every one of his hospital patients. In 12 years' experience I have never met a patient with whom it was impossible to do this sort of personal Christian work.[41]

Because there was no native Church, i.e. no indigenous Christian congregations, it was perhaps more true of Arabia than other mission fields that they concluded evangelistic work could not be separated from the educational and medical ministries. The sole purpose of the schools was to instill Christian ideals and principles in the minds of the children. The twofold purpose of the medical work was to heal the bodies and the souls of those who came to the hospitals and dispensaries. The main object of every endeavor was the spreading of the news of the Christian Gospel among the Arabs. In short, it was all pioneer work.

One Muslim-background believer church plant happened in Oman during the beginning of the 1930s, growing out of a school for boys and girls and mostly the fruit of Paul Harrison and Dirk and Minnie Dykstra. The church was located on the compound of the mission hospital, which was later called Omani Christian Fellowship. When the mission gave up control of its medical institutions to the government of Oman in 1973, the community continued to worship but by then the majority of believers were migrant Christian workers from Syria, Lebanon and Egypt.

In 1966, missionary Jay Kapenga obtained permission to rebuild a Bible shop in Muscat's old bazaar. His opinion of these shops was that in reality, they were "dialogue shops...where local Christians could and did sit with local

Muslims and make their confession."[42] Kapenga viewed these shops as an important aspect of mission to Muslims.

In 1974, missionary Jim Donham attributed the friendly relations between believers from Muslim and Christian backgrounds to the fact that both wanted the comradeship of mission personnel. However by 1977, the Omani Christian Fellowship had begun to quietly fade out of view. Why did this happen? The profession of faith in Christ by Omani believers was taken as sincere by the missionaries as they witnessed the cost paid for their decisions. Christians from Muslim backgrounds demonstrated great courage against opposition and although some may have been attracted by employment at the hospital, the general conclusion was that the Omani church dissolved because their ex-pat missionary support group left the country. By the time Alfred Samuel came from Egypt to take over the Arabic language ministry in 1984, the cultural gap between the simple Omani Christians and the sophisticated Egyptians was just too great to bridge. Another factor may have been that the children of the converts put pressure on their parents to draw away.

Whatever the cause, several of the fellowship's leading members ostensibly returned to the Muslim fold and by the mid-1980s nothing was left of the church community. Midge Kapenga of the Arabian Mission wrote:

Our last years in Oman, we would have Arab church with only two or three Omani Christians present. They were joined by expatriate Christian workers from Egypt, Palestine, or Lebanon. Things were never the same again. Most of us missionaries suffered a deep sense of failure. We examined ourselves and what we had done, looking for mistakes. But I wonder if we could have done differently.[43]

Yet even in the face of realistic despair, there is still reason to celebrate, and for Midge, one of those reasons was Miryam Mas'ud:

The wife of Oman's first convert Marash, [Miryam] was led to Christ by her husband and baptized by Gerrit Van Peursem in 1923. When her husband died in 1930, she defied local custom and refused to go into mourning, declaring in the face of a crowd of angry Arab men that she was a Christian and believed in the security and peace of her husband's soul. Her idiosyncratic way of life made her a person who sustained relationships throughout the society of Muscat, taking in orphan children and raising them. She became the powerful center of the Omani Christian community that later developed. She died in 1972.[44]

Country Snapshots: Yemen

In 1839, piracy provoked the British to annex the port of Aden which opened the door a crack for missionary involvement. By the early-mid 1880s, Britain divided the Persian (Arab) Gulf into British and Ottoman spheres of influence, negotiating agreements with local rulers from Muscat to Bahrain. With support from the Free Church of Scotland and inspiration from his friend C.T. Studd, Ion Keith-Falconer adopted this British base to evangelize and from there, along the southern coast to Muscat. In 1885, after teaching himself medicine, Falconer chose the town of Sheikh Othman as base for the mission. He felt there was a need for a medical program combined with proclamation to remove from the Arab mind misconceptions resulting from the "evil example" set by many Europeans. He recruited surgeon Stewart Cowen and was soon gathering small groups for Bible readings in homes and coffee shops. In the puzzling will and wisdom of God, 32-year old Falconer contracted malarial fever and died in May of 1887. His determined colleagues pressed on with the medical ministry until 1920 when their educational program opened another front. Their stated aim was "to preach Christ to Arabia by word and deed by every means within our power... the real hope of winning Arabia lies in the creation of the indigenous native church."[45]

The next wave of pioneers included Dr. Lionel Gurney and his teammates in the Red Sea Mission, who arrived in Aden in the 1950s. Their story begins with Alfred Buxton, who had gone out to the Belgian Congo with C.T. Studd in the 1920s. He later served in Ethiopia with the Bible Churchman's Missionary Society (BCMS). In 1934, Buxton returned to Britain to challenge young people to work in Abyssinia, hoping to recruit eighteen new workers. One of the few who responded was his distant cousin Lionel Gurney. Gurney had just qualified in medicine from Bristol University and was recruited by the BCMS, then loaned out to the Church of Scotland mission hospital in Aden. Gurney was introduced to work among Muslims at the age of twenty-three, and after spending a year in Aden, he joined Buxton in Ethiopia. But seeing there were a number of mission agencies working there and many churches already established, Gurney was challenged by Buxton to go where Christ was not known.

Gurney's next challenge then was the totally unreached (and quite fanatical) Muslim tribe of the Danakil (Afar) who dwelt on both sides of the Ethiopia-Eritrea border. Although the BCMS had no missionaries available to pioneer among the Danakil, 35-year old Gurney sensed the door was opened because of a malaria epidemic among them. After spending six months learning their language, he realized no one would join him because he had no mission agency for them to join and no clear plan.

During this period, Italy had invaded Ethiopia and missionaries were expelled. Gurney knew at that point that his call was to the vastly neglected Muslim world. Yet, it would be another twenty years before he would be able to take up residence in Eritrea among the Danakil. After being expelled from Ethiopia, he was sent to British Somaliland to minister to Abyssinian refuges. He managed to get back to Britain on a war ship as WWII was starting in 1939.

Gurney was able to complete a diploma in tropical medicine at the University of Liverpool while the war was raging. In 1945, BCMS reopened the work in Ethiopia with David Stokes commissioned as field leader. While waiting for permission to enter into the region of the Danakil, Gurney formed an evangelistic team of Ethiopian believers (graduates of BCMS' Bible school) which focused on prison ministry. Some of the prisoners who came to the Lord became lifelong friends. During this waiting period, Gurney sensed a call to establish a new mission agency that would focus on Muslims in the Red Sea region. Consequently, he resigned from the BCMS and took a position again in the Church of Scotland hospital in Aden for a year.

Back in Britain at the Keswick convention in July of 1951, Gurney met 33-year-old bachelor and chemist Bevan Woodhead who had recently given his life to Christ. Gurney immediately challenged Woodhead to accompany him to South Arabia. In addition to Woodhead, polio victim Miss Gypsie Perkins, who had served in India for several years as secretary to Dr. Brown (the founder of the Ludhiana Mission Hospital), convinced Gurney that God had called her to now to look after the home end of the new mission. Gurney replied that he did not have a mission and that there was no "home end" to oversee! However, she insisted that the Lord was telling her to do just that. Before Gurney and Woodhead left for Aden (via Marseilles, Beirut, Alexandria, Baghdad, Kuwait, and Bahrain because there were not many passenger ships in 1951), Gurney had also recruited Jack and Kathleen Budd from

England and Bruno Herm from Germany. These six, plus Marian Thomas, a qualified nurse and midwife from England, made up the charter members of the Red Sea Mission team, a British Charity which still wasn't officially registered when they launched out.

The RSM team's inaugural ministry was to the Muslim Arabs of Aden, then a British protectorate, teaming up with the Danish Mission which had been there since 1904. By 1953, the Danish Mission had a school of about 120 Muslim girls utilizing several Muslim lady teachers on their staff. They also had a hand-weaving and handicrafts school, mainly for providing divorced Muslim women a means of earning a livelihood. The Church of Scotland hospital, taken over by the Danish Mission, saw the first church established there after a man named Mubarak was baptized. The house church went in and out of existence depending on the courage of the handful of believers. Woodhead writes of the birth of an indigenous church in Aden after 67 years of mission work. In the various efforts, there had been one or two converts every few years. The believers vacillated from standing their ground and living in victory to hiding in fear. Sadly, the majority turned back to Islam.

In the spring of 1955, there were only one or two converts attending the Sunday Arabic services of the Church of Scotland served by the Danish mission. When the words "Son of God" were spoken, some would spit, get up and walk out and maybe throw stones back into the meeting place. There were some weekly investigative Bible studies with Muslims, but reportedly, no real fellowship times for building up believers in the Faith. Woodhead challenged one local Christian, a man named Marouf, to gather some Muslim-background believers together without the missionaries present. Seven responded to this challenge and met together for the first time on the evening of May 29, 1955. Suddenly, as they were able to do things their way and encourage one another without being shamed, they seemed to have a new power to witness and withstand fierce reactions. So by the time the Red Sea Mission staff left Aden in July, 1956, there were seventeen Muslim-background believers in that fellowship; a year later, it had grown to twenty-seven.

As is so common in mission history to Muslims, fearful opposition caused several of them to be fired from their jobs and even have their lives threatened. Marouf with his faithful wife Suad was considered a Moses, bringing the believers through a wilderness of testing. They were even sheltering and feeding some of them in their home. Just when it seemed that they were going to overcome the opposition of the outside, Satan succeeded in tearing the church apart, dividing the attenders into two groups over the issue of infant baptism.

Still, Gurney excitedly wrote in 1969 that he was witnessing "wider open doors into Muslim hearts than we have ever known."[46] It was easy for Gurney to realize that if the Muslim world was going to be continually confronted with the claims of Christ, there needed to be a lot more workers among them. To his delight, he received an invitation from SIM inviting him to the USA and Canada for a speaking tour to share the needs of the Muslims in the Red Sea area. Although he was greatly disappointed with the lack of response to his recruiting efforts, it did give his burden visibility. A few prayer partners and donors enabled him to continue in the Red Sea region, and at least a few courageously joined the effort there. Dick Hildebrand related this story to Woodhead many years after the fact: "At a meeting where Dr. Gurney spoke, I enthusiastically introduced myself to him at the end, blurting out that God had called me to be a missionary." "Oh," replied Gurney suspiciously, "Where?" "To South America," declared the unsuspecting Hildebrand. "Why? Have you not heard of the Muslim world?" exhorted Gurney dismissively.[47] Hildebrand was so upset with this missionary statesman's lack of encouragement that he went back to the Lord of the Harvest and found himself directed to Morocco where he labored for years.

While Gurney was recruiting in America, the early Red Sea Missions team almost split, largely because of a lack of leadership. Gurney, was away from the field for two years pouring out his heart in Bible schools all across North America and Europe in order to raise up laborers for the Muslim world. He also highlighted the need for coaches to be in place on the field to help new workers.

Unsung Heroes: Female Missionaries in the Arab Peninsula

From the 1890s on, as reported earlier, the primary Western missionary presence in the Arabian Peninsula had been the American Reformed Church medical mission, with stations in Bahrain, Muscat, and Kuwait. They had opened a hospital in Kuwait in 1914 and a separate women's hospital there in 1927. The Muscat station included a school and a hospital that opened in 1934, and the missionaries also provided some medical services to the royal family of Saudi Arabia during their allowed short visits. The interwar period (1918-1938) saw the beginnings of tremendous change on the peninsula and in the Gulf with the discovery of oil. Americans began to establish a special relationship with the Saudis, although the Wahhabi rulers of Saudi Arabia did not permit any Western religious personnel to be active in the Kingdom itself.

However, medical work for women in Muscat was opened in April 1914 by Dr. Sarah L. Hosmon (who would later pioneer female medical missions in the United Arab Emirates). For two months in 1916, Dr. Hosmon took an extra load in Basrah after Mrs. Bennett died. She was called upon during her stay to inoculate ninety women and children for cholera in the house of the sheikh. It was not an easy task to use such a means of preventing a disease among so many ignorant and frightened women, most of whom had to be literally dragged to the end of the corridor where Dr. Hosmon stood with her syringe and needles! As missionary Midge Kapenga would later attest, Dr. Hosmon was a formidable woman who would not back down to the devil in the fight to win souls:

Wadi Sulayman came to work as Dr. Hosmon's cook. By that time he was married and soon had three sons. During his years with Dr. Hosmon, he got to know about Christianity and, by 1930, claimed to be a believer. But he hesitated about baptism until, according to Mission legend, Dr. Hosmon locked him in a room and told him to make up his mind. When he came out of that imprisonment, he had decided to be a Christian and never deviated from his new faith. Immediately his wife divorced him and took the boys.[48]

After resigning from her mission agency in 1939, Sarah Hosmon established a hospital in Sharjah and, ever the sly evangelist, was known to wrap Gospel tracts around dispensary drugs for her Muslim patients.

No record of medical work for women in Arabia would be complete without highlighting the often thankless toil throughout the years by other noble trained and untrained "nurses." Whether married or single, they often carried on the hospital work without the aid of a doctor. Mrs. Zwemer, Mrs. Cantine, Mrs. Van Peursem, Mrs. Harrison, Miss Holzhauser, Miss Van Pelt and Miss Dalenberg, all at times, with or without a doctor, did heroic medical work for women when there was no one else to do it. Sadly the norm, especially with the second generation of missionaries and those who followed them became the majority of the missionaries who recommended restraint. The distribution of Christian literature and the teaching of the Bible to Muslim women and children was considered manipulation. However, some old-timers who knew the language and local culture well found opportunities for friendly conversation on the claims of Christ and even read some of the Bible to those befriended. Yet as time went on, fewer Muslims were challenged with the claims of Christ and even fewer underwent baptism.

Another ministry for the women was the opening of a trade school in the Gulf. The native embroidery work was sufficiently in demand and could be taught, thus avoiding the frequent complaint of the Muslim mothers that though their daughters were learning to read and write, they were learning nothing that did anybody any good. A direct Gospel talk was given each day, accompanied with the reading of Scripture and the attendance at these training sessions was often greater than at the medical clinics. A few whispered that the local women actually came primarily to hear the Bible teaching. Even in the medical clinics, the missionaries sensed some women were coming only for a social hour away from the drudgery of home duties since they had no ailments that required the attention of the medical staff.

Schools were more intentional in their evangelism as the missionaries sought to influence the Arab Muslims to think about the claims of Isa Al Masih. Mrs. Zwemer founded the first school which was simply English lessons for two hours each morning (with her baby at her side) to a Jewish girl and boy and some local Arab boys who wanted to learn English. Not many Arab girls were allowed to attend school. Attendance by Bahraini boys was irregular due to suspicion that they would be infected by the Christian religion. Nevertheless, the educational ministries grew and Arab Christian teachers from Palestine and Lebanon were recruited as the years went by. Determined to see women receive quality education, Mrs. Zwemer opened a small girls' school in Bahrain in 1900, and classes were held in the mission house. It did indeed look as if "the dayspring from on High" had visited this barren and neglected spot when such a miracle as a Christian school for Muslim girls, however small and rudimentary, became possible. By 1901, Amy Zwemer had gained a welcome through the school and in other services, into thirty homes in which she had sometimes as many as eight or ten pupils. In those homes, Gospels and leaflets were given out to those who could read, or where the men could read to them. Occasionally, she was ordered out of a house by the owner who feared that his women were being unduly influenced. Once, instead of leaving, she engaged the man in conversation resulting in him assuring her that henceforth his house was her house! Friendly relations grew as more than two hundred women visited Amy Zwemer in one year alone on some pretext, many simply from curiosity. Of course, she welcomed them no matter what their motivation might have been for coming.

With few exceptions, the Muslim women seemed incapable of independent thought. Their hearts and consciences were atrophied. The missionaries concluded that meals, sleeping, sex, child-rearing and unprofitable gossip formed the sum total of their existence. Lydia was an exception and proved a great help to Amy Zwemer in those pioneer days. Lydia and her three children had been sent away quietly from Baghdad where the Muslims were trying to force her into a new marriage after her own husband was imprisoned for becoming a Christian. Lydia and her children were baptized in July 1899 and she became Mrs. Zwemer's most competent assistant, managing the financial support provided by the Reformed Church Woman's Board. She gathered women together for prayer, and in January 1902, Amy and Lydia held the first women's prayer meetings for Muslim women in Eastern Arabia, with Lydia actively praying and explaining the lessons.

Mrs. Marion Wells Thoms, M.D. went out to the Persian Gulf with her husband S. J. Thoms M.D. in 1898. Many suffering Muslim women were persuaded to avail themselves of her skill while Amy Zwemer made herself available when assistance was needed. Sadly, they were usually not summoned until the native practitioners had done their worst. Even then the female patient was so surrounded by a host of protesting family members that there was very little chance for rational treatment. Mrs. Thoms' dispensary was one room for drugs, examinations, treatments and operations! Treating patients in the Arabs' own homes was even more unsatisfactory because of the number of women who gathered about the patient trying to prevent, if possible, the doing of anything which they thought strange. A not very clean room in which five or six other people were living was hardly an ideal place in which to recover from a serious operation. Yet in spite of all this, Mrs. Thoms' efforts saw not a few women on the way to recovery. As a display of the gratitude felt toward her by the entire country, Bahrain opened a new hospital in 1926: The Marion Wells Thoms Memorial Hospital.

Amy Zwemer's school continued irregularly, the children coming and going without any sense of obligation or particular goal. Mrs. Zwemer considered it progress when they came at all! In 1901 there were seven Christians, four Jews and five Muslims in her informal school. By 1915, there were twenty girls enrolled in the Bahrein Girls' School including nine Muslims, eight Jews and three Christians. Arabic, English, Arithmetic, Geography, Physiology and History constituted the curriculum. Mrs. Zwemer also introduced industrial work in the school, as well as teaching the pupils to wash and iron their own clothes, sweep and dust a room, and to do other domestic work for themselves.

As the school had no equipment, books, maps, globes, charts or pictures, teaching was clearly a creative art with constant challenges. For starters, the house where the school was held was considered by the locals to be haunted by *jinn*. Mrs. Dykstra found herself dealing with panicking young girls. In fact, to win any group of Muslim women was a daunting task. The non-Muslim Indian coolies were weeded out to get Muslims to attend, but a sudden fever or a death in any family would empty the school at once. Opponents were constantly at work inventing excuses to keep the girls from attending. Another difficulty in recruiting female Arab students was that most of them married as young teenagers. Some in the lower classes were more motivated to be taught, assuming a little schooling was the first requisite to advancement in society.

The work called for faith, perseverance and immense patience as they experienced only a few encouragements. Owing to these adverse conditions and to the scarcity of teachers, the Bahrein Girls' School was discontinued in 1917, not to be re-opened until 1922 when Mrs. Dame undertook the challenge. A small Arabic Sunday School was organized which opened twenty new homes to them. That they could report that 125 visits were made to these homes is evidence how they kept close track of their ministry days.

Eventually some sheikhs in Bahrain were befriended who encouraged the women of their families to increasingly invite the female missionaries to spend a week visiting among them, even to bring their books and have discussions! More than once they were kept busy reading and answering questions all day long. They had taken their sewing with them, thinking that an all-day visit might be difficult, but the Muslim women usually insisted they put their sewing aside, preferring instead to be read to and engage in discussion. At least once, the lady missionaries had an audience of about fifty women for what was practically an all-day "Gospel service;" a truly marvelous occurrence in the Gulf in those years. Working as a team, all four female missionaries felt there had never before been such a day in Bahrain.

Questions to Ponder

Women such as Amy Zwemer, Elizabeth Cantine, Marion Wells Thoms and Sarah Hosman had significant opportunities for ministry, even in the early years of the 20th century. How can women of the 21st century carry on their legacy and wage war against the Kingdom of Darkness in ways unattainable to men?

What advantage is there in reaching children with the Gospel as a first priority? What are the disadvantages?

Hardship: Reality of the Call

GEORGE STONE DIED on the field in 1899 and Zwemer spoke at his funeral,

We lived together in the same cramped quarters in Bahrain. He had no romantic ideas of mission work but took hold of grim realities with a grip that meant business. Although life in the Arab Gulf was more primitive than other stations, he fell in love with the new environment and laughed heartily at the idea that it was a sacrifice to live in Bahrain.[49]

Actually, plague and small-pox were rife, sometimes breaking out simultaneously. When there were epidemics of plague, cholera, smallpox and flu, all mission personnel were mobilized into action. The missionaries courageously visited the plague and small-pox patients in their homes, giving them food and medicine twice a day. Their courageous action and obvious sacrifices led to relationships with the communities becoming so solid that, for example, a series of rulers in Bahrain continue to give support to The American Hospital to this day. In April, 1905, Marion Thoms died of typhoid fever literally laying down her life for Muslim women. Her dying request was, "Have them send more missionaries to take the place of those who fall by the way."[50] Nine months later, Mrs. Jessie Vail Bennett was also taken home to glory, another victim of typhoid fever. Death from illness was not relegated to adults, often snatching the firstborn child of a new missionary couple. Samuel and Amy Zwemer buried their two young daughters, dying eight days apart from each other, and inscribing on their tombstone: "Worthy art thou, Lord, to receive riches."

Questions to Ponder

What does the epitaph on the tombstone of Samuel and Amy Zwemer's daughters tell you about the theology of their parents? Would you be able to respond as they did?

6

PALESTINE

ALTHOUGH PALESTINE, WITH ITS 650,000 INHABITANTS, HAD BEEN geographically and ethnographically a province of Syria (Mesopotamia), it deserves to be separately treated on account of its unique place in the history of the world, the Christian religion, and of Protestant mission. To Jews, Muslims and Christians alike, it is "the Holy Land." The longing to be near and have a share of the sacred places has attracted members of a great number of varied religious communities. Perhaps it is a desire for physical reminders of their heritage and/or hoped-for future. There, especially in Jerusalem, the mixture of churches and various religious sects is greater than in any other part of the Near East. Historically there has been considerable tension between Roman Catholics, Greek Orthodox, and Russian and Armenian Orthodox, for influence and supervision of the ruins of supposed biblical sites. Nestorians, Jacobites, Abyssinians, Copts, Maronites, etc. established a presence there long before Protestant churches existed.

Palestine, as it was known when the first Protestants ventured there, drew pioneering missionaries to the Middle East because their theology included the conviction that they might hasten the return of Christ by winning Jewish allegiance to Him as the Messiah. However, few welcomed the Protestants to join the already jostling religious groups, each claiming they were Christ's true church. In addition to hostility from various Christian sects, there was the majority - the Muslims, mostly Arabs, who inhabited Palestine. Kept aware of belonging to the race of the Prophet, the Arabs were angry that they should have been robbed by the indolent Turks of the supremacy appointed to them by Allah to rule Jerusalem. Many dreamed of a great Arab Empire that would embrace all Arabs, with Mecca as its capital. However, the Arabs shared a certain commonality with the Turks: contempt for the Christians and Jews. This, understandably, created a huge antipathy and hindrance to evangelical mission among Muslims.

1800-1850

The ABCFM and Samuel Gobat

In 1818, the ABCFM (American Board of Commissioners for Foreign Mission) decided to launch a mission to Palestine. Two young Andover graduates, Pliny Fisk and Levi Parsons, were chosen to lead the way. After a year spent traveling around the United States raising funds and founding "Palestine Societies" to support them, the two set off for Jerusalem in November of 1819. Fisk and Parsons were tasked with scouting out the land to discern what ministry attention should be given to Muslims, Romans Catholics, and members of the Eastern churches, but especially to the Jews. They landed on Turkey's coast in 1820, staying for a brief time in Smyrna before moving on to Scio. There they studied Greek (spoken among the Greek community there) and produced a small evangelistic tract which they distributed to local Muslims. From Scio, they travelled through Asia Minor and eventually parted ways, Fisk returning to Smyrna and Parsons continuing to Jerusalem where he died in February of 1822 – a missionary career of less than three years. Fisk decided to base in Malta where he was eventually joined by Jonas King. They toured Upper Egypt, crossed the Sinai Desert, and reached Jerusalem before the end of the year. They faced rejection by those in authority, instigated by Roman and Maronite Catholics and the Syrian Orthodox patriarch. In the summer of 1824, Fisk and King toured the major centers of "Greater Syria," changing their base to Beirut. Fisk died nine months later in the spring of 1825, having nearly completed an Arabic-English dictionary.

By 1827, the ABCFM incorporated Palestine into a broader "western Asia" mission that included the entire eastern Mediterranean region. No ABCFM missionaries had actually resided in Jerusalem since 1822 (the brief settlement by Fisk) until William McClure Thomson and his wife Eliza were sent there in 1834. Eliza died soon after and her husband was forced to evacuate the city when the Egyptians attacked Jerusalem as part of their campaign to occupy Mesopotamia. Over the next several years other ABCFM missionaries arrived, but almost no one stayed long. In 1843 that American mission in Jerusalem was handed over to evangelical Anglicans. They found in the remotest parts of Palestine a desire and demand for this never-before-heard Message by at least the poor Orthodox Christians. Not a few Muslims bought portions of the Scripture in Arabic, the first religious books they could possess.

In 1846, King Frederick William appointed Samuel Gobat to be the Protestant Bishop of Palestine. Gobat had recently returned to Europe in shattered health after his efforts to establish a work in Abyssinia and Malta (where he had been the principal of a mission college). Upon his acceptance of this commission, he was made Bishop of Palestine, Syria, Egypt and Mesopotamia, though in reality he had only one parish in his diocese, located in Jerusalem, weekly hosting forty or fifty communicants. Truth be told, Gobat was less interested in converting Jews than with bringing Arab Christians and (theoretically) Muslims into the Protestant fold. A French-speaking Swiss, he spoke Arabic fluently, having spent considerable time in Palestine, Lebanon and Egypt.

Whether Gobat deliberately changed policy or not, he focused on Eastern Christians rather than Jews or Muslims, believing his task was to create a Protestant people in the Middle East. The glaring question: how would he accomplish this? Mission work amongst the "Muhammadans" was out of the question because of the suspicious vigilance and oppression of the Ottoman Turkish government. The earlier distribution of Scripture by the Americans had spread some knowledge of biblical truth in the Holy Land, though the Roman Catholics had induced the Turkish authorities to forbid the selling of Bibles. They even demanded any copies that might be found should be burned because only their priests were allowed to interpret the Scriptures. The tensions between the Protestants and the other churches raged fiercely. Who then could focus on the Muslims?

In 1848, Bishop Gobat received a letter signed by several Greek Christians in Nablus, declaring their resolve to leave their Church since they were being kept in a state of ignorance. Bishop Gobat exhorted them not to take such a step without earnest consideration. As soon as this defection became known in Nablus, a storm broke out. Two of the leading Arab Protestants were imprisoned and condemned to death. Gobat rescued them utilizing the influence of the Governor of Jerusalem. The Greeks eventually turned back, deciding that the cost of being Protestant was too great. Imagine what that message gave to the on-looking Muslims who dared to be interested in the missionaries' Gospel?

The few oppressed Palestinian Protestants were always on the lookout for help from a powerful friend who could protect them against the Turks. Bishop Gobat, making use of their mixed motives, hired people who were able to read, without demanding of them that they should leave their own churches. He commissioned them to go through the country reading the Bible and talking with the people about what had been read. The fruit of this scheme was surprising. It was reported that as soon as these simple "Christian" Arabs opened their Bibles in the streets or public places in the towns and villages, people crowded around them to listen and often showed signs of being touched. Individuals often came in the evening to the lodgings of Bible-readers, confessing their sins with tears in their eyes, and asking to be instructed in the way of salvation.

Question to Ponder

The example of Samuel Gobat using oppressed Palestinian Protestants as itinerate evangelists may surprise some, especially as it seems that Gobat may have manipulated them in some way. Yet the results were very positive in terms of the Gospel taking root in the Palestinian countryside. Reflect on God's over-ruling flawed motives for the advancement of His Kingdom.

GOBAT ALSO SUCCEEDED in setting up English schools throughout Palestine which were utilized by Jews and Arab Christians, the ones who responded. Schools were started at Nablus, Nazareth, Jaffa, Ramleh, Bethlehem and Ramallah. These schools created a strong nuclei of evangelical belief within the Greek church. Muslims boycotted the schools, not wanting their children to be deceived by Christian teachings. Thus, Bishop Gobat and the Anglicans "reaped" where the Americans had sown, but none of the schools knowingly produced disciples from amongst the Muslim population. Nevertheless, the history of Gobat's thirty-plus year episcopate (1846-1879) is admirable. Whatever Protestant missionary work there was in Palestine by 1910 could be traced directly or indirectly to Bishop Gobat.

1850-1900

Gobat's English school system grew. The teachers proved themselves to be steadfast. Their Catholic opponents established opposition schools and searched for Bibles in the houses of any Catholics associating with the Protestants, extorting fines from the people who had possessed them. If these measures failed, the Greek Bishop excommunicated those in Bible studies. Bishop Gobat collected the excommunicated into a Protestant congregation. Throughout the Holy Land similar developments took place. When the people had been thrown out of their churches, there was nothing left but to receive them into the Protestant Church and form them into congregations.

Almost more disquieting and threatening, however, was the unexpected opposition and disapproval among the non-evangelical Anglican Church leaders in England. No wonder there was little time to consider the needs of the Muslims. Gobat naturally turned for assistance to the evangelical Church Missionary Society (CMS), in whose service he had been for twenty years and with whom he felt himself most closely related in faith and practice. He was all the more encouraged to do this because the CMS had, almost from the time of its inception, been carrying on mission work in the Near East. Much to Gobat's disappointment, this very fact caused the CMS to hesitate in granting his request for more missionaries for Palestine. How could they continue their work in Palestine when their ministry in Syria and Egypt was about to be abandoned, having accomplished so little in spite of the large sums spent upon it and the able missionaries that had been employed?

They must have responded in the end, for Gobat launched the CMS Palestine Mission, which greatly strengthened the Anglican arm in the Near East. Under Henry Venn's direction, interest grew in having a policy which endorsed proselytizing to Muslims. The CMS Annual Reports from 1851 onward reveal statements declaring an aim to "enlighten" and "evangelize" Muslims: "Whereas the Mediterranean Mission had restricted itself to reviving the Eastern church and ministry to the Jews, the CMS Palestine Mission began to give attention to Muslims."[1] However, as might have been anticipated, the first converts from Islam (e.g. Muhammad Amin Al-Qasim of Nablus) and the new initiatives of Protestant mission activity following the Crimean War, incited a wave of Muslim hostility and violence. Although the results were limited to scattered individual converts (who often had to flee for their lives), at least some of the CMS workers were making an effort. At the Anglican Conference for Missions to Muslims, which was held in London in 1875, it was "agreed that Islam must be confronted at its center in Palestine and the Arab countries." We also read this from a CMS report from 1880:

I have visited thirty-five stations and outstations and I say without hesitation that the CMS is saturating the villages with Gospel knowledge, but High-Low church controversy in our church and Anglican-Lutheran tensions tend to dominate discussions causing great damage to Anglican efforts among Muslims.[2]

Christian Fallscheer

A locksmith by trade, Fallscheer arrived in Jerusalem in 1862. After helping Bishop Gobat in the diocesan school on Mount Zion, he was sent by the Bishop to Nablus in 1864 to one of the most fanatical Muslim towns in Palestine; no European had been able to live there earlier. In spite of many hindrances, Fallscheer settled in the town, and by his patience gained a footing for the mission. He succeeded in building a church and a parsonage, thus opening the way for the single lady missionaries. He was also granted government permission to build a mission hospital. Little known or noticed outside Palestine, Fallscheer was celebrated throughout the region for his hospitality and selfless service to the peoples. Because of this overt humility and piety, he won the respect of all. When he died, Christians and Muslims alike said with tears in their eyes, "Our father is dead and we are orphans."[3] Muslims even requested the honor of carrying his coffin from the church to the cemetery.

Questions to Ponder

What contributed to Fallscheer's success? How can this challenge us today?

Vartan and Zeller

Most of CMS missionaries working in Palestine were actually German, not English. Johannes Zeller, a man of great intellect and talent, arrived in 1857 and married Hannah Gobat, the Anglican bishops' daughter. They labored for forty years in Nazareth where he had the first church building erected. There he assisted Kaloost Vartan to open the English hospital. The Zellers ministered in Jerusalem until he reached the age of 71. Although he didn't focus much on the orthodox Muslims, he was something of an expert on the Druze community, a secret Muslim sect.

Pacradooni Kaloost Vartan, a son of a poor Armenian tailor, was born in Constantinople in 1835 where he attended the city's first American missionary school. After witnessing the dreadful inadequacies of battlefield medical facilities during the Crimean War, he resolved to become a surgeon, training in Scotland under the auspices of the Edinburgh Medical Missionary Society (EMMS, founded in 1841). He married a Scottish nurse named Mary Anne Stewart and immediately after the wedding he and his bride left for Palestine where they founded the Nazareth Hospital under EMMS, to whom he reported every quarter. Birthing the first hospital in Ottoman Galilee was not an easy task, but the young couple persevered despite constant rejection due to the peoples' unshakeable dependence on utilizing leeches and bone-menders, plus their prejudice against Protestant missionaries.

When Kaloost and Mary Anne arrived in Nazareth in 1861, the average life expectancy was twenty-two years for males and twenty-four years for females. The first floor of the house he rented in the old souq (marketplace or commercial quarter) housed the dispensary, with a separate room with four beds. After many difficulties, they purchased land in 1906 where the present hospital still stands. Kaloost died two years later. They might not have persevered those forty-seven years except for the assistance from Pastor John Zeller's church there.

Henry Tristram, the canon of the Durham Cathedral, once said of Zeller that he was "the only European who could venture to pass through the whole of Palestine without a military escort."[4] He was known by many, distinguished from Greek and Latin priests as the "priest of the Book." When Tristram told a sheikh that Zeller was his friend and brother, the reply that came was, "then you too are one of the Bible Christians."[5]

Practical Danger

The missionaries were constantly exposed to the attacks of predatory neighbors. For example, the Reverend Ludwig Schneller, who first moved to Jerusalem in 1854, was returning home from the city in company with another missionary when they were beaten and robbed, even stripped of their clothing. Later, he was attacked again in his home by robbers. The windows were smashed in, the doors broken with stones, and seven robbers armed with swords and guns burst into his room. Schneller was bidden, with a sword at his breast, to hold a light till they had taken all the clothes and articles of furniture. Finding little money, they struck him several times on the back with a sword in order to terrorize him into giving them more money, which the poor man did not possess.

Five months later, the robbers came again, thirsty for blood and death. Due to their homicidal resolve, Schneller was compelled to shoot at them, intending to do whatever was necessary to protect his wife and child. His marksmanship caused the wounded robbers to flee. The Schneller family had to abandon their home and take refuge within the walls of the city, but not for long. The Syrian massacres in the 1860s created thousands of widows and orphans. Schneller hurried into Syria, collected Maronite orphans, and brought them to Jerusalem where he placed them into his newly established home for orphans, aptly named the Syrian Orphanage. Beyond basic education, each boy learned a practical trade or farming skills, and the girls were educated in basic nursing wherever there was a mission related medical outlet. Sadly for the goal of indigenous evangelists witnessing to their fellow countryman, the most gifted of these young people eventually emigrated to the West.

Questions to Ponder

Do you agree with Reverend Schneller's decision to defend his home with violence? Is this type of response becoming of a follower of Christ?

FURTHER WORK by the CMS

In 1875, General Lake, an influential member of the Church Missionary Society, called a conference of CMS members who had a burden for the Muslims. Up to this time, ministry to the Muslims was unthinkable, not considered possible. Lake died before any definite plans were made, so the impetus which he initiated was threatened with extinction. Still, the CMS recognized that Palestine was a strategic land for such an undertaking among Muslims. They abandoned their plan of restricting the work to Christians after Bishop Gobat's death, therefore sensing God leading them toward more direct evangelism to Muslims.

Their first venture was to establish several schools for Druze children, but that had to be abandoned when Turkish opposition thwarted the effort. The Turkish authorities were continually throwing new obstacles in their path. For example, the Turkish Governor placed soldiers on sentry duty at the gates of churches to prevent the entrance of any Muslim. Undeterred, the CMS next set up a hospitality center for the pilgrims who passed by on their way to Hajj. Sadly, lack of funds compelled the CMS to abandon that ministry project.

Meanwhile, the Keswick Conferences in England responded to the request from CMS missionaries in Palestine to send single lady missionaries. In the late 1880s, missionary vision was reaching unprecedented heights and women came in ever-increasing numbers. Between 1888 and 1894, thirty single women uprooted to Palestine and thirteen of them were self-funded. These women established schools for girls (both day and boarding schools) and were indefatigable in visiting the homes of the people. They endeavored in every conceivable way to gather round themselves groups of neglected women and girls. Sometimes the Muslim women were astonished at their foreign visitors. "What do you want to teach us?" asked one woman, "We are after all only goats and asses."[6]

Visiting from house to house was indeed trying on their patience. One female missionary wrote the following account of what a typical visit was likely to encompass:

Picture a courtyard, which is entered by a shattered door, and, round this court, perhaps five to seven houses. In the summer time, the women, when not engaged in the fields or vineyards, congregate together in a courtyard to do their daily household work, such as sifting the corn, cleaning the grain, basket work, cooking, mending their one garment, combing their hair, and so forth. Into this court the missionary enters, Bible in hand, ready to speak to any one she may find, and as she enters her eye gladly and quickly sees a little group of women sitting quietly together in the center of their courtyard and she is apt to think what an especially good opportunity has fallen to her! Yet, after she has been speaking a few minutes, and the women seem to be listening, as she is anxious to drive the lesson home, suddenly the quiet and attention are broken by the shrill scream of a rooster, repeated and repeated, and the hens begin to cackle. The dogs start barking, for some stranger has come to beg a piece of bread, or a neighbor wants to buy some eggs. As the afternoon wears on, the husbands and the elder boys return from the fields, bringing with them herds of goats and sheep and oxen, and the whole little company must get up in order to make room for them to enter. By the time we settle down again, the thread is broken, and the children cry, and the women have only a scattered recollection of what has been taught them earlier.[7]

Yet the idea of education for females was beginning to be accepted by more progressive Muslim families; some sent their girls to learn reading, writing and needlework. Arithmetic was not desired however, since it was assumed women would never get involved in business, nor did they require geography since it was assumed they would never travel.

The greatest response from Muslims was due then to the introduction of medical work. At first, people distrusted the simple medicines of the missionaries. To make sure that they were not poisons, a dog was often subjected to the first dose before a Muslim would allow the medicine to enter their own body. Other times, the cross would be cursed immediately preceding an operation so as to ward off evil influences that may affect the outcome of the medical care. Be that as it may, the calm, patient, self-denying work of the missionary eventually triumphed over such fears. A single hospital had, in one year, 1,200 inpatients and 30,000 outpatients. Whether in the consulting room, the wards, or simply standing in the open with a medicine chest beside them, the medical missionaries found opportunities for giving Isa Al Masih the credit to any receptive persons. During medical treatment, even fanatical Muslims would listen to words which, if spoken in any other place, or by a non-medical person, would fill them with rage. The largest mission hospital of the Church Missionary Society was in Nablus, home of the most stringent Muslim population. Normally, providing medical help had a quieting influence both in Nablus and Gaza. In Es Salt, Kerak, and Acca, the Church Missionary Society stationed medical missionaries where local's houses served as clinics.

Archibald Forder

In 1891, Archibald Forder and his wife left England bound for Moab. For the next thirteen years they lived among the Muslims of Palestine, faithfully sowing Gospel seeds into the rough, trodden earth. He recalls numerous instances in his memoirs of opportunities to tell Muslims about Jesus Christ and their need for His perfect atonement. Occasionally, he was able to witness results. One day after departing from Hebron, he arrived at a village called Dawimee and found himself afforded the opportunity to preach inside the local mosque. However, his life was quickly threatened. He might have been killed if not for a kind man who offered Archibald sanctuary in his home:

He put me in a corner of his yard, and as it was sunset I had my supper. After this my host and his uncle came and sat down with me and I began to tell them of Jesus the Savior. For two hours they listened very attentively and asked many questions. On into the night we talked. They said, "We never knew these things before, now we have no excuse; we are glad you came; there is no way but Jesus." The next morning early I lay as they thought asleep, I heard them telling others all I told them, so my visit was not in vain.[8]

1900-1978

The "Preparandi Institute" (a seminary) was attempted in 1905 for candidates for ordination as pastors, but the lack of students led to its closing. A boarding-school for girls was opened in 1892. Then in 1902, this school was merged with the Syria and Palestine girls boarding-schools which were taken over from the Female Education Society based in Bethlehem. By 1910, CMS had fourteen couples serving in Palestine, five of whom were medical missionaries, plus thirty-one unstoppable single lady missionaries in their mission stations. The members of their congregations numbered 2,323, having doubled since Bishop Gobat's death in 1879. However, as Richter wrote in 1910, "It cannot be said how many of them are converted Muhammadans."[9]

An ordained missionary, whether European or native, soon finds that his efforts to reach the people are limited by barriers which have not been broken down. "A catechist, employed to follow up cases that have been in the hospital by visits to the villages from which these cases come, has often told me how exceedingly limited even his work is."[10] An occasional visit may be satisfactory, but, as soon as it is repeated, say once a month, the people wander away, having nothing to say to their visitor.

Reverend T.F. Wolters, a CMS official, wrote: "Whether the day of visitation for the Moslem has come or not, the hard fact, as far as my observation and experience lead me to judge, is that the Moslem is still very far from being accessible to direct effort, except when he is under medical care."[11] Still, the Anglican Church members in Palestine doubled in size between 1879 and 1910, and many who contributed to that number were Jews and even former Muslims. Rev. C. T. Wilson gave this optimistic report:

As to the work among the Muhammadans, it would seem as if the day of grace were about to break. Our medical missions remove prejudices, overcome opposition, and open a way to many hearts that have been hitherto closed to the truth. There is encouragement, but the red of dawn must not be mistaken for the full light of day. Our experiences can again point to the fact that, before the day can come, many social and political limitations have to be removed which hinder Moslems from making an open confession of faith. How and when this will come to pass, no one can say. It may mean enduring painful conflict, yet it may happen overnight. Who knows? Grateful for the dawn, we are waiting patiently until God reveals His purposes of grace.[12]

Then he added:

Palestine is the stoniest ground to cultivate by missionaries, especially because the opposition of the Turkish authorities is so deeply rooted there. Equally distracting is the never-ending tendency of the church members in Palestine to make large demands on the mission. It seems particularly difficult here to educate the people to aspire to become financially self-supporting. It is a fact that Christians of all confessions in Palestine have been spoiled by the competition among foreign governments and churches in the effort to win them, so that all benefits bestowed are accepted as a matter of course. And, if one congregation is thought to be treated more generously, the others at once become jealous.[13]

James Addison's perspective in his mission history book in 1940, *The Christian Approach to the Moslem* was that

the Arab Moslems are the most backward people in Palestine. However, thanks to British rule, Hebrew energy and the activities of Christian missions, the three chief elements of the population are well supplied with educational facilities. There are over 1,400 schools in this small country. In the 402 schools maintained by the government, the great majority of the pupils are Muhammadan. The 193 Christian schools care for most of the Christian children, with a substantial Moslem minority in the few secondary schools.[14]

Addison continued, writing about Palestine:

For the last twenty years, an emphasis upon a direct approach to Moslems has steadily grown, because of the greater religious freedom with the lands being freed from Ottoman rule to European rule. What was reported in 1927 is still true: "Evangelistic work with Moslems meets with far less hostility than at any other period in Protestant mission history. However, greater readiness to listen does not translate to the Muslim becoming a Christ-follower, thus converts were few."[15]

No doubt Catholic and Protestant apprehension over the future of mission and Christian institutions in the Holy Land was alleviated in 1922 when the League of Nations approved the establishment of the British Mandate over Palestine. Suddenly, the land was flooded with missionaries and "religious workers" of many stripes. The mainline American churches had not been particularly active in Palestine before World War I, leaving that field to the British, but now evangelical American Christian organizations, including the Southern Baptists, the Assemblies of God, the Church of the Nazarene, the

CMA, the Society of Friends (Quakers) and the YMCA all took up residence in the land. During the 1920s, more than thirty Protestant missionary societies from different countries, in addition to Catholic and Orthodox missions, became active in Palestine. Various methods were employed: evangelism, both public and personal, the sale and distribution of the Scriptures and other Christian literature, schools of primary and secondary grade, medical work in the hospitals and dispensaries, and social services, including work with young people rendered by the YMCA and YWCA

Different Articles, Different Approaches

In 1923, an article appeared in *The Moslem World* by Archibald Forder entitled "Evangelism in Palestine." Forder laments the present situation missionaries face in Palestine due to an increase in Muslim education throughout the land, which has the backing of the government.

The Moslem is more and more satisfied with his own system of religion, and more against the preaching of Christianity, thus religious meetings are not frequented as they were before the war, and it is becoming more and more difficult to get Moslem boys and girls into Christian schools.[16]

Forder goes on to argue that the printed page is now the optimal option for evangelism to Muslims in Palestine:

During recent years there have come into active existence agencies for the printing and circulating of printed matter especially to meet the present difficulty, and it is possible to evangelize the Moslem in a quiet way by means of the printed messenger, for the average Moslem will read if the material is put in his way, but is not anxious to look such up for himself.[17]

Sixteen years later in the same journal, E. Theodore Bachmann published an article entitled: "Mission Frontier in Palestine." Bachmann argued that education, not literature, was the greatest tool that a missionary could utilize, and an orphanage was the way to do it!

Why a Syrian Orphanage in Palestine? Once the boys and girls have entered they receive, among other things, a sound Christian training. When you hear them recite Bible verses, sing hymns, answer questions on the catechism or about the right way of life, you know that their teachers have been effective. Their religious education reaches its climax in confirmation. Although this rite is voluntary, most children desire it. Moslem youngsters would first have to be baptized. But generally they do not venture to take this step, owing especially to the death penalty - or at least the social pressure for any one breaking with the faith.[18]

Bachmann admitted that even with this "Orphanage as School" model, very few converts from Islam had been witnessed by the missionaries.

Question to Ponder

Looking at the articles in *The Moslem World* by Forder and Bachmann, which opinion do you agree with? Defend your answer.

BAPTISTS IN PALESTINE

Dale Thorne, who worked at the Nazareth Baptist School from 1966 until 1983, offered me his recollections about the school and other Baptist ventures in Palestine:

From its founding in 1948 the Nazareth Baptist School has enrolled Muslim students. When I worked with the school from 1966 until 1983 the ratio was roughly 10% Muslim to 90% Christian. Today their 1,000 member student body breaks down to 25% Muslim and 75% Christian. However, as throughout the history of the school, all the students are required to partici-pate in all activities of the school including the Bible classes and chapel services which contain a strong evangelistic element. They are also involved in summer camps run by the school at the Baptist Village Camp and Confer-ence Center. I know of no notable conversions by students in the school but the Muslim graduate community strongly supports the ministry of the school. In the 1960s, Southern Baptists operated a vocational training boarding school at the Baptist Village. The majority of the students were Muslim, coming from the Bedouin families of the Negev and the Circassian villages in the Galilee. This was a rather unique school which was run by Christians with mainly Jewish teachers for Muslim students. The school closed in the late '60s when it was unable to obtain government recognition of its program and the facilities were changed into a camp and conference center. From the 1950s until the 1980s Baptists operated the hospital in Gaza that was leased from the Anglicans. The ministry there also included a nursing school and a school of allied health sciences that taught medical lab work and physical therapy. Some of the workers and students became believers, but I do not know the number or names of them.[19]

End-of-Chapter Reflections

Ray Register is the name that comes to mind as I ponder ministry among Palestinian Muslims. Indeed, Dale Thorne referred to him as "the Baptist representative most active in personal evangelism among Muslims"[20] during the middle of the 20th century. He argues that from his experience, the majority of Muslims who came to know the Lord do so because of the personal witness of close friends and family. Some of the first ones in the chain of events even had a visitation of the Lord Jesus in a dream or vision. I can testify to this reality and a common factor seems to be the yearning for a faithful "friend who sticks closer than a brother."

Muslims are not mavericks. They live their entire lives dependent on the guidance of those they most trust; those whom they sense care deeply for their welfare. When they experience seeing the love and commitment within a group of Christ-followers, they can sense that they will have a family that won't desert them. That is the point of birthing a house fellowship. One Muslim said to Register, "I can't leave my old family's demands until I have a new family to catch me."[21]

Register continues,

If God opens their minds to grasp that Isa Al Masih is alive and still forgives sin, removing shame, and promises eternal life without fear of Hell, we don't need a lot of technique to see them call on the Lord and be saved. However, becoming an open disciple is quite another mountain to climb, especially if he or she doesn't run away but stays close to the clan.[22]

Concerning discipling a Muslim convert to Christianity, Register recommends reading with them from the Bible, starting in Genesis or Psalms and Proverbs from the Old Testament. The books of John and Acts also provide the believer with New Testament models.

From a conference in Canada, Register "registered" nine factors that others agreed God has used in drawing Muslims to Himself:

1. Reading the words of Jesus in a Gospel.
2. Sensing a visitation by Jesus in a dream.
3. Being freed from demonic oppression by calling on Jesus' name.
4. Believers helping one get free from an abusive relationship.
5. Disillusionment with society or their own religious experience.
6. Desire to be free from an immoral lifestyle.
7. Freedom from the fear of death and the Judgment.
8. Women discovering how Jesus honors and values women.
9. Having a history from childhood of having personal contact with Allah.

Register sums up his experience with four different types of MBBs:

1. Grateful believers: those who realize Christ set them free forever!
2. Switching converts: they found Islamic religious practices boring, unfulfilling and desired "western freedom."
3. Hateful converts: they suffered under a cruel teacher or religious relative, but could not live without believing in God.
4. Converts who are seeking material benefits or help to get to the West.

That said, Register agrees that God's people must continue to pray with expectation. He WILL draw a remnant from EVERY background, tongue and people to Himself. Keep looking until you find the "man of peace" (c.f. Luke 10:6) who will start the chain response among those who respect them, as illustrated by Lydia and Cornelius in the book of Acts.

Questions to Ponder

What percentage of the Muslims described by Archibald Forder were accustomed to learning through the medium of written text? Might leisurely reading clubs with tea and snacks (for example) yield more robust reflection on the claims of Isa Al Masih? What about your Muslim friends where you are?

One might have thought that a significant number of Palestinian Muslims, who felt deserted by other Muslims but who were befriended and provided with services from Christians, would have bowed the knee to Isa Al Masih. Why do you think so few actually did?

Why have the multitude of Christian schools in Muslim countries over the years been almost universally unfruitful in seeing Muslims decide to follow Isa Al Masih?

Ray Register has argued that Muslim-background believers should marry another Muslim to whom he/she has been perfectly clear regarding living as a resolute obedient follower of Isa Al Masih. Doing so has the best chance of affecting others in the clan. The potential mate should be well acquainted with the Christian friends of the believer, not jealous, or resentful of them. Do you agree with this strategy? Why or why not?

7

EGYPT

Pre-1850

FOR FIFTEEN YEARS (1768-1783), THE MORAVIAN CHURCH IN EGYPT conducted an important mission, not directly to the Muslims, but to the Coptic Orthodox Church, endeavoring to see them become more evangelical; a more effective witness to the Muslim population. Dr. Hawker, who had failed to gain entry into Persia, acquired residency in Cairo but he and his three teammates did not attempt to convert Muslims, apparently with one exception. That exception was Weiniger, a German tailor, who was approached by an educated Muslim who said:

"I prayed to God and God promised to send me a man who would tell me how to be saved. You are the man so speak plainly to me."

"No," replied Weiniger, "you know that I dare not speak about religion to a Muhammadan."

"Yes," said the mameluke, "I know that if the authorities heard you, you and I would be put to death. But fear not, I am an honest man and I promise not to betray you."[1]

Thus encouraged, Weiniger spoke of Jesus crucified and resurrected while they sat under a fig tree in a garden. The mameluke, faithful to his promise, remained a loyal Christian, though in secret, at least until the Moravians left Egypt.

In 1825, the Church Missionary Society (CMS) sent workers to Egypt and the American Presbyterians followed in 1854. However, both agencies concluded that reaching Muslims directly was problematic. They reasoned that it would be more fruitful in the long run to see God revive the Coptic Church so that they could engage in Muslim evangelism. The Anglicans encouraged Copts who experienced redemption to stay in the Coptic Church as "salt and light." The American Presbyterians, however, after getting blocked from teaching Scripture, encouraged the Copts who were coming to their Bible studies, when threatened by the priests, to form Bible-based Protestant churches. Either because few Muslims came to faith via anyone, and/or because CMS workers in Egypt died or left without replacements being available, that British mission's work was shut down less than 10 years later.

1850-1900

Sa'id Pasha (1854-1863) was a progressive wāli (leader) eager to establish greater religious liberty in Egypt. This opened the door for the American Presbyterians, who were nearly all evangelical at that time in their history. Entering Egypt in 1854, they soon became the largest Protestant mission endeavor in the country. James Barnett (1817-1884) and Gulian Lansing (1815-1892) transferred from Damascus to join new recruit Thomas McCague and start the Presbyterian efforts. There, Scottish missionary John Hogg was added in 1859, and Andrew Watson arrived in 1861 to make up their early team. Other notables were B. F. Pinkerton (who later broke off to start a Plymouth Brethren work), Miss M.J. McKnown, and the more renowned Charles Watson, who founded the American University of Cairo in 1912.

Initially, effort was exerted to witness to Muslims in the missionaries' earliest months. However, there was soon a consensus that two things must precede any wide spread response from Muslims. First, the Coptic Church and other Christians in Egypt must be revived. Second, God must change the political, cultural and economic grip of Islam upon the peoples of Egypt.

Many obstacles littered their path. Egypt's intense heat, disease, and overwork snuffed out the lives of many missionaries. Others left ill or to early retirement, deciding they should minister back home. The Crimean and American Civil War brought added hardships, including financial support periodically cut off. But those difficulties were not as depressing as the lack of religious liberty to declare the Message among Muslims. Missionaries, especially Lansing, spent much time battling to gain equal rights for Christians and to secure those same rights for the scattered converts from Islam between 1858 and 1864. At times it was feared that open Muslim hostility might replicate the mutiny that occurred in India against the British.

From the very beginning of missionary work in Egypt, there has been the hope in the hearts of the missionaries that Muslims would eventually "bow the knee" to Isa Al Masih, despite their deep-seated prejudice against Christianity. This prejudice on the part of the Muslim, and hope on the part of the missionary, is reflected in a letter written by pioneer missionaries Rev. and Mrs. Thomas McCague. In reference to their teacher of Arabic, a learned Muslim sheikh, they wrote:

Sometimes when he is reading the Bible, he will often appear struck with some passage, and stop and say "Beautiful." But because death is the penalty which the Moslem law inflicts upon any apostate from their faith, that's as far as it goes. But we hope this state of things will not long continue.[2]

Another letter, written in 1856 reads:

I must commence preaching in Arabic before long. But there is a hindrance to my preparation. Our teacher is a Moslem and if I write a discourse and wish him to criticize it, he is unable to enter into the spirit of Christian language, and furthermore shuts down, thinking I want to convert him to my faith instead of wanting help criticism.[3]

That this prejudice was often unsettling was further aggravated by the fact that in certain localities in Cairo, Christians were at times harassed while walking on the streets with Muslims. An example is detailed in the following incident related by Mrs. McCague:

One day we went to the bazaars to do a little shopping, with Mr. Barnett going along as interpreter. I had become accustomed in the street to sometimes hear the children say, "You Nazarene, you dog, you pig," but this day men muttered and scowled. Mr. Barnett said, "It is your dress." I thought I was looking very nice in my pretty green cashmere. I hurried home and never again wore my green dress in the streets of Egypt. Green is regarded by the Moslems as a sacred color and none but the descendants of Muhammad are permitted to wear it.[4]

These pioneers soon found that Muhammadans (as they referred to them) were not yet open to biblical truth, concluding that their work must begin with the Copts. However, concern for the Muslims was not in short supply, as evidenced by their purpose statement: "To gather in converts whose lives should be an incontrovertible proof to the Moslems of the divinity of the Christian religion."[5] This is also seen in a report by Dr. Barnett (a transfer to Egypt from Syria) published in the November 1857 edition of "The Christian Instructor": "These Christians must be changed before their moral influence can be brought to bear upon the vast numbers of Muhammadans by which they are surrounded. And who stands responsible for this great work more than we do?"[6] He then adds,

Now, Muhammadans there are listening to a Muhammadan brother preaching Christ. People at home must be patient and remember that work in the north [Middle East] has been going on for a number of years; here in Egypt, it has scarcely had a beginning. Revive these dead formal Christians and the surrounding Muhammadans and Jews will take knowledge of them that they have been with Jesus and seeing their good works and their holy lives, they, too, will fall down and worship God.[7]

Questions to Ponder

What was Barnett thinking? Would non-believing Muslims and Jews "fall down and worship God" purely as a result of seeing the good works and holy lives of those who already called themselves Christians?

IN AN ARTICLE WRITTEN for *The United Presbyterian,* entitled "Egypt Revisited," Dr. McCague wrote the following:

From the beginning of our mission, we were privileged to carry on our work with but little, if any, open manifestation of opposition or trouble from the outside. Little ripples on the sea, however were enough to show us that opposing elements existed, which would only require a disturbing cause to raise a storm.[8]

But through the warnings of danger from foreign consuls and through their influence, the Pasha assembled the sheikhs and with a firm hand warned them that if a Christian was touched, their own heads would pay the penalty. This had the desired effect and all passed off quietly. To quote from a letter written at this time,

The Moslem excitement is all passed by...two of the highest officers here were executed and others taken prisoner to Constantinople. This will teach the Arabs a good lesson that Europeans are not to be promiscuously slaughtered at their will. Perhaps you may think it strange to hear me, a missionary, plead for immediate justice to be administered by the sword upon this poor, degraded people. But I tell you, to make every murder they commit a speedy example by the executioners is the only way to keep this people in peace with Christians and especially with European Christians.[9]

Missionary uneasiness was understandable when taking into account the dreadful eruption of Islamic fury in Damascus the following year, when five to eight thousand Orthodox Christians were massacred in Syria.

The firm position taken by Sa'id Pasha in Egypt removed immediate danger from such an outbreak of opposition there, though the laws clearly favored Muslims and made life difficult for the Christian minority. Government regulations required all hostility between Europeans and natives to be settled before an Egyptian court, while evangelistic services were forbidden to be held outside of designated buildings. Muslims were understandably very hesitant to send their children to mission schools, although one school had nine girls from a Muslim family. Although some of the missionaries wrote home discouraged about making spiritual progress with any Arabs, Mrs. McCague did not waver, saying: "We are working for a good and faithful Master, who is ever jealous of His own cause, and who will assist all who labor for Him. The silver and gold and the hearts of all men are in His hands and if we are faithful He will help us."[10]

A marked feature of the educated people of Egypt, namely their disposition to read and discuss religious truths, was recognized by the early missionaries. Accordingly, stress was laid on producing literature as the best means of reaching the Muslim population. From the beginning, a considerable number of Bibles were distributed and usually sold for a small sum. A reading room had been opened in a missionary's house where natives could discreetly peruse and discuss religious matters away from snooping relatives. The following year a shop was rented on one of the main streets in Cairo, with Awad Hanna, a Coptic convert, in charge. Bibles were obtained from the British and Foreign Bible Society at Malta, while books and tracts were donated from the American Mission Press at Beirut. Passers-by would enter the shop often to talk with the shop keepers and thumb through Christian Scripture. Another book shop was opened in Alexandria.

In addition to this seed-sowing in the cities, attempts were made in those early years to bring the whole population of the country within reach of an evangelizing influence. A system of colportage was commenced among the chief towns of the Delta and later, on a more extended scale, throughout the provinces of Upper Egypt. The first itinerary in the Delta was made in April 1860, by Rev. McCague, who was accompanied by Mr. Awad Hanna. They spent three weeks in Tanta at a Muslim festival celebrating the life of Ahmad al-Badawi, as well as the Coptic festival of the Lady Damianeh on the borders of the "Eastern Province," that is the ancient Land of Goshen. In a letter from Tanta, after describing their room which overlooked a small court containing two buffaloes, a cow, a donkey, a mare, a colt, turkeys and chickens, plus recounting their host's kindness in giving him a first portion of meat with his own hands, McCague joyfully claimed they sold 1,750 piastres worth of books: mostly Scriptures.

The extension of the work in the Nile Valley had become so important that Lansing, Hogg and McCague purchased a boat, The Ibis, in which to journey up and down the mighty river. On the first trip, Rev. and Mrs. McCague took four Egyptian assistants with them and twelve boxes of Scriptures and other books on the Christian faith. During their five-week trip, they sold many more books than they expected, all the while establishing two new mission stations in Assouit and Luxor. McCague, assisted by Awad, loaded a donkey with Bibles and went through the streets crying aloud that the Holy Bible was for sale! In his book *Egypt's Princes*, Dr. Gulian Lansing describes the second

Ibis trip when $1,000 worth of books was sold. As can be imagined, this confirmed in their minds that literature distribution, as the method for proclamation, was truly the Lord's leading.

Shortly after the forced return of Reverend and Mrs. McCague to America in 1861 on account of his wife and son's threatened blindness due to ophthalmia, they received a letter from Dr. Lansing telling of his negotiations with the Egyptian government for the purchase of the government press at Boulak. He wrote: "We trust this will put us in the way of supplying Egypt with a Christian literature." A month later he wrote, "We are not to have their printing press. The Counsellors stepped in and said they could not allow this press, which had been a fountain of Islamic learning, become Christian."[11] Still, the work of the Nile Mission Press patiently making the case for Christ's sovereignty gave hope to the missionaries that there would eventually be a gathering of Muslims into the Kingdom.

In the correspondence of those years, there is a very evident note of joy at each indication of the gathering of a Muslim into that Kingdom. Dr. Hogg wrote that the boys in his school at Alexandria "are beginning to search for themselves at midday, whether these things told them in the morning are so." He adds, "May the Spirit lift up the veil and show them the loving heart of the despised Nazarene."[12] Scottish missionary John Hogg accepted appointment to join the Presbyterians and Andrew Watson arrived in 1861. Their policy from the start was to proclaim the Gospel to the whole population of Egypt. However, it was soon agreed that two things must precede a widespread response from Muslims (as mentioned earlier): first, the Coptic Church and other Christians in Egypt must be revived. Secondly, the political social and economic grip of Islam on Egypt must be minimized.

Still, there were encouragements. Ahmed Fahmi, a Muslim student who became a teacher at a Presbyterian school, was baptized on November 26, 1877. Progress toward religious liberty in those years of ferment, 1822–1922, were advanced most by liberal Muslims and evangelical Christians. Nevertheless, foreigners increasingly bore a stigma that they were government agents of their home countries, which curtailed their contribution to the cause of religious liberty. The government wasn't the only problem. John Hogg wrote that a great stumbling block in the way of doing much among Muslims is the Coptic church. Muhammadans have not the means in this present time of knowing what Christianity is. The missionaries continue to visualize their work among the Copts as instrumental to what God was going to do among the Muslim populace.[13]

Dr. Lansing emphasized that everything they do must aim at attracting and training nationals to take up a ministry. This included taking Egyptian Christians with them on the boats up and down the Nile to sell literature and attend church meetings, while encouraging isolated believers to become part of that training. At first, the Protestant missionaries tried to avoid head-on collision with the Coptic Church by attending their worship services then conducting evangelical services later in the afternoon. Sometimes, however, angry Copts and Muslims joined forces against these Protestant intruders, initiating book burning and boycotts of the schools. It is easy to see why the Presbyterians decided they must form separate Protestant churches. As in Armenia, mobs stirred up by the priests attacked Protestant homes and outspoken evangelists were driven out of town.

Heather Sharkey, Associate Professor in the Department of Near Eastern Languages and Civilizations at the University of Pennsylvania, wrote an article in 2005 entitled: "Empire and Muslim conversion: Historical reflections on Christian missions in Egypt." Sharkey's thesis is that Anglo-American Protestant missionaries encountered fierce resistance from Muslims despite the small number of Muslim conversions and how they inadvertently galvanized Egyptian anti-colonial nationalists with Islamist movements. She admits that it is difficult to assess missionaries' motives, social influences, and the legacies of centuries of history between Christians and Muslims which portray Christian missionaries as neo-Crusaders posing a continuing threat to the integrity of Muslim societies.

The 1875 Anglican Conference for Mission to Muslims including Bishop Gobat (Palestine), Koelle, Zeller, Robert Bruce (Iran) and Bishop French (India), decided ministry must concentrate on the Arabs who most influence all Muslim peoples. This prompted the CMS to re-enter Egypt to focus on Muslims. That mission-minded Christians focused on the redemption of Muslims in the world at all, was a result of the decade of the 1880s. The student-led Christian evangelical movement on college and university campuses in America and Europe ignited educated, talented, and ambitious men and women to choose missionary careers in subsequent years. Suddenly, finances for Protestant foreign missions became available as never before in history. This enabled mission agencies to send out more people, buy properties, and develop social service institutions including schools, hospitals, bookstores, and conference centers. The Student Volunteer Movement inspired Christians to believe that Muslims would finally come into the kingdom. Mission leaders also became more optimistic because of the expansion of railways, telegraphs, steamships, and communication which made overseas missionary enterprises more logistically feasible than ever before.

Thus, beginning in the 1880s, a new burst of European expansion in Africa and Asia was paralleled by an upsurge of support for foreign missions from North America and Britain. For the first time, Anglo-American Protestant missionaries began to promote evangelization of Muslims. From North Africa to India, missionaries offered social services, specifically education and medical care, accompanied by distributing Christian literature, initiating conversations about the claims of Christ, and sponsoring public lectures. Although their efforts gained relatively few Muslim converts, it did inspire a backlash among some anti-colonial nationalists and Islamic religious loyalists who rallied fellow Muslims by denouncing missionaries as cultural imperialists. Furthermore, continued ministry became increasingly untenable as decolonization became political policy of the Western nations.

Back in Egypt, however, by 1880 Hogg was giving more attention to Muslim evangelism in his theological classes and prepared a booklet under the title *Neither is there Salvation in any Other.* He taught in the seminary because he contended that the answer to Islam must be demonstrated in the church's life. In a pastoral letter he wrote:

"The work for which the church exists is that for which the Son of God became incarnate. As Christ's work was not completed by his incarnation but only then begun, the work of the Christians is not completed when you become an organized congregation; it is only begun."[14]

In another letter, he wrote that it was not so much the number as the nature of the churches that would determine success or failure of the mission to Muslims. He urged the evangelical church to activate itself in reaching out to its Muslim neighbors and prayed for a baptism of the Spirit on the congregations.

In the early 1880s, something of a movement took place through the inquiries made by Muslims who were disgusted with Islam. In the twenty years leading up to this, the American Presbyterian Mission had baptized twenty-six Muslims. Between 1881 and 1882, twenty-two more professed their faith in Christ, and Muslim students attending mission schools became general knowledge among government officials. In some places, Muslims even attended Protestant church services. Hogg wrote: "If Egypt is given religious liberty worthy of the name our success amongst Muhammadans will soon surpass that amongst Copts."[15]

That "if" was never fulfilled. Mission agencies assumed religious freedom would increase under British control to the point that Muslims would be willing to openly become disciples of Christ. However, family retribution and British government restrictions on the missionaries (to prevent riots) continued to hinder evangelism among Muslims. Yet, as so often has been the case, the Holy Spirit moved despite human opposition. By 1895, the American Presbyterians had baptized nearly 100 converts from Islam. New mission stations were set up in Tanta in 1893, and Benna, Zagazig and along the Red Sea in 1894. Giving a condescending nod to any non-denominational faith missionaries which were emerging in the latter part of the 1800s, Richter wrote: "For such patient work and preparation, one is inclined to feel that even freelance missionaries may be useful if they are not too fanciful and sectarian in their views."[16]

Thornton

In 1898, Douglas Thornton, who was a top recruiter for the Student Volunteer Movement (SVM) in Britain, chose Cairo over India and China as the greatest need for world evangelization, arriving later that same year. He was a pioneer in Egypt with a vision for the entire Muslim world; a man of one idea: reaching the whole world for Jesus! Thornton was a son of an evangelical Anglican vicar whose family had been leaders in the great evangelical revival of the 18th century. He was known at Cambridge as having a fiery devotion to the Lord Jesus and the work of influencing others to faith in Christ as well as to the cause of world mission. He was nurtured under Charles Simeon of Holy Trinity church who gave him vision for worldwide mission, as Simeon had done for Henry Martyn. Thornton was very involved in the Student Volunteer Movement and organized the first SVM conference in England in 1896. Their aim was to send out 1,000 men (including 150 from

Cambridge) into pioneer missions as a result of the conference. Before he went to Egypt, he was urging each denomination to seriously plan how to send out thousands of workers to the mission field. While his goals were ridiculed by some, his reply was always that the church of Jesus Christ is involved in so many secondary issues that distract from the major call to the church to evangelize the world.

Thornton was a missiologist before the word was coined. He was stunned that spiritually-minded pastors gave almost no thought to the world outside of the West. In July of 1897, he applied to join the CMS and although he was aware of opportunities in China and India, he increasingly saw Islam as the greatest strategic spiritual stronghold resisting Christ. Thornton highlighted the three key areas: India, Egypt and what he called Hausaland (northern Nigeria, Cameroon, and Senegal) but decided that a breakthrough in the Arabic-speaking lands would influence the entire Muslim world. He considered the key Arabic-speaking centers to be Mecca, Damascus, Jerusalem and Cairo, with the most influential being Cairo. In August 1897, he wrote to the CMS: "I feel that the hardest spots in the Muslim world really do need proportionally more attention than CMS has been able to give them even in the last 30 years."[17] He received his assignment to Cairo in December of 1898.

Thornton believed that marriage was a ministry enhancement. He found a like-minded woman named Elaine Anderson whom he married in Cairo in 1899 after declaring to her:

I will not by the help of God allow the world to dazzle me in wealth, in popularity, or the soul I see before me to divert ways. The one is that of settlement and ease the other data pioneering as a preacher – profit all the time I do not believe that God wants me to live comfortably in the sense of settling down. I trust you my fiancée will always stand in readiness to bear separation if the Lord shall cause it. Maybe we shall stay in Cairo many years. It may be that we moved to Sudan of the Hausaland; I trust you will not think me selfish if I work at night in years to come, for I fear there will be very little sitting room time in my active life. God willing, Cairo must undergo a spiritual transformation and how to bring this about calls for our constant prayers. It must be done![18]

Two years later in 1901, Elaine gave birth to their son Cecil.

Upon his arrival to Egypt, he drew up a strategy paper listing five separate goals: 1) evangelistic meetings for Muslims, which will in the future have Egyptians running them, 2) training classes in English for teachers or young men, 3) Bible classes for Coptic and Muslim teachers, 4) development of apologetic, devotional literature and Bible study materials, and 5) establishment of Christian schools. He confessed that he did not have time to think through medical work or how to reach women. Believing in thought through methodology, Thornton worked hard at learning Arabic and grew a mustache and beard as he was committed to becoming an insider in Egyptian culture. Reportedly, his colleagues thought him rash because of his self-abandonment to this rather eccentric labor for the kingdom of God.

Thornton wanted Cairo to become a center for training workers with Muslims because, in his mind, it was the best place to learn Arabic and it was a healthy place to live, with substantial toleration by the Muslims and the British-influenced government. He particularly targeted the educated Muslims of Cairo, introducing investigative Bible classes, evangelistic lecture series, and one-on-one discussions. It was his great confidence in the power of literature which led to a literature conference for the Muslim world.

He also wanted to set up a hospital to better equip Arab Christians learning how to make disciples among Muslims, as well as a training program for workers in residence in Cairo. He read theological, historical and scientific books in Arabic to widen his vocabulary and read the Arabic daily newspapers, as well as spending much time visiting Egyptians for discussions. He even had open air meetings by the Nile in the evening because the British had guaranteed freedom to propagate religion within limits. He would rig up a sheet and have a lantern show, explaining the Gospel to the boatmen as he sat on their boats.

At Easter 1901, he had the joy of baptizing two Muslims, one Egyptian and one Syrian, having spent many months discipling them both. He felt they should stay with the Copts, not the Presbyterians, so that they could influence the Coptic Church to take interest in making disciples among the Muslims. He also started a small fellowship in his house led by Sheikh Boulos and a Jewish believer; it was called The Society of Faith which reportedly had four branches in the city. One of his favorite ways to spend his time was in the bookshop near Al Azhar University, which became a center for religious discussions. The bookshop had a separate entrance for the upper-class educated Egyptians who didn't like to mix with the Al Azhar students, whom they probably viewed as too dogmatic.

After mastering the language, Thornton produced a 500-page Arabic prayer book, spending hours with the Muslims in the printing press until they had a good understanding of the Gospel. But soon he realized that the Muslims needed different literature than the Christians, so he started a new publishing house even though perhaps only 6% of the Muslims in Egypt were literate. In reaction, Muslims also started publishing books to counter the Christian claims.

He gave six reasons why literature was even more important than personal witness in pioneer situations with Muslims: 1) street preaching is not permitted because it raises angry reaction, 2) full-time missionaries find it impossible to gain entrance into middle-class homes except for doctors, 3) visits by full-time missionaries to Muslims in their shops, factories or offices creates deep suspicions of the owners, 4) evangelistic gatherings in homes only work if the host does the inviting of his friends, 5) Christian schools have many limitations, and 6) Thornton never found distributing Arabic Bibles to be well received by the Muslims.

As a practitioner of what he taught, Thornton started *The Orient and Occident* magazine. "Each edition had a Bible passage with a simple study. There were drawings to illustrate. There were articles on aspects of faith, often in a question and answer format."[19] Initially, 7,000 copies were printed and mailed throughout Egypt and Sudan. After a time, it was not uncommon for people throughout both countries to pay for a subscription. Thornton however was not a natural business man and continued to gravitate toward public meetings and face-to-face interactions with Egyptian Muslims. Trying to maintain both was exhausting for him as no reinforcements were sent his way. One of his friends wrote about him: "He's tired, with a worn expression and a face so palpably thin – writing in his study, unable to do anything but think of the work and its needs and too tired to stop thinking."[20]

In 1907, Thornton contracted dengue fever and yet he refused to slow down. The hurried pace only weakened his immune system further, and in September he was further diagnosed with pneumonia and typhoid. Elaine and his friends cared for him and Scripture was often read aloud at his bedside. Sometimes he would speak with great clarity to both Elaine and Cecil, and other times he would ramble incoherently as the fever took its toll on his body and mind. "Sometimes he seemed to be preaching a sermon. Once he shouted out, 'wonderful opportunities!' And another time, 'joy in service.' As he died, he said quite distinctly, 'Yes, Lord!'"[21]

The Egypt General Mission

The Egypt General Mission (EGM) started with a group of university students and businessmen from the university in Belfast, Ireland. The group was formed to encourage one another to follow the Lord fully, including inviting missionaries to their weekly meeting. That led to them spending half the night in prayer once a week. On February 16, 1897, during one of these half-nights of prayer, there were thirteen people present. The need of the foreign mission field was brought so convincingly to their hearts by the Spirit of God that before separating, those present were constrained to draw up and sign the following declaration: "Lord I am at thy disposal for foreign missionary work as soon as, and when, where ever thou callest."[22]

It was laid on the heart of a Brother Cleaver that God wanted to send out a group of seven together. They then went to a student missionary conference in Derbyshire where they heard Miss Van Sommer, a missionary recruiter, plead the cause of Egypt. Amazingly, they discovered that she had been praying for exactly a group of seven to go to Egypt! One of the seven got his call confirmed while visiting short-term in Algeria; another through a pamphlet entitled *A Challenge to Faith*, by Lilias Trotter. Another, while waiting to visit a pastor, read on his office wall the text of Genesis 45:18: "Come unto me and I will give you the good land of Egypt and you shall eat the fat of the land."

Arriving January 31, 1898 in Egypt, the group of seven was introduced to the other missionaries by Miss Van Sommer, which helped their acceptance. They also represented five different denominations. God led them to use suitable language teachers and by visiting Syria they were able to get coaching by workers there. They rented a small room for Bible studies which were frequently broken up by fellows bearing overripe tomatoes, their favorite weapon. Still, a small number of Muslims became interested and one of them, Hafiz, profess faith in Christ. For a while all went well, but as the only son, home life pressure proved too much for him. He eventually ceased to have any communication with the missionaries. "Of the others, we kept in touch with some through our Arabic Gospel magazine and have occasionally met with others. Some of them are undoubtedly no longer Moslems, but neither have they been willing to pay the price of coming out on the side of Christ."[23]

Typically missionaries want to do something of evangelism from the beginning of their time in a country, and these brothers were no exception. Thus they translated a tract by a Dr. Rouse, entitled *Which of the two: Muhammad or Christ?* They distributed them partly from a book depot and partly in the streets. It was in the streets that they first came into conflict with "the powers that be." Crowds began throwing stones, which led to the British police asking them to minister indoors.

George Swan of the Egypt General Mission wrote:

The whole question of the attitude of missions to governments is a most difficult one in Muhammad Don's lands. On the one hand, the crowds are so inflammable that those in authority have to keep a most vigilant eye upon every source of possible opposition, and because the ultimate authority in Egypt is in fact though not in name British, it follows that British subjects have less independence of action where missionary obligations come into conflict with government views of what is expedient than do other nationalities. The authorities rightly press upon us the necessity of not offending Muhammadans' susceptibilities but Muhammadans' susceptibilities are such that one can never tell when they will be offended or when they will make vigorous complaint, for the very presence of Christian missionaries is an offense and the bare statement of the most substantial of historical facts that Jesus Christ was crucified on the cross, is the greatest offensive for it gives the lie direct to Muhammad and to the Quran.[24]

Although at that time there was technically freedom of religion and freedom to propagate one's faith, any Egyptian so doing was not given any protection against the mob. We and they all struggle for grace to "obey God rather than men." Cleaver and Thompson decided to base in Belbeis, a reasonably healthy town with an almost exclusively Muslim population. Bradley and Logan decided to minister from an Egyptian village that had a large percentage of Coptic Christians.

At Zagazig, Logan gave some vendors a few copies of an Arabic tract published by the CMS which the Muslim boys could sell. Imagine their surprise however when they heard the boys announcing the headline "the death of Sayyida Isa" as if it was the breaking news of the day! All the copies were quickly sold.

1900-1978

Egypt, which had a strong missionary presence, became in the 1900s both a center for anti-colonial nationalism and a launching pad for global Islamism with its emphasis on Islamic law, government, and social behavior. The ministry of the missionaries, particularly in education, ignited an abundance of anti-missionary treatises in the Arabic genre. The majority of historians agree that British missionaries were often agreeable to British Imperial expansion and even felt a degree of national pride in their country's growing power and prestige. American missionaries also brought Western education on the presupposition that "thinking" Muslims would undoubtedly find the Christian faith more sensible than Islam. This is well-documented in their own reports to agency leaders, as demonstrated above. Middle Eastern leaders on the other hand also welcomed Western education, but more on the presupposition that it would help them to rise to the same economic and military levels of the West. Sadly, cooperation from Arab governments came with the proviso that evangelization among Muslims was out of bounds since it would represent an assault on Islamic values which assumes that Islam superseded Christianity. Thus, the missionaries focused on stimulating a "Protestant Reformation" among the ancient Christians in the Middle East.

In 1900, John Mott proclaimed that the political conditions were finally optimal for worldwide evangelization.

The influence and protection of Christian governments is an immense help to the work of missions. In no age in the past could the ambassadors for Christ carry on their work with such safety. Over one-third of the inhabitants of the unevangelized world are under the direct sway of Christian rulers. Moreover, the Protestant powers are in a position to exert an influence that will make possible the free preaching of the Gospel to the remaining two-thirds of the people of the earth who have not heard of Christ.[25]

However, freedom to teach the Christian faith and freedom to respond to such teaching are two different things. For three years beginning in February 1900, Muslim boys every morning were instructed in the Christian Scriptures by EGM missionaries, faithfully memorizing the texts by heart: "But to our regret there is no boys of whom we can point and say with certainty that boy entered eternal life through the school at Belbeis."[26] As has been the case through the years, missionaries, sometimes out of desperation, have hung on to the promise that "God's word will not return to him void." This may be more faith than accurate exegesis and probably does not include every piece of paper or book or even a printed New Testament which is not read. God must love his servants who do not doubt, but continue believing!

Whenever a boy would begin to take a stand for Christ, or even show more than usual interest in the Gospel story he was taken away from us at once. Most have had their minds poisoned and others disappeared possibly because their bodies were poisoned! Still we thank God for the great privilege of sowing the seed of the word in the hearts of the many hundreds of Moslem boys who passed through our schools in these 13 years; yet the same time we've never ceased to long for more definite fruit and to search ourselves, in the presence of God, to find if there were any hindrances to blessing in ourselves.[27]

At least they were comforted that before that time, everyone where they lived was entirely ignorant of the claims of Christ, whereas after thirteen years, there was a near universal knowledge of His claims.

Among the many tasks undertaken by workers of the Egypt General Mission, they started a school for girls and a monthly magazine for Muslims. They also set up a base with the British and Foreign Bible Society in the Suez where no other missionary had ever settled before; thus, the residents came across as very suspicious and unapproachable. For Logan throughout his first five months there, "the heavens seemed of brass and the earth iron."[28] Some comfort was felt by the missionaries who produced literature which, though not fully accepted in Egypt, was dispatched off to ministries as far away as China. In the Suez, they were gratified that at least some Copts and a few Shi'a/Sufi Muslim visitors, as well as Armenians, Jews, and Maronites from other countries, came to a biblical knowledge of Christ through discussions in their reading room.

In 1909, W.H.T. Gairdner, a British missionary in Egypt with the CMS, argued that the paucity of Muslim conversions did not diminish the value of the effort or justify the reallocation of funds and workers to China where prospects for mass conversion were brighter. Kenneth Cragg, an Anglican

Bishop, agreed: "There is a Christian obligation to Islam that neither begins or ends with how Muslims respond. It is rooted in the nature of Christ and his Gospel."[29]

Questions to Ponder

Do you agree with Kenneth Cragg's statement? How should one view their ministry if, year after year, no conversions are witnessed?

EVEN IF COLONIALISM had benefited missionaries in the Middle East by providing them with protection of Western powers and associated legal and operational privileges, why did they stay when decolonization had the opposite effect after World War II? It wasn't with political leaders, with whom they readily had an adversarial relationship, that the missionaries consulted to press on at the impossible task, but with each other, meeting for conferences hosted in Egypt, inviting some of the most prominent mission leaders and thinkers including scholars specializing in Islamic and Arabic study. Egypt emerged as the center of Protestant missionary publishing and collaboration to devise strategies for evangelizing Muslims from Algiers to Turkey, to China and Indonesia.

Discouragements

There were several disappointments along the way. A huge blow was Hanna Butros, who professed to be a Muslim convert, serving with Mr. Logan for three years while at the same time defrauding people of money and ending up in prison. Swan's reflection on this event was as follows: "It is a great trial for the missionary that he must always fight against the tendency to suspect alternative motives in every inquirer. Missionaries need to grow not suspicious and distrustful but stronger in spiritual discernment."[30]

Habib Abdel Masihi, a Moroccan returning from Hajj, became a Christian brother and co-worker after passing through Suez and reading the sign on a bookshop "Come unto me, all ye that are weary and heavy laden, and I will give you rest." Baptized in 1905, he worked several years in the outstation of Tell el Kabir, then felt he could be a better witness as a tentmaker independent of the mission. The missionaries, however, suspected that he was led by a desire for greater income and independence.

Question to Ponder

If the ministry needs initiating and entrepreneurial MBBs with gifting to make disciples among their fellow Muslims, why should we expect them to work for or under a foreign agency or missionary?

FURTHER SORROWS MOUNTED as boys who professed the Lord were said to be dead when inquiries were made to their families.

There is much evidence that the missionaries from the different societies were mutually interdependent. For example, one of the original seven joined the team of the American Presbyterians in Zifteh, and the following year married Mary Harrison, an Australian nurse at the CMS hospital in Gaza. The missionaries of the Egypt General Mission often felt their lives were barren and monotonous, making no impression on the district they adopted. One in a letter back home compared himself with a "blinded Buffalo, yoked to an irrigation wheel, eternally tramping round in a circle but seeing no result in for labor."[31]

When Elias Thompson died in Egypt, the Rev. W.H.T. Gairdner of the Church Missionary Society, a close personal friend, declared:

He went about doing good, so he was loved intensely by all who knew him well; which were perhaps few. For many weeks at a time, he was alone; the only Englishman in the town facing the discouragements which must be the lot of all pioneers. He laid down his life for the people of his adoption.[32]

Question to Ponder

Why did some missionaries "miss" the obvious: that Jesus sent his apostles out two by two? There is little discussion by the early missionaries of the different giftings which need to be combined in a church planting effort. Paul's church planting teams were of course larger and when he was alone, he pled for co-workers to join him.

OUT OF JEALOUSLY, shame, or simply to draw Muslims away from the missionaries' clinics and schools, the Egyptian government, pressed by Muslim sheikhs, opened up both clinics and schools. This successfully led to the closing of those founded by the missionaries. Where they could keep a school open, Mr. Swan leaked out the complaint: "The funds at the disposal of most missions for school work are ridiculously inadequate."[33] Occasionally a Muslim father would bring his son back to them because of the more positive effect on the boy's character which had been produced at the mission schools. What they could feel good about was:

Without intermission since 1900, every village, every hamlet, every farmstead has been visited, and the Gospel message clearly proclaimed. Although many are fearful, and others liars and adulterers, we missionaries cannot but have an intense sympathy for them as we come in contact with them, for we consider ourselves and wonder what we would have done in their circumstances?[34]

Of course it were a few, especially boys, whose eyes were opened and were able to flee to the missionaries who baptized them, gave them Christian names and provided them with a Christian education, all while living at a Christian boarding school.

Question to Ponder

Regarding these boys who fled to the missionaries, what did that do for their witness to their families?

IN ZEITOUN, a suburb of Cairo, a retreat center was built for bringing people apart for a while to meet with God. A joint committee of missionaries invited all the known Muslim converts to come for three days to meet together on June 16–18, 1909. Thirty attended, which started a pattern for the years ahead.

By 1913, those in the Egypt General Mission were confirmed that their calling was not to plant churches but to introduce the Christian faith among those who are without access to a witness, especially the most neglected Muslims. They began to realize that there were different ministry gifts and therefore they earnestly prayed for more evangelists, i.e. "many-tongued men with a soul-winning gift."[35]

Because the missionaries established higher education and taught the Arabs how to use the printing press, Egypt in the early 20th century had become the intellectual pacesetter of the Arab world. Nevertheless, a vigorous early nationalist movement voted for the Egyptian government to clamp down on evangelism among Muslims. At the same time, Egypt was achieving prominence from other Muslim countries as missionaries themselves of Islamic reform and "evangelism." They commonly emulated the methodology of the Western missionaries. Thus it was Christian mission which stimulated the early development of Islamic movements including the Muslim Brotherhood, which organized conferences and organized YMMA (Young Men's Muslim Association) to counteract Christian evangelism. On the other hand, the Presbyterians and Anglicans failed to motivate many of the Christians to attempt evangelizing the Muslim majority. In 1908, C.R. Watson echoed John Hogg, who warned that prejudice against Islam and Muslim converts was the greatest hindrance to the church influencing Muslims toward Christ, thus missing her true calling to become a national church.

The first conference of missionaries to Muslims was held in Cairo in 1906 and was something of a fresh beginning. The call extended to Samuel Zwemer by the United Presbyterian Mission established Cairo as a place to train workers among Muslims. Zwemer and W.H.T. Gairdner would usher in a new era and were instrumental in developing the Cairo School of Oriental Studies, the Nile Mission Press, the Inter-Mission Council, the Near East Christian Council and the Fellowship of Unity (founded by Bishop Gwynne in 1921). Many of the missionaries attending the Cairo conference were from other parts of the Muslim world and were encouraged to know other workers and what they were doing.

Also from these years we learn about the death of Pastor Ziemendorff, the director and father of the German Sudan Pioneer Mission and the first German missionary to work among Muslims in Egypt. For more than twenty years he was a pastor and chairman of the annual conference for the deepening of the spiritual life at Wiesbaden. His home became the center of his blessed work and God also called him to prepare women for the service of the master, helping them to go out under the Sudan Pioneer Mission. Scarcely ever has a mission had to battle greater difficulties than the Sudan Pioneer Mission in its first beginnings. They started a school for Muslim children in Ascalon, but their missionaries passed through a severe crisis of skepticism when even experienced missionaries of ten years looked upon the mission among Muslims as utterly hopeless.

The following seven years, God granted his servant to see some fruit – new stations were founded in Assuan, Daraw, and Edfu. Baptism was given to two grown children of the Nubian evangelist. He continued traveling, recruiting Germans to join him. He went home to heaven from Fairhaven in the presence of his replacement – the "beloved head of the mission," Miss Annie Van Sommer.

Bright Hope for Tomorrow

The following was written in first edition of *The Moslem World*:

After long and careful preparation, eleven adult converts from Muhammadanism were baptized last year in the Egypt Mission of the CMS. The Rev. Canon MacInnes writes: "Certainly three of these men were first influenced towards Christ by others than members of our own Mission."[36]

There was abundant proof in the early 1900s that a new day was dawning. Among the most significant of these was a small conference held in Minich, in Middle Egypt, on April 23-24, 1912. For some ten years, an annual prayer conference, having its origin from the Egyptian Evangelical Church itself, was held for the deepening of spiritual life. The last of these, held in Sanabu, took for its motto "Egypt for Christ." The program emphasized the duty of evangelizing Muslims. At one of the sessions, an influential pastor asked how many would join him in a covenant to labor personally for the winning of Muslims to Christ. About forty rose to their feet.

The conference at Minich was a calling together of this forty for a comparison of experiences and for mutual counsel and encouragement. Nearly all were present, and a number of others who wished their names added to the list. There were missionaries, pastors, merchants, farmers, and others. Each gave his personal testimony concerning his efforts, covering a large variety of methods used. Among the attenders was a pastor who had visited the houses of students to converse with them about spiritual matters. Others had preached in the trains, in the shops, in the homes, and in the fields, as well as in more public places. Some had distributed literature while others told of the effect of Christian example. A note of strong encouragement pervaded the testimonies. All had found an open door and no reason to fear. One pastor said: "If the evangelization of Moslems is yet distant, the reason is in us, not in them."[37] A convert from Islam, who was a graduate of the Al Azhar, spoke of the changing attitude of Muslims during the last dozen years: "Leading Moslems are now saying there is no difference between Islam and Christianity; tomorrow they will be saying that the Christian faith is the nearest way to God and before long, that this is the only way."[38] Among those present was a pastor (Egyptian?) who had recently resigned his charge to give his whole time to working among Muslims. Small though the gathering was, it made the day seem nearer, when "the Lord shall be known in Egypt," and Ishmael shall live before him.

From 1930, efforts to slow down witness increased until 1956, when Gamal Abdel Nasser continued a popular drive to minimize or nationalize missionary operations as part of its move toward foreign investment. Missionaries were ordered to replace themselves with citizens, not a few who took the job for less than biblical motives. Mission schools were also nationalized. From the 1940s, the schools which resisted nationalization were forbidden to teach the Bible to Muslims, often even requiring them to teach the Qur'an. The Presbyterians and others not only complied, but ironically, as missionary visas became more difficult to obtain, it was generally the Western missionaries who opposed their home governments' policies regarding Israel. In the mid-1950s the strong public pro-Arab stance helped save the American University in Cairo from nationalization.

During the Suez crisis, the Egypt General Mission had one of its schools seized and refashioned as a government institution with its bank assets frozen and all its missionaries deported, which led to the mission dissolving. In this context of nationalization, other Protestant organizations in Egypt began to question the feasibility of continuing Christian mission in Egypt and several began to dismantle, transferring authority and property to local Protestant pastors.

In 1953, one American missionary estimated that there were perhaps 200 Muslim converts among the tens of thousands of Egyptian Protestants from Coptic Christian background. More evangelical mission agencies on the ground began to develop programs with the goal to evangelize the Middle East from remote bases such as France or Cyprus. By the 1960s, however, American Presbyterian church leaders shifted their concept of mission to matters of common human concern instead of confronting Muslims on matters of theology. The title missionary was replaced by fraternal worker. More evangelical churches simply shrugged their shoulders and turned their efforts toward peoples and places that were friendly to missionaries, which obviously excluded Muslim regions.

Thus evangelism among Muslims, never a major activity in Egypt, became visibly extinct by 1970 except for the silent witness or an occasional humanitarian intervention. Some workers with Operation Mobilization were opposed by the Egyptian churches who feared they would be victimized by the government in retaliation.

8

NORTH AFRICA

IN 1960, missions historian Willy Heggoy wrote:

When the results of the Christian missionary endeavor among Muslims are compared to those among Animists, Hindus or Buddhists, the missions among Muslims appears to be vain efforts. There is no example of large success of Christian missions among the Muslims of the Arab or Arabized heartlands of Islam.[1]

Heggoy continues with his blunt prognosis:

Experience reminds us that the Muslim world still is a hard mission field, and that converts are few. Because missions among Muslims have produced so little fruit in terms of converts in the past, questions have been raised not only as to the advisability of the continuation of missions to the Muslims, but even of the justification of such missions. If statistics alone were the basis of judgement, nobody would dare to argue against the objections and hesitations expressed in the questions just mentioned. Missions to the Muslims would then be a large-scale waste of time, effort, intelligence and lives.[2]

Yet, even in the revelation of such a harsh reality, Heggoy injects the type of hope that missionaries for centuries have clung to: "It is something else to know that God is there, and that God wants missions to the Muslims, even when there is nothing to show as far as numbers go, and there is no exterior sign of success."[3]

Morocco

The 19th century saw little progress made in the way of evangelization vis-à-vis Moroccan Muslims. This was mostly likely due to family loyalty and hostility to foreigners. The most that can be said is that Catholics and Protestants were able to establish some schools and medical clinics, yet as this book can testify, starting a school is much different than actually making disciples among Muslims. In the 1880s there were a few foreign missionaries sent to the Jews (who were abundant in North Africa having been expelled from Spain 400 years earlier), but as far as Muslims were concerned, North Africa was still outside the sphere of the Protestant missionary vision.

Of course not every agency ignored the Moroccan Muslims. In 1881, the newly established North Africa Mission opened their first clinic in Tangier. Yet on the whole, Morocco was still widely regarded by evangelicals as beyond the range of the Great Commission, even though the country was comparatively near Britain. Those who did find residency in Tangier quickly discovered that the locals were only interested in medical relief. The British and Foreign Bible Society were able to hire a few colporteurs who cautiously found recipients willing to receive portions of Scripture, though curiosity and not spiritual hunger was probably the driving factor. Few at the time were even literate.

Not much is known of the Central Morocco Mission founded by the English Presbyterians or by some efforts of intrepid individualistic Plymouth Brethren. What is known is that nearly all the response to the efforts of the

Protestant missionaries up until World War II was limited to Europeans. Nevertheless, God kept calling (particularly British) pioneers to sow. Mission stations were opened in Mogador and Tangier 1884, Rabat in 1888, Tetuan in 1889, Fez in 1890, Casablanca and Marrakesh in 1891, Safi in 1893, and Laraehe and Mekinez soon afterwards. Such an advance could not be expected to pass unchallenged, for an orthodox, despotic sultan still reigned in the land. Accordingly, in the spring of 1891, all missionaries were asked to withdraw from his dominions. Women workers in the north were charged with entering the houses of the people and corrupting the women's minds with strange doctrines. In the south, men predominated; and in Marrakesh they were accused of giving the people money in order to change their religion and also of seeking to entice the boys and corrupt their minds.[4]

Early Workers

E.F. Baldwin, the first American missionary to Morocco, was a Southern Baptist preacher from North Carolina. When he was holding meetings in Virginia in 1883, he read in a London magazine about the need among the Kabyles of North Africa. Believing God was sending him and his family of eleven there, he presented his burden to the Southern Baptist Board of Foreign Missions who sent him to Algeria to scout out possibilities. When he returned with a plan, he found the board had decided instead to extend their work in Mexico. So Baldwin left the Baptists and wrote to England to join the new enterprise called North Africa Mission.[5] They then departed for Morocco, arriving in Tangier in November of 1884.

Over the next two years, eight more missionaries would arrive in Morocco to partner with the Baldwin family.

Work began in Arzila in 1886 and two women workers obtained entrance into numerous Muslim homes. The missionaries claimed that several persons died trusting in Christ. Three Englishmen, William Summers, Jeremiah Edwards and C. Mensink, began work at Tetuan in 1889, but left after encountering many obstacles – they were replaced by two women, Frances Banks and Alexis Bolton, both of whom rendered distinguished service through the years. The men went to open a work at Casablanca in 1890.[6]

Mrs. Baldwin was the daughter of a doctor, so with her limited understanding of medicine they opened up a clinic which later evolved into the Tulloch Memorial Hospital in Tangier. After three years, the pioneering Baldwins (for unknown reason) resigned from NAM to begin an independent work in Fez where he assisted the first recruits of the newly-formed Southern Morocco Mission from Scotland. An enthusiastic, if not overly discerning evangelist, Baldwin reported results everywhere he went. It was said of him not altogether facetiously that he "preached to men on Friday, baptized them on Saturday, admitted them to the Lord's table on Sunday, and then sent them out as missionaries."[7] He also gained some measure of notoriety when he demanded that missionaries live without any certain income or possessions or even provisions for health, and that they must deny themselves time-consuming social friendships.

Another mission operating in Morocco at this time was the newly formed Central Morocco Mission, started by Robert Kerr "after expressing disappointment with the lack of missions enthusiasm for North Africa on the part of the English Presbyterian Church."[8] Kerr remained in Morocco for seven years, engaged in medical ministry to both Muslims and Jews. Yet, at the end of that time,

he could not speak of great results, meaning conversion to the Christian faith. He did mention the conversion of an Arab girl named Iness and an Arab youth named Hamed. Both conversions were from the early years of his missionary work, 1887 and 1888 respectively. Later, he was satisfied to record that several, both Jews and Muslims, "believe in their hearts...like Nicodemus."[9]

To any report of conversion, Willy Heggoy is slow to celebrate, reminding the reader that "the reports from the interior [often were] exaggerated and some were entirely false. Of the converts known to the missionaries, very few remained faithful."[10] Still,

some missionaries could tell of professed conversions that led to public baptisms. Brave were those Moroccans who dared to be baptized by the missionaries, as these missionaries insisted on public baptism. Even when the convert was the only disciple in the place, his baptism had to be a public event, which meant that it had to be done in the presence of witnesses, more than likely hostile Muslims.[11]

In the spring of 1890, E.F. Baldwin wrote a letter back to his superiors in which he said:

Arabic is the language of the great Muhammadan nations. These all lie in great darkness and almost wholly unevangelized. Muhammadans are still fast bound in the chains of their religious delusions and in the dense darkness that envelops them. Five years ago, I began in Morocco as the only missionary to the Muhammadans. Now, thank God, in both Northern Morocco, with Tangier as its base, and Southern Morocco in Mogador, there are thirty devoted missionaries. It is well known that I have advocated and sought to practice simple and self-denying methods of mission work, as the most effective means, although hard to the flesh. I drew them from the Lord's instructions to His first missionaries as recorded in Matthew 10. Practically speaking, following out these principles leads those pledged to them to live upon the level, in material things, of the people to whom they are sent, as far as is consistent with health and cleanliness. Missionaries should live outwardly as they go, two by two on foot, carrying only the Gospel message, unimpeded by anything which excites the envy or cupidity of the natives.[12]

Questions to Ponder

What above can you appreciate? What might you avoid or alter?

IMAGINING he had completed all he had to do as a foreign missionary, Baldwin and his family left Morocco for Syria, however before he left, he was at least able to report the privilege of personally baptizing Muslim converts to Christianity.

Initially journeying to Morocco with the Baldwins was Miss Emma Herdman, who hailed from a wealthy home in Belfast. She was one of the most unusually gifted missionaries in NAM's entire history. Emma was a skilled communicator, fluent in six languages in addition to knowledge of Latin, Greek and Hebrew.[13] In Fez, Morocco, she developed an exemplary ministry training Moroccan believers to use the occupation of colporteur as a means to evangelize their fellow countryman and distribute literature: "[Emma] always kept in view the importance of circulating the Holy Scriptures, and encouraging the more educated inhabitants to give them their careful study."[14]

Emma maintained an unshakable hope that, like the walls of Jericho, "Muhammadism in Morocco will thus fall"[15] and she was able to witness first-hand the power of God over and against the fragile walls of Satan's kingdom:

One of our men, at a place two days from Fez, found a shereef (noble) who had become a Christian. He had received the Gospel through one of our men. That night the shereef sent out his slave, and gathered twenty of his converts out of the village. Four had New Testaments of ours, and were able to read them, and sixteen were able to give good account of their new lives, and faith in the precious blood of Christ.[16]

Without doubt, few women possessed her combination of intelligence, imagination, leadership, and confidence in God. Emma Herdman died on the field in 1899 after a fierce illness.

The Gospel Missionary Union [17]

On January 9, 1895, a small band of Americans under the leadership of Rev. Albert Nathan, a convert from Judaism, landed at Tangier's port warmly greeted with cries of "Welcome to Morocco! Praise the Lord!"[18] This party from the newly organized Gospel Missionary Union in Kansas City, led by Rev. Nathan, declared as they departed from the United States that they are going forth "to a strange dark land—a land of filth, dirt, and pestilence, a land of 'Darkness, despair and death!"[19] Nathan reminded the faithful on his team and those who supported them that the coming of the Lord was near and that they toiled among a people probably doomed to damnation, reminding themselves that martyrdom was the seed of the church and it was likely that some of them would lay down their lives in Morocco. With those presuppositions of the task before them, the Gospel Missionary Union began its work as the first American religious organization in Morocco.

At first, Tangier was considered to be the most desirable base for a mission as it was the supposed key to Morocco. Near the city market, a refuge was opened where transients were given refreshments and a place to sleep, while each evening the missionaries preached to them. By 1898, over seven thousand had lodged there and the GMU reported at least two bonafide conversions. From Tangier, the missionaries planned to carry the Gospel into the interior to Meknes, a large city without a single witness of the cross. In 1895, Nathan and another missionary named Hammer set out from Tangier to gauge possibilities during an inspection trip of the interior. The estimated costs for four donkeys and a good tent would be about one hundred and twenty-five dollars, while travel and food were anticipated to run about two dollars a day.

Traversing the dismal roads in a land totally lacking in modern transportation, they made their way to Meknes and Fez, preaching in the villages along the way. The anti-foreign attitudes of many Muslims, as well as hostility from government officials, was readily apparent and in fact would remain a persistent obstacle through the years ahead. Much of the difficulty was due to the endemic disorder in the land and the inability of the sultan to exercise authority throughout his domain. Despite these problems, the GMU gradually extended its operations placing twenty missionaries in Morocco during their first ten years in the country. Nathan was also able to translate the Gospel of Luke into Moroccan Arabic.

As in other parts of the Muslim world, however, some Moroccans were open to friendship when touched by the compassion of the missionaries for their medical needs, despite the fact that few of the missionaries had medical training. Other initiatives included a farm that was purchased by Jeremiah Edwards in 1897. Named the Raymond Lull Orphanage, it was established to care for neglected boys and was eventually operated by an independent Canadian missionary named Herbert Elson. Unfortunately, reported by Francis Steele, "the boys had been so seriously affected by their environment, they were disinclined either to work or study, much less obediently follow Christ."[20] Still, the workers persevered and by 1900, Fes, Tetuan, and Casablanca had missionaries dug in with long-term intention.

In 1901 the GMU decided to concentrate its evangelizing efforts among the Berber mountain tribes, especially those south and west of Meknes and Fez. The missionaries therefore began to study the Shilha Berber language as well as Arabic. That itinerant work was physically demanding to say the least. The missionaries

camped for a few days near each village and then repacked and moved to the next one several miles away, usually up the side of a mountain or down into a valley. The heat, the weariness, the impure water, and the sticky flies all combined to bring sickness to one after another of the team—headaches, nausea, diarrhea, chills and fever, drained every ounce of strength from their bodies.[21]

Wherever they went, their main interest was to proclaim the Word of God, usually as they walked through the streets of the bazaars preaching to the shopkeepers and shoppers despite warnings by Moroccan officials of possible dangerous reactions.

The work of the missionary women was different. Restricted by Muslim custom from preaching to men, they walked the streets, knocking door-to-door seeking contact with the women in their homes, offering Scriptures. Frequently well-received on their first call, they might be repulsed on subsequent visits after the Moroccan women's husbands forbid further contact. In the towns where the GMU was well-established however, children regularly came to the mission house and were taught Bible verses and hymns by the women there. "The [Muslim] women differ from the men," said Maude Cary, "in that they have little to say when the Truth is presented to them—no arguments to bring forth—their minds being so unused to thinking of anything above their duties in everyday life."[22] Within a few years after their arrival, the American missionaries were preparing colloquial translations of the Bible and other religious writings in Arabic, Berber, and even Hebrew for befriended Jews.

One-half of the GMU missionaries who served in Morocco between 1895 and 1912 were women. True to the governors' warning, the missionaries were often harassed. Elizabeth Tryon wrote: "the children in the streets often revile us and even spit on us, or worse, throw stones. In some houses, the Muslim women frequently said they'd like to kill us or burn us alive if they dared."[23]

The American missionaries were criticized for their involvement in political issues, for their adoption of Moorish garb, or for their overzealous proselytizing. It was argued that their "harangues" not only antagonized the Moroccans whose souls they were attempting to save, but also seriously disturbed the European residents who, believing that the Moroccans would be incited to violence, feared for their own safety and endeavored to halt the evangelizing by the missionaries. Years later, George Reed would state in his memoirs that "the Allah of the Koran is Satan's distortion of the God of the Bible; Muhammad is Satan's substitute for Christ, the true mediator;

the Koran is Satan's parody of the Bible."[24] By such outspoken convictions, it is not surprising that the missionaries found the Moroccans fiercely resistant.

Questions to Ponder

Do you agree with Reed's convictions and/or how he expressed them? What type of offense should be expected and avoided when communicating the Gospel to the unsaved?

IF SUCCESS IS to be measured by how many Moroccans were converted to Christ, the results were most unrewarding. Despite their dedicated efforts, the GMU missionaries were no more fruitful in making disciples among the Muslims than evangelical missionaries focused on Muslims elsewhere. By 1912, after seventeen years, the GMU workers had baptized only two or three Muslims, and evidently no Jews. Missionaries with the Southern Morocco Mission of Scotland had a similar story. After years of weary, disheartening efforts to make the Good News "sound" like good news to the Moroccans, they felt they were only beginning to see a clearing in the dense jungle of Islamic superstition, only finding patches here and there on which they could sow some seed and then wait and hope.

Yet good work is being done in a quiet way, and substantial progress has been made. Through medical work, probably 100,000 hear the Gospel every year; the attendance at one dispensary in Southern Morocco last year was over 22,200. Thirty years ago no one heard a doubt expressed as to the perfection of Islam. Now they are accustomed to hear of its defects, and to have a new faith extolled as the only way of life…true, we cannot speak yet of numerous baptisms, nor of churches filled with worshippers every Sabbath morning, but faith can see them. The work has already demanded, and will yet demand, precious lives gladly laid down; days of hard toil and patience; nights of strong crying with tears to Him who is able to save from discouragement and surrender; also a large expenditure of money will be required; but the foundations have been deeply laid, the structure begins to appear, and its completion is only a question of time.[25]

Heggoy also reports that, while the missionaries themselves may not have seen much fruit, that does not mean that fruit was non-existent, for the Moors were carrying out extensive behind-the-scenes evangelistic efforts among Muslims:

"We hear of a Sharif who had bought a New Testament from one of the colporteurs and had become a Christian, and who since had baptized twenty-two believers. We hear of thirteen baptized students in a Muslim college. We hear of three men baptized in the Tadla, and of at least thirty unbaptized believers in different locations. All this work was done by the Moors themselves."[26]

Questions to Ponder

What are the pros and cons of indiscriminate distribution of Scriptures? Should they be sold or given away for free? Do you agree with those who argue that only hardcover elegant versions should be used because doing so increases respect for the Holy Book? Should one book be handed out at a time? If so, which one? A gospel?

The Bible is Working in Morocco

Missionary to Morocco Robert Steven wrote: "I am often asked the question: 'Do the people in Morocco want the Bible?'" He then relates the following two incidents which he hopes will answer that query:

In Fez, we stood on the spot where in 1903 a North Africa Mission worker lost his life, and offered to the people as they passed, the Word of God. The first day I sold over 400 Arabic portions, the second day over 200 Gospels and so on. We were just behind the Great Mosque and better class Moors on their way to prayers at midday bought portions of the Old and New Testaments, put them inside their *libdas* and entered the revered mosque to pray! I tried to imagine these worshippers bowing, and praying in the name of the False Prophet, yet having the book under them which could lead them to Him who is the Way, the Truth, and the Life.[27]

He adds,

In Tala, we found untrodden ground for the Bible seller and missionary. In less than an hour, I sold out the stock I had brought with me surprised that the demand was greater than ever. "Come back again soon and bring a greater supply of books with you," they yelled. It was an exciting scene. Algerians, Sousis, Moorish soldiers and others all crowding round, and late comers, when they learned the nature of the books, tried to press through, holding up their pennies over the heads of those in front calling out "Give me one." My bag carrier, a Moor, was absolutely astonished and kept saying "Ahjoobah! Ahjoobah!"[28]

Steven also comments about the spiritual productivity found in Moroccan prisons:

For debt, a Moor found himself in prison; no uncommon thing in these difficult days. A lady friend, who visits the local prisons regularly, gave him a copy of one of our Maghrebi Gospels. On regaining his liberty, he sought out the lady to thank her for her kindness in giving him such a book and wished to have further enlightenment upon certain truths. She gave him a note of introduction to me, and one day, the week before last, he came to the Bible Depot. After about two hours, reading and explaining he said, "This has been the very gate of heaven to me, from this time forward I build my hope of pardon for my sins on the Lord Jesus. I believe He died for me, and that His blood cleanses me from all sin." He was awakened to his need of a Savior in prison through reading the Word of God. The Bible is working in Morocco.[29]

More to be Done

"Sixty-eight missionaries were working among the Muslims of Morocco in 1912-13. By 1925, the number had increased to 78 and by 1931, to 96."[30] Heggoy reports that in 1931 there was a Moroccan church that was welcoming eight converts from Islam into the service every Sunday morning. The GMU continued to expand not only their geographic footprint but also their impact of ministry in the years leading up to and then succeeding World War II. Between 1947 and 1949, the first ever recording of the Gospel was produced in Moroccan Arabic, and in 1957 GMU missionaries began distributing a Bible correspondence course. To their delight, and with aid from an OM team, in 1962 over 50,000 Moroccans had enrolled although perhaps less than 5% completed it. Those were years when Moroccans wanted contact with the West so they were liable to write off for anything, especially if it was free, and sometimes if only to simply display an educational certificate. A fraction of the small number who finished a course responded to an offer to have a teacher visit them to speak of spiritual matters, even if it was done surreptitiously. The missionary presence of NAM during this time numbered sixteen missionaries on the ground in Morocco with five on furlough. The Southern Morocco Mission similarly reported having fifteen workers in five different cities.

Questions to Ponder

What is the role of correspondence courses, by post or online in ministry with Muslims? There are many hundreds of thousands of Muslims who are not likely to ever have a face-to-face meeting with a caring follower of Jesus Christ. Is something better than nothing?

IN 1966, the opportunity came about for the GMU to partner with Trans World Radio to produce a Gospel program for Morocco. The messages were prepared by missionary Maynard Yoder along with a young Moroccan convert. In September of that year, a new radio program entitled "The Voice of the Word of Life" first aired across the country. Through that program, hundreds of Arabs made a profession of faith in Christ. This alarmed the government to the extent that the Gospel Missionary Union was officially expelled from Morocco in 1969. They transferred their base of operations to Málaga, Spain.

Notable Women

Many brave women have set out for Morocco as missionaries to Muslims, so it would be appropriate to close this section by mentioning a few. Kansas native Maude Cary, feeling God's tug at a young age, moved to Morocco in 1901. She immediately began journeying out to villages, sharing the Gospel with any native Muslim women who would listen until the men returned. Maude worked hard learning Berber and Arabic. Though she eventually became engaged to fellow missionary George Reed, it is suspected that she was too independently strong-minded, leading to the marriage never taking place.

After twenty-three years on the field, Maude returned home for her first furlough! What had she accomplished in those twenty-three years? Had churches been founded? Were mission schools overflowing with eager students? Were converts winning their own people to Christianity? In terms of outward lasting fruit, very little had been accomplished against the fortress of Islam and the stronghold of Moroccan culture. Of the handful of converts, the most promising ones turned away from following Christ when faced with persecution. Were her years of investment then truly worth the sacrifice? Maude was convinced they were. Pressing on, in 1951, fifty years after her debut, she helped organize a Bible institute to train young Moroccan disciples.[31] Working alongside fellow female pioneer Ila Marie Davis, they also produced handwritten Arabic hymnals and Bible lessons for both children and women who were illiterate.

Failing health forced Maude's retirement and departure from Morocco in 1955, which coincided with the end of the French occupation of Morocco and an exciting new era of relaxed restrictions against the missionaries. Maude Cary died in America in 1967, but during those twelve years after she left the field, until 1967, the missionaries worked openly and freely among the Muslims. Some thirty thousand Muslims felt free enough to enroll in Bible correspondence courses and small Bible studies multiplied.[32]

Questions to Ponder

What do we learn from the life of Maude Cary in terms of giving our all, and perseverance to the end?

How does one know if they have a trained disciple? What is the evidence?

ANOTHER HEROINE of the faith was Patricia St. John, an English nurse who spent twenty-five years (1950-1975) working as a medical missionary in Morocco. She wrote this about her place of employment, the Tangier Hospital:

The work of the hospital carries on year after year. There was faithful sowing and little reaping, and the fruit was indeed handpicked. Through the witness of the medical work and the daily preaching of God's Word among the outpatients and in the wards, Christianity is respected in Tangier today, although the hospital, as we knew it, was shut nearly 20 years ago.[33]

She also wrote the following about the Muslim patients under her care:

While they were with us, they seemed to respond to the Christian teaching, but I was still only beginning to discover the stranglehold of Islam and the spiritual warfare involved in the release of its followers. Of those who have stood firm and become recognized as active disciples of Jesus, I cannot write, as they are alive and vulnerable. But there are those few from among the student nurses and those who worked for us in the hospital who have remained true and for them we thank God. Of these, some have left the country and can live openly as Christians and others serve in the quiet, limited way which is at present all that is possible to a Christian woman living in a 100% Moslem country. Only a very few have let their light shine more clearly and have suffered.[34]

Questions to Ponder

Suffering for the Lord Jesus is normative, but what is the value of suffering that does not result in disciples? Is this normative in the New Testament?

FINALLY, we have Miss Margaret Chipperfield, affectionately called "Chippy" by those who knew her the best. Going to Morocco with Emmanuel Missions in 1931, she served as a nurse for forty-five years. In addition to medical services, she also taught Bible classes for girls. One of her co-workers, Selma Mills, wrote the following in Margaret's obituary: "Many hundreds of girls passed through her hands and heard the Word of God. Contrary to the usual response in Moslem work, a fair number accepted the Lord as Savior."[35]

Questions to Ponder

What action hits you as relevant for today? What have you gleaned from these early pioneers to Morocco?

Algeria

THE TREND SETTERS

A report from Algiers in 1739 described that for about six months,

Abraham Richter worked, not among the Muhammadan traders, but among their heathen slaves. He preached in public on Fridays, visited the slaves in their bagnios, and attended the sick free of charge. At this point, however, there broke out such a terrible pestilence that the number of deaths was 30,000. Among the victims was Richter himself, and no successor was found.[36]

In 1838 when a Roman Catholic Bishop was finally appointed for Algiers, there was in all the French colonies in North Africa only a few priests and sisters. The first Bishop, Antoine Adolf Dupuch, was dismissed by the civil and military authorities because he wanted to do mission among the Muslims. His replacement, Bishop Pavy, founded forty-three new parishes, established between 1846 and 1850. Before he died, that number increased to 273. Thus the Muslims were getting acquainted with Roman Catholicism from afar, not failing to notice the "Christians" praying to "idols." Protected by French administrative control, some mosques were taken over to become church buildings; a move which could hardly endear the Christians to the Muslim majority.

Pavy was succeeded by the renowned Charles Martial Lavigerie, who created the White Fathers as a mission agency. He was made a cardinal and ultimately given the title of Archbishop of Carthage and Primate of Africa. Lavigerie required his first seven missionaries to conform as far as possible to Arab ways and even gave them a modified form of Arab dress as their official garb. The White Sisters were later added for enterprises appropriate for women. Very soon however, the White Father priests were diverted, looking south beyond the Arab and Berber Muslims who lived north of the Sahara. Their main vision was to cross the desert to baptize the sub-Saharan pagans. Lavigerie did appoint three priests to be missionaries to the Muslims, but they were only allowed to teach the Bible to Muslim orphans; the idea being that the orphans would grow up and become priests to the Muslims.

In 1858, John Furniss Ogle arrived in Oran and began a self-supporting mission work near the city:

On arriving in Algeria, Mr. Ogle found a state of things which led him to contemplate a prolonged stay in that country...what weighed most of all with him was that it appeared to present numerous openings for the Gospel. He felt that the hand of God had led him hither, and in this conjunction of favorable circumstances he heard His voice bidding him remain and labour here.[37]

Ogle was a passionate evangelist, driven by a deep sorrow in the knowledge of how lost mankind truly is.

Question to Ponder

To what degree do you sense that present would-be disciple-makers among Muslims stay conscious of the fact that the Muslims around them are headed for an eternity of miserable separation from the Creator?

ONCE IN ALGERIA, Ogle spent countless hours sharing the Gospel with everyone who would listen:

The hours of rest from labour afforded him many openings for conversing with Spaniard, and Moor, and Arab on divine things, and making known to them the Savior. And when the working-day was ended, it often happened that many remained with Mr. Ogle until far into the evening to unite with him in prayer, and to receive instruction on the things of the kingdom of heaven.[38]

The results of his labors will certainly be known only by the Savior that he so mightily cherished. Ogle was killed in a shipwreck in 1865.

This same year, J. Bagdon, an Anglican chaplain and member of the Moslem Mission Society, reported that Mustafa Musa Ben Yusuf, a native Algerian, had converted to Christianity and was baptized.

North Africa Mission (NAM)

By the 1880s, Protestant missionaries began to trickle into North Africa. George Pearse, the English founder of North Africa Mission (Arab World Ministries/Pioneers) was particularly gifted as an initiator who was keen to explore pioneer areas. He stirred others to birth the first efforts to evangelize the Muslims of North Africa. He had been a founding member of the Chinese Evangelization Society which in 1853 sent out young Hudson Taylor. Later, the two men traded ideas, which Taylor utilized when he left that society and founded the China Inland Mission in 1865. Fortunately or unfortunately, depending on one's view, Pearse was as much interested in reaching French soldiers in North Africa as he was the Muslims. This precedent may have worked against full focus among Muslims during the first seventy years of NAM's existence in North Africa.[39]

In 1880 George Pearse and his wife Jane decided to move to Algeria at the urging of Henry Grattan Guinness, the grandson of brewer Arthur Guinness. From Grattan Guinness, the Pearses also received the first ever offering given for missionary work among the Kabyles of Algeria: "Humanly speaking, it seems probable that but for Dr. Guinness, the work of the North Africa Mission would never have been founded. God worked through him to initiate the work."[40] Guinness, spent the last fifty years of his life deeply involved as a promotor and financial backer of missionary enterprise. In fact, Guinness founded the East London Institute which prepared 140 men for overseas missionary service even before he was persuaded to serve on NAM's Board of Directors. Soon Guinness was asked to be the Director of NAM for the next forty-three years.[41] In 1880, at the age of sixty-five, George Pearse and his wife Jane became the first unofficial NAM missionaries.

Question to Ponder

What stands out regarding the roles of George and Jane Pearse and the work of Henry Grattan Guinness?

MORE A RECRUITER THAN A CHURCH PLANTER, George soon returned to England hoping to birth a mission agency specifically to the Kabyles. "In his pamphlet, Pearse called for immediate action to provide the Kabyles with 'this great and inestimable boon [i.e. Algeria opening to the Gospel of Christ].'"[42] On the trip back to England he found his first recruit, a young Swiss man Henri Mayor. In addition to trying to learn the Kabyle language, Pearse wrote a booklet *Mission to the Kabyles* in an effort to recruit new missionaries. He then returned to Algiers in November 1881 with their second co-worker, a Syrian named Selim Zeytoun. Pearse also recruited Edward Glenny.[43]

On November 5, 1881, the first NAM team, composed of Mr. and Mrs. Pearse, Edward Glenny, Henri-Samuel Mayor and Selim Zaytoun, all landed in Algeria, but it seems they were hindered from the start. Henri Mayor was harangued by the local French administrator and unable to dedicate his time to first-aid medical work and leading classes for boys. Within a year, Selim and Henri both resigned after finding the pressure from the French authorities too difficult. Mayor returned within a year as an independent worker, choosing to "start up his own mission in the small village of Moknea. One may wonder at this choice, the smallest of the 31 villages of the tribe. Was he still so inexperienced that he believed a polite invitation to be an honest invitation?"[44] Next on the field in Algeria, to "restart" the mission, was Mr. and Mrs. Alfred Lamb, plus Eugene Cuendet of Switzerland. Finally in 1888, the North Africa Mission was officially established.

An outside witness, Douglas Thornton, with the Church Missionary Society in Egypt, wrote in his book *Africa Waiting* (1897) that "The North Africa

Mission deserves our attention. Originally called 'Mission to the Kabyles of Algeria,' they will soon have a hundred workers on the field. NAM is responsible for almost all the interest lately aroused for that long neglected field."[45] Thornton concluded that Arabs and Berbers were not found altogether unapproachable, observing that hospital and dispensary work had opened some otherwise closed doors. He also highlighted that "the British and Foreign Bible Society" in 1896, distributed 15,000 portions of the Scriptures in Algeria and Tunisia in various languages.[46]

Two years after the founding of NAM, Pearse turned over the leadership to Edward Glenny, a 29-year-old disciple of Dr. Henry Guinness. Upon doing so, he returned to England, sick and too aged to continue. He wrote to the NAM headquarters in June of 1902: "I hope you will see that the Kabylia is cared for!"[47] He must have found great satisfaction in the outworking of that request, for during the next decade most of the major Algerian cities had missionaries residing within them.

In 1910, a Kabyle woman was baptized in Algeria by NAM missionaries, the first time in recorded history of a Muslim woman being baptized in that country. Heggoy also reports that two lay-preachers, Said Flici (Kabyle) and Muhammad Beddai (Arab), were both converted under the ministry of North Africa Mission. The year of 1911 saw NAM establish Field Councils which were elected by the missionaries in their regions to give oversight to the placement of personnel into new mission stations. By 1913, "total evangelical missionary strength to Muslims is reported to be ninety-seven."[48]

Part of the rationale for Field Council oversight was likely a response to criticism of all inter-denominational "faith missions." "Faith" appeared to be reckless. True enough, there was commonly a lack of planning, coordination with other workers, or provision of coaching, finances, or member care which was built into most denominational agencies. On the other hand, pioneer types tended to shy away from the cautious rules decided by non-missionaries who were deliberating far from the areas of ministry.[49]

The work continued to expand as help was continually arriving, both from abroad and within. "In 1919, there were 13 North African lay preachers in the Methodist Mission. J.J. Cooksey reported in 1925 that there were 123 missionaries in 34 stations."[50] By 1931, it could be reported that "there were more missionaries in Algeria than in any other part of North Africa."[51]

Summing up his thesis, Heggoy writes:

The year 1931 was a milestone for Protestant missions in North Africa. It was fifty years since the first organized missionary endeavor had been launched among the Kabyles of Algeria. The goal had been to plant an indigenous church in North Africa. The goal had been reached, although in all weakness. There was an indigenous church in North Africa. The sum total of baptized Arabs and Kabyles and other Berbers after fifty years of missions was more than three hundred in good standing. Some small indigenous congregations had been established with ordained Arab and Kabyle pastors.[52]

Lilias Trotter

One of the most revered pioneers in Algeria was Lilias Trotter and her Algiers Mission Band of single women which she launched in 1888 after she, because of health issues, was rejected by the North Africa Mission.

Writing of her call first to follow Christ, then to declare him among the Muslims, she describes the instant when she received the call to missions from our Lord in 1878:

I had two friends with whom I was working and they had both taken to heart the outer darkness of heathendom. They said nothing personally to me about it, but one felt it when around them. They were all aglow and after a time I began to feel that they had a fellowship with Jesus that I knew nothing about. I did love him but not wanting to be "out in the cold," I began to pray, "Lord give me your burden about the heathen that you have given to those two." Not many weeks later, a great barrier between me and Him had been broken down as a strange, yearning love was given to me for those who were in the land of the shadow of death.[53]

Lilias Trotter knew that God wanted her to serve as an overseas missionary, but her question was where? She attended a three-day mission conference where she met Mr. Glenny, who had recently returned from the Kabyle mountains of Algeria giving out literature "where Christ was unknown." From those four words Lilias knew that God was calling her.

In March of 1888, Lilias and her two friends, Blanche Haworth and Katie Stuart, left London for Algeria, arriving in Algiers several weeks later. The language was unintelligible to them; the climate was brutal, but the women persevered. Despite long, exhausting days, Lilias wrote: "the first months were full of the joy of new beginnings."[54] In 1893, five years later, the women expanded their ministries to the Arab women by renting a house in the Arab quarter of Algiers. Lest they leave their supporters assuming they now had a cheap vacation getaway, the ladies wrote: "The air here is stale and bad, the house damp and draughty."[55]

There was much heartbreak to be found in Algeria, particularly among the children. The women started a group aimed at getting Muslim children together to scrapbook, read Bible stories and sing hymns. They often saw a child's heart beginning to turn to the Lord, only to be "snatched back irrevocably into the darkness."[56] It was a pattern to be repeated countless times; so many bright responsive children, loved and prayed over, were taken from them and never seen again.

But the Lord continued working despite their discouragement. Yamina was one of their first converts and her child Attiqua regularly attended their gatherings: "More and more they became part of the household, gradually recognizing and learning to love the one who so manifestly dwelt among them."[57] Soon there were quite a few children attending their meetings, yet as far as they could tell, "none of these children grew up to be followers of Christ."[58] A number of adult women did leave the prison of Islam; some because of the testimony of the three missionary ladies, and at least one because of a dream where she saw Jesus. "Frail and timid as these believing women were, some were beginning to walk the elementary lessons of the Christian life."[59] Their first baptized convert was Ahmed, a young boy, who feared for his life after being attacked following his conversion. He moved to Tunisia. After their first eleven years they had four male converts, and after the thirteenth year, five females worshipping Christ Jesus. Yamina was the first female to be baptized: "The seed of that tiny church had been sown, but only the Holy Spirit could make it grow."[60]

Opposition was incredibly fierce, and as one professing believer after another fell away they became conscious as never before of the power of Satan. Lilias wrote: "The powers of evil feel the shock of battle that has been re-awakened in the heavenlies by our cry down here and set themselves to hinder the fresh tide of victory that has been set free."[61] The demonic oppression was sudden and devastating. Attiqua, whom Lilias had loved and nurtured since childhood, was drawn away by sorcery. Soon Yamina followed her daughter's defection, abandoning her husband and her Lord. Taitum, whom they had considered a true follower of Christ, was exposed as living a secret life filled with lies and immorality. Trotter wrote: "Taitum we had loved and trusted has been swept out of existence, and this one can have been nothing but the utmost dishonor to Christ's name. Our ministry seems like some horrible nightmare from which we must wake up."[62]

Still, hope was not lost. God brought Fatima into contact with the female missionaries after giving her vivid dreams of Jesus: "When I slept, Jesus was there. He said to me, 'I am always here, Fatima, and I always hear you when you call to me.'"[63] There was also Sherifa, who first heard the Gospel through missionary Helen Freeman. About her, Lilias wrote: "Although she can seldom join the little Bible study group, in the brightness of her face, Christ in her is much more evident than in any other."[64] Because of her testimony, Sherifa suffered longer than other converts. Her family disowned, sued and threatened her, but she remained steadfast. Patrica St. John, Trotter's biographer, wrote: "There are many pages in Lilias' diary that tell of Sherifa's struggles and persecutions and the efforts made to force her to marry a Muslim, but, for many years, she found work and was able to support her child herself."[65] At the end of 1905, Lilias wrote:

As the new year dawns, there is a great sense that God is very near to us; a new hunger in our meetings, a new liberty, a new cry for the power that Jesus promised…and today, a new joy, as, for the first time for years, we have met at His table with a few gathered out of enemy territory.[66]

As a talented artist, Trotter spent hours writing and illustrating tracts with Arab backgrounds and cultural themes. These were printed on their rather primitive duplicating machine and distributed, once a month, in the cafes around the towns. The New Testament was also translated during this time into colloquial Arabic by Swedish missionary Martin Nystrom who had worked earlier in Palestine. The missionaries received copies of Luke's Gospel to distribute at the end of 1908. By that time, the Algiers Mission Band was becoming a well-recognized and appreciated small mission with twenty-three members in four stations.

Lilias stayed in Algeria for the remainder of her life, continuing to focus on the publication of literature and ministering to Muslim women and children. Battling heart problems in the last few years, she went Home to her Lord in 1928 after forty years of non-stop witness.

Questions to Ponder

A theme that is certainly present in this section but also throughout the book is converts who fall away from the faith, i.e. apostates. Are there any factors that you can identify as contributing to this? Can you identify ways to safeguard against the backsliding of professed believers?

WORK AFTER TROTTER

In 1942 those reporting on Algeria stressed four "successful" methods of reaching Muslims:

Direct evangelism: Following in the footsteps of early missionaries, many today emphasize the direct approach to the Muslim with the message of the Gospel, that is, by direct evangelism. Though public preaching, for the most part, is not feasible, the evangelist may hold meetings in mission halls, talk to gatherings in private homes, engage in conversation in cafes, markets and other public places.

Furthermore, classes for children in private homes or mission halls, with creative varied programs, serve the same purpose of introducing the Savior. The message itself constitutes the driving motive and the central theme. Some of our most faithful native evangelists today are men who were won to Christ in this way before they were sixteen.

Visitation in Muslim homes: Women missionaries, after having won the friendship, respect, and confidence of the indigenous population, may obtain entrance into Muslim homes, particularly in times of illness, misfortune or special need. While ministering to a sick child or giving a word of advice or hope to a sorrowful mother, the women have the opportunity to speak of the Great Physician; the Light of the world who dispels all darkness of mind and soul.

Whatever the action performed or the word spoken, the primary purpose and hope is that Christ may be exalted.

Literature: Missionaries in Algeria have always believed that the masses of the people should have the Christian Scriptures in their own heart language. A translation of the New Testament into colloquial Arabic, the tongue used by the majority of the population, was begun by a pioneer missionary before WWI broke out. Although portions of it have been published, much remains to be completed.[67]

Question to Ponder

How would you utilize, revise or avoid any of these four recommendations?

IN THE 1950S AND 60S, Ruth E. Stewart, a member of Campus in the Woods, helped to host Christian summer camps for Muslim students at the University of Algiers. We find much cause to rejoice in the reports she sent home to her family and supporters. For example, in August of 1962 she mentions working with another (likely) single female missionary named Marge Ballard. In connection to the expected reopening of the University of Algiers, she writes:

What a privilege it is to minister to them [Muslim students], but we would find the responsibility crushing were it not for the call and promises of God. Do pray that the seal of His approval might be upon our ministry and that we might see some Muslim students turning to the Lord Jesus Christ for salvation.[68]

In June of 1964, as she recalls the previous summer's girls camp, she writes: "One girl from Bordj-Bou-Arreridj who accepted Christ during this camp has made steady spiritual progress during the year. Her baptism at Dar Naama in May was a spiritual highlight."[69] Also, in recalling her trips with Marge into small Algerian villages to visit Bible correspondence course students, she writes: "We were amazed at how many had clearly grasped the Gospel, and some confess belief in Christ."[70] She also wrote about two more conversions in June of 1965. Ruth celebrated twenty years in Algeria in June of 1974.

In the 1960s, when the North African countries were getting their independence, missionary visas were becoming extinct. Bill Call, having lost such a visa, visited his friend in the foreign office who had issued his "missionary visa" in the past. Now he was asking for a visa to teach English. "Why," his Tunisian official friend asked, "I thought you were a missionary. Did you lose your faith?" Bill laughed with him, retorting, "Your government won't allow me to be one anymore!" Not only did Bill and his wife Peggy stay in country, but starting with high school students who came to their reading room in the capital, they were instrumental in discipling four Algerians boys right through university. Those four became elders of the first Arab church among the two million Muslims in Algiers. One of Peggy's disciples, a strong-minded Kabyle *hajji* lady, raised her four daughters in the Lord, then overruled her husband and arranged for her four daughters to marry the four elders! In that same decade, Don Rickards of NAM, attested that hundreds of Algerians were introduced to the message of Christ through massive distribution of Bible correspondence course invitations. It was so "successful" that most NAM missionaries were expelled from Algeria and they went rejoicing.

By the near the end of the 1970s, there were ninety believers between the age of 25-40, the majority baptized, who met in three different homes. About 65% were Kabyles. The church assumed responsibility for its own meetings, finances, and continued witness. The university-educated among them preferred to study the Bible in French, rightly or wrongly holding rather Western-style services as their sought-after audience was more likely to be more acquainted with Sarte than the Sermon on the Mount!

Section Reflection

Having met Ruth Stewart and five other single women of NAM who ministered from the 50s to the 70s, I was deeply impressed by their effective ministries. I surmised that single women missionaries historically have been among both the best and the least effective missionaries overseas (not the same ones, of course).

Tunisia

NAM, still called Kabyle Mission, entered Tunisia in 1885, led by Frenchman Jocelyn Bureau. Tolerance in Tunisia was surprisingly high and Algerian converts were even sent to Tunis for baptism in the early days of the mission...the missionaries had a professed convert as early as 1891; in 1897 they speak of two converts and in 1898 a young sheikh was converted. In 1903 a young woman professed conversion and gave the missionaries much joy.[71]

Heggoy further reported that "in 1925 the Methodists had seven missionaries working among the Muslims in Tunisia."[72] Nothing else is known about their work or the results of it.

Helen Morriss [73]

Helen Morriss was born in Kairouan, Tunisia, Islam's third most holy city, where her father had been the first male Protestant missionary in known history. Her father Evan ministered there for twenty years despite food being scarce and fleas and flies being abundant! Helen remembered boys in the street cursing her parents, even throwing rocks at them. Yet, with patience and love, her parents would put drops in the eyes of the children gradually gaining the trust and affection of many of their neighbors. Not unlike Samuel Zwemer in Bahrain, Mr. Morriss opened a little bookshop where he could have discussions or at least read the Scriptures to those who were illiterate. In the evenings he would hold "magic lantern" meetings beginning with a parable or an Old Testament story.

Helen returned from England to Tunisia in 1927 to minister for ten years. It was frustrating in that young girls would come her lessons but by the time they were reaching ten or eleven years old and when their minds were beginning to really be receptive, they would apologize to Helen saying, "My father says I mustn't go out of the house anymore." She shares further challenges and encouragements:

It was difficult to accomplish anything in their homes as there was no privacy. Several families sharing one house meant chaos and inability to give religious instruction to the women and girls. Even they would confess, "We are donkeys. We don't understand anything so we're not told anything." Their only religious outlet was to make a pilgrimage to a saint's tomb.

Going into the mountain villages to visit the Bedouin women was more encouraging. Once you got past the fierce dogs, the country people were usually very warm and friendly, but one wonders how much they could grasp of our message. During the two world wars we had to return to England, but when we came back the French were gone, Tunisia had gained its independence, and the present good standing on France has completely opened all the schools for women. Even gave them the vote! Finally women were able to open their minds and they were finally able to read the Scriptures! Not a few were even to come to a Friday afternoon girls club where we would have discussions after doing their needle work, or whatever they wanted to learn, settling down for an hour of Bible study, singing Arabic songs and discussion with them about the claims of Christ.

Twenty years later in 1957, Helen returned to be principal of a school for girls in Tunis until her retirement in 1971.

North Africa Mission (NAM)

In 1977, the USA base of NAM rallied behind the call from General Director Abe Wiebe who set as a goal the planting of twenty-five Muslim convert-led fellowships in Morocco, Algeria, Tunisia and Libya. Along with my sending base team, we went into action, recruiting ninety-five new missionaries from North America to help fulfill that goal. Nevertheless, the expulsion of missionaries from North African soil meant to many of the veterans that the church-planting goal was unrealistic. We therefore concentrated our personnel and finances on the Radio School of the Bible in Marseille, France.

Missionary J.J. Cooksey wrote in 1924 that

Our most notable service contribution of recent years, the founding of Christian homes for orphan and friendless children, was realized only after twenty years of patient, loving service. English and Scottish missionaries succeeded in winning the confidence of the Muslims by slowly overcoming their age-long hostility towards the Christian faith. The missionaries' patience seemed futile, but at the long last, Christ may soon see "the travail of His soul" and be satisfied in Tunisia with some "first fruits." Six have asked for Christian baptism in our native church and a seventh informed us that he would have been baptized but for the opposition of his father. His letter, however, concludes with the words, "I am, and I shall always be a Christian, and carry engraved on my heart these words: Christ is my Savior."[74]

Libya

In CMS missionary Douglas Thornton's survey book on Africa, *Africa Waiting* (1897), he makes this comment about Libya:

Tripoli, a province of the Turkish Empire, has chiefly Arab tribes, with a few Berbers inland. Not much can be said about the country, except that Tripoli and Benghazi are the outlets for Sudan's trade which are chiefly in ostrich feathers. The powerful Moslem sect of Senusi is a great obstacle to the progress of the Gospel in Eastern Tripoli.[75]

In 1912, "Missionary News" from *The Moslem World* reported[76]:

Since the rule of Christian powers, it has been the boast of Tripolitan Moslems that it was one of the very few remaining lands of Islam having no native Christians and being still governed by the true believers. They have been considered more fanatical than the rest of their brethren in North Africa, and were considered hopeless for Protestant missionaries to attempt to settle amongst. That all changed when Edward Glenny, honorary secretary of the North Africa Mission, paid a visit to the capital. In spite of much advice to the contrary, he decided to send missionaries to open a medical mission as the most effective means of disarming opposition, winning the confidence of the people, and drawing them within sound of the Gospel.

Thus in 1889, Dr. George Michell and Dr. Henry Harding were sent to Tripoli. A house was rented and it quickly became known that an English doctor had come and was giving free medicine. His fame soon spread and people, chiefly men of all classes from the very poorest to the well-to-do Arab gentleman, might be seen sitting together in the waiting room listening to the Gospel message. The work at the dispensary prospered under Mr. Harding, who worked alongside Michell until 1892 when the latter departed Tunisia and was replaced by Mr. and Mrs. W.H. Venables. The number of registered attendances rose to 10,000 a year, the patients including Muslims of all classes and from every part of the Vilayet, and even from the Sahara and the distant Sudan. Some of them heard the Gospel often enough to become familiar with its essentials, and some asked for and were supplied with New Testaments or Gospels, which found their way to distant parts where no missionary could penetrate.

Along with the work of healing and preaching at the Mission House, the women have been visited in their homes and taught by the mission ladies while the men were visited in the shops and cafes in an unostentatious way so as to avoid attracting the attention of the authorities or rousing their opposition. In 1896 a Bible depot was opened, and though sales have been very few, some thousands of Bibles, New Testaments, and Gospels in Arabic have been distributed.

About the same time a girls' class was started, and did a good work in a very modest way. This is the only effort that has been made in the direction of education. From the first, missionary work has been restricted to the capital, which covers an area of nearly a square mile, the missionaries not being allowed to go into the interior. The reason given for this restriction is that the government could not be responsible for their safety. Although the influence of the medical mission has, through the individuals who came for treatment, extended to every part of the Vilayet, it may be said that no missionary work has been done outside the capital. A good work has been done and much prestige obtained, but at least 90% of the population remain untouched by the Gospel.

Addison estimated that in 1911 Libya had a population of fewer than one million, of whom 87% were Muslims. Latourette agreed, stating simply: "Christianity was weak in this vast area."[77] An anonymous missionary who spent twenty years in Libya wrote in *The Moslem World* magazine in 1912, deploring the fact that "Tripoli was practically unknown to even the general public of Europe, except by Christians concerned for the Jews of North Africa."[78] Students of mission in 1912 suspected that Islam used Libya as the road to evangelize the sub-Sahara countries to the south; a vision that Colonel Qaddafi revived after 1970.

I suspect those hopeful writers in *The Moslem World* magazine, like us today, might have been tempted to put a positive spin on how much "preaching went on at the Mission house." NAM doesn't record such a mission house as existing, but it is likely that the wife of each doctor did visit some homes of the female patients, sometimes alongside the doctor when he could get free from the clinic. That the three NAM doctors "wore out" is certainly understandable.

Dr. Francis Steele, in his history of North Africa Mission *Not in Vain*, confirmed that Tripoli was the only location ever occupied by any Protestant missionaries in Libya. Although there were sometimes gaps of a few years, a clinic was reestablished in Tripoli by a Mr. Reid. When he left, it was taken over by James Liley, and then, in the 1960s by Drs. Pat and Patsy McCarthy until they were expelled in 1969 by the take-over of Omar Qaddafi. Not easily thwarted, the McCarthys went to Egypt and applied for visas to be a private government physician, which enabled them to carry on for nine more years!

Questions to Ponder

As exemplary as that was, how realistic was it for the McCarthys to think that one couple could establish a fellowship of Muslim-background believers with their own elders that would persevere? Is the same mistake being made in some Arab cities today?

EXCEPT FOR THREE different Protestant couples attempting a medical clinic ministry in the capital, Tripoli, with gaps of years in between, mission work was limited to Bob and June Douglas of the Church of Christ and some short-term experiments by the Southern Baptists until an OM team traversed the country distributing Gospels of Luke and correspondence invitations in 1972.

This team, comprised of two Americans, a Lebanese and a Belgian, was arrested and sentenced to eight years in prison. Although they were released after eight months, Libya was considered "off limits" by nearly all mission societies to engage in evangelical proclamation to Muslims after that.

Although this record normally stops at 1978, some might be aware that in 1982 four Campus Crusade (CRU) graduates from Penn State University agreed to "try again." Their story of getting jobs for the 1980-81 school year as "the English Department" of a technical university in Tobruk is amazing.

Because they were single men they could live in the men's dormitory, having on-going conversations with the students and showing the Jesus Film when invited to the students' homes during the breaks. Although they were limited by not knowing Arabic, the fact that they obtained residency as teachers and were not prevented from witnessing manifested that it was indeed possible to get in, stay in, and sensitively share the claims of Isa Al Masih.

Then, missionaries with the Christian Missionary Alliance of Canada spent some years teaching in the capital, seeking to encourage the Indian and African Christians working secular jobs there to befriend their Libyan neighbors.

Mauritania

In 1977, the year before this account draws a line, some university students challenged me to consider that this desert country was entirely devoid of any known evangelical witness. Once more the Lord of the Harvest birthed apostolic pioneers to a land where there were zero fellowships among the 99.5% Muslim population. The following years changed that, but for the purpose of these historical sketches the question must be asked: Why did it not happen until 125 years after pioneers went to other Arabic speaking peoples? What happened, after World War II, to the apostolically-called pioneers? Did they get detoured by the wars or no longer believe that bringing the only message that leads to eternal life was worth risking one's life?

Thankfully, the Lord of the Harvest once again met mission leaders at the North American Conference on Muslim Evangelism held at the Navigators headquarters in Colorado in 1978. Directors of mission agencies realized that the Bible did not say to go and make disciples of all peoples except if they are Muslims or unless one can get a missionary visa. Once again God would call a new generation to go and do what it takes to see the Church of Jesus Christ become a lighthouse where Christ was unknown. They are among those of whom the world is not worthy.

APPENDICES

APPENDIX 1: NEAR EAST CHRISTIAN COUNCIL INQUIRY ON THE EVANGELIZATION OF MOSLEMS

By Henry Riggs, 1938

ABOUT THE AUTHOR: Rev. Henry H. Riggs was born in 1875 in Sivas, an Armenian region of what is today Eastern Turkey, to a family of Presbyterian missionaries stationed in the Ottoman Empire. In 1852 the ABCFM (American Board of Commissioners for Foreign Mission) had established a theological seminary in Harput, Turkey to educate clergymen for the budding Armenian Evangelical Church. It expanded in 1859 and became American Harput Missionary College. However, to meet the growing demand for general education in the English language, the school's program was extended in 1878. Once again the school was renamed, this time becoming the Armenia College. Ten years later the Ottoman authorities demanded another change: Euphrates College.

To build the college, $140,000 in funds were raised from the USA and $40,000 from the local people. This occurred in 1875, the year Henry Riggs was born there. The facilities at the college expanded to include a hospital and an orphanage, in addition to the theological seminary and high schools for Armenian boys and girls. In 1895, Kurds looted and burned the Armenian villages on the Harput plain and eight of the twelve buildings on the campus were burned down.

In 1915 several of the leading Armenian members of the faculty were arrested, tortured, and executed on trumped-up charges. The college buildings were then occupied by the Ottoman military and initially used as a training camp, later as a military hospital. Euphrates College was officially closed shortly after the founding of the Republic of Turkey in 1920 and nothing now remains of its buildings.

Riggs grew up in the area, traveling to the United States to attend Carleton College in Minnesota and Auburn Seminary. He came back to be president of Euphrates from 1903 to 1910. In 1912 he witnessed the near annihilation of the Armenian people that he, his brother, and parents had come to serve. He carried on as a teacher and evangelist among Armenian refugees in Beirut from 1923 to 1940, dying in Jerusalem in 1943.

The following text is from his 1938 report. Be amazed at how Riggs was thinking far ahead of his day.

REPORT

Nine-tenths of non-Christian people in the Near East are Moslems, the Near East is the home and the base of Islam. Hence the concern which has prompted this inquiry. Feeling that missionary work among Moslems has not produced the results that ought to be expected from so much sacrifice and labor, the Near East Christian Council has undertaken to study the causes of the relative sterility of this field, and to discover if possible ways of making these efforts more effective.

Part I is an effort to state, in very brief compass, some creative suggestions which have grown out of this Inquiry. For the form of this statement of findings the writer is alone responsible, as he was asked to conduct the Inquiry. But the many hours of earnest study that have gone into this Inquiry, and the thoughtful letters that have embodied the results of that study, are the joint contribution of a large number of busy and earnest people directly engaged in the effort being studied; the aim of this report is to make available for all some of the fruits of this sacrificial effort.

I have conscientiously omitted from this report many of the most stimulating suggestions because they are merely a fresh statement of principles on which all are agreed; I have tried rather to give a fair idea of some of the positive and original suggestions which have been put forward,--not what is already accepted as common practice.

Whether or not they shall be so accepted depends on whether in the light of practical and prayerful thought and experiment, these suggestions prove to be sound and worthy of application. But I think it is only fair to say that if the findings thus presented are valid and right, there must be some definite and perhaps radical changes in the attitudes, methods and thinking of many Christian workers whose main business is the presentation of Christ to the Moslem, and who either have not yet thought these things through, or have felt in duty bound to follow the traditional lines of presentation. It would be a sad miscarriage of all this costly effort if this report is merely read with approval or disapproval and filed away. Its most fervent purpose is, after calling attention to what is wrong with present methods, to stir Christian workers to press on till they themselves discover the actual paths that can avoid that wrong.

Part II. Limitations of space and of the patience of readers have dictated the selection of a few quotations from the very large amount of available material. The effort has been to present samples of all the various lines of thinking, but no effort has been made to indicate the proportion of answers showing each trend. As a matter of fact, the answers that have pointed out objections to the new suggestions are quoted in much greater detail than the very much greater number of replies which indicated general agreement. Nor have I tried to decide which is the *best* statement of any point of view, but have rather selected the briefest.

Because in some cases it would be unwise to publish the name of the contributor, I have very reluctantly omitted all names in quoting the comments. Henry H. Riggs

PART ONE FINDINGS

The Inquiry has brought forth many practical suggestions for the improvement of missionary methods. But the main value of the discussion has centered around two questions, and the answers that have been offered to them. 1. "What special hindrances make the work for Moslems less successful than similar efforts for other people?" and 2. "What changes in our methods or line of approach offer hope of better success?"

The replies received have had a cumulative effect in focusing attention upon two special hindrances, which appear adequate to explain the lack of success pointed out:

A. *Christian teaching does not mean the same to the Moslem that it does to the Christian.* The Moslem mind has been conditioned by definite teaching against a distorted conception of Christianity; so that some of the most essential elements of the Christian message mean to the Moslem things that are repulsive to him, and would be *equally unacceptable to the Christian* if he saw them in the same way. What is divine truth in the mind of the Christian worker, as it reaches the mind of the Moslem listener is a falsehood which he rightly rejects.

Illustrations.

a) The Christian believes that Jesus is the Son of God, and this is frequently regarded as the crucial test of the acceptance of Christ. To the Christian this means something about Jesus. He is that kind of a being. His character, his power, his peerless teaching proclaim a being who, in that peculiar sense, "came forth from God." The Moslem thinks of none of these things. His mind turns to the question "Can God beget children?" For him to say yes means degrading God. He insists that God is not carnal but spiritual and absolute.

b) Christian faith centers around the belief that Christ is divine. The more intimately we come to know Christ, the more vivid is our conviction that He is "God made flesh." But the Moslem, when he hears of the deity of Christ, is immediately driven away from a consideration of his wonderful person, because his mind is filled with the thought, "God is one, not two or three." And to even think of any other as divine is the horrible sin of "shirk." Similarly and for the same reason, the blessed and mighty work of the Holy Spirit can mean to the Moslem nothing of what it means to the Christian, as a part of the doctrine of the Trinity.

c) The terrible pollution of sin, power to overcome sin, and the forgiveness of sin through Christ; these things are tremendously real to the Christian. But the Moslem is not impressed by our message about sin; first because of the different words used by the Moslem and the Christian and also because, to him, sin is a matter in an entirely different sphere; to be forgiven, to be freed, means to him merely a relaxation of the strict requirements of the Absolute Sovereign.

d) Similarly the Moslem who hears of the Atonement cannot think of "God in Christ reconciling the world unto himself." He has been taught to deny the death of Christ on the ground that it would be wrong for God to permit a sinless person to suffer for others.

B. *In the thought of the Moslem a change of religion is primarily a change of group-connection and group-loyalty.* "Every convert to Christianity is a dead loss to the community." "The Moslem Community is a noble and sacred thing, a social-political-religious fellowship for which the believer is willing to give his life." "The greatest handicap against which the Christian missionary has to strive is the power of Moslem solidarity." "There are thousands of men and women who believe in Christ and are trying to follow him, but they cannot bring themselves to face the break with their own community."

The great fact pointed out in these statements is very evident. But is this unwillingness to break with their own community due only to lack of courage or conviction? Not always. Many cases have been reported of true believers in Christ who have refused to break with the Moslem community because they wish to live among their own people, to make Christ known to them.

But even where the deterrent is fear or unwillingness to take the consequences, it is still true that this bond of Brotherhood is one of the strongest bulwarks of Islam; and so long as the Christian missionary undertaking appears to be a frontal attack against this great and (to the Moslem) precious fellowship, so long that powerful instrument will effectively oppose the progress of the Gospel.

We cannot forget that the sad history of the conflict between Islam and Christianity, past and present, makes it inevitable that the Moslem should see in our missionary zeal, merely a part of the imperialistic arrogance to which he has become accustomed; and with his mental equipment we cannot expect him to distinguish between the political and the spiritual elements of imperialism. It is a very sobering thought for all of us to reflect that possibly, if we could see our own spirit as it actually is we might find that the Moslem is not altogether wrong in sensing a spiritual arrogance in our effort to bring him to leave his own group and join ours.

These two major obstacles, then, loom up as the answer to our first question. In answer to the second question, "What methods or lines of approach offer hope of better success?" suggestions have been mainly along two lines.

The first is, "The way to overcome these hindrances is more devotion, more effort, more prayer, more faith, and above all, more love." Many and moving expressions of this convictions have come in, and point to the fact that we who would win others to Christ must look first of all to our own faithfulness and consistency as witnesses for Christ.

But other suggestions have come in along quite another line. "We must try to find a way *around* these obstacles," so that we shall not be in the position of attacking Islam frontally, and at its strongest points. These suggestions involve very serious changes in our approach, and should be studied with particular care, keeping in mind, of course, that differing conditions due to political situations and cultural background in different parts of the Near East make the answer found in one area perhaps inapplicable in another.

These suggestions are based upon the belief that it is possible and it is necessary to recast our message and approach to Moslems so that, without relaxing our effort as messengers of Christ, we may win them to Him without directly overcoming the special obstacles described. Our aim is one—to bring men into direct and personal relationship with Jesus Christ, as Teacher, Savior and Lord. If this is accomplished, all else can be left to the guidance of the indwelling Christ, whose Spirit works such "diversity of manifestation."

The following proposals are put forward for study, prayer, and experiment, as possible ways to attain the goal:

I. *To avoid the obstacle of the Moslem antagonism to the main Christian doctrines.*

1. A sympathetic understanding of the mind and heart of the Moslem is a prime necessity for anyone who would bring to them the message of Jesus Christ. Anyone who unthinkingly presents the Gospel only from the point of view of the Christian, without understanding what it will mean to the Moslem, becomes responsible for results which in many cases have proved to be absolutely the opposite of what was intended.

2. Our one effort must be to make Jesus Christ effectively known to the Moslem. Islam has already provided imperfect knowledge of Jesus, and a

certain reverence for Him. But we must start with that very imperfect knowledge and proceed to enrich it from the Gospel story and from the experience of the Christian life, till they can see Him as He is. We must guard carefully against the premature introduction of thoughts which will divert the attention of the inquirer from Christ himself. His reverence will grow to adoration as he becomes acquainted with Christ, and with His power in the life of those who surrender to Him.

3. In view of the almost certain misunderstandings resulting from the discussion of doctrines, doctrinal questions need to be handled with extreme care, remembering that Christ's method left his own disciples to formulate the deepest truths for themselves under God's guidance, and He himself said, "Upon this rock will I build my church." Public proclamation of our most cherished beliefs to those unprepared to understand them too often leads to an indignant rejection which closes the heart to the appeal of Christ himself.

4. Get the inquirer to study the New Testament, and especially the Gospels, as the adequate and original source and authority for the understanding of Jesus. Do not urge him to accept our interpretations.

II. *To avoid the obstacles which result from the ancient jealousy between the Christian and the Moslem group-organizations.*

5. Remembering that deep suspicion separates these two groups, we need to overcome that suspicion by a frankness and absolute honesty in which acts and words conform to what we profess to hold as our purpose. At all costs we must avoid anything which the inquirer or his neighbors may interpret as clandestine efforts to alienate him from his own people. In this matter the circulation of literature other than the Scriptures should be done with understanding watchfulness.

6. It is the conviction of large number of workers among Moslems that the ultimate hope of bringing Christ to the Moslems is to be attained by the development of groups of followers of Jesus who are active in making Him known to others while remaining loyally a part of the social and political groups to which they belong in Islam. The ideal is that there should thus come into being a church whose only head is Christ, and which does not carry the stigma of being an alien institution, drawing men away from their natural social and political connections. In spite of the stupendous difficulties in the

way of such an outcome, many workers are convinced that only as the spiritual significance of Christ is thus separated from external and unhappy connections in past and present can the way be opened for the power of Christ to do its work in the Moslem world.

7. To such followers of Jesus the term "secret believer" has been applied, sometimes with a degree of deprecation. To clarify our attitude towards such believers it might be stated that we lovingly encourage secret believers to go forward in the Christian life without publicly professing themselves as Christians in the sense of separation from the fellowship of their own people. But the purpose of such a course is to make possible a more effective witness, in life, in words, and in the reading of the Gospels, to the power of Christ in their own lives, among their own people. Experience has shown that unless such effective witness develops into a *group* of such believers, a solitary believer seldom survives. The essential function of the church can never be ignored. The aspiration here expressed is that the church of Christ might take root within the social-political body called Islam, and not as an alien body encroaching from without.

8. If such a line of effort is to be followed, certain very practical questions must be met. The first is that the name Christian, in the Near East, has almost exclusively a racial, political and social group-connotation, and does not suggest either a new way of life nor a spiritual rebirth within. If a group of believers is to grow up as indigenous and not alien, they cannot take on themselves that particular name. Some other terminology must be developed.

9. Similarly, baptism is almost universally recognized as the sign of the definite transfer to a new group-connection and is thus the inevitable signal for casting out the convert from the fellowship of his own people. It does not mean, to the Moslem, as it does to the Christian, repentance, a new birth, and a total surrender to our Lord. There are some who believe that some spiritual equivalent of baptism, free from the false significance which has grown up in the thought of the Moslem, can and must be devised.

10. The Moslem community life includes such matters as marriage and divorce, inheritance, etc. Unless a convert is officially transferred to the Christian registry, he is confronted with serious problems in reconciling his new life with such non-Christian relationships. Faith and great patience, with God's guidance, must solve these and many other problems of personal status.

11. But the greatest unsolved problem in this connection is that of providing spiritual fellowship and nurture for believers who thus remain a part of their Moslem social-political group. Without such fellowship and nurture the new believers seem doomed to lapse into the old way of life and thought. The hope for such a solution seems to lie along two lines: 1) That indigenous Christians develop such a loving and sympathetic relationship with their neighbors that such spiritual fellowship might grow up without raising the question of propaganda and the transfer of group loyalties. 2) That young missionaries, in the spirit of self-emptying which brought our Lord into this world, might overcome the barrier between Christian foreigner and Moslem native by "growing up" among Moslem people. Remember the words of the almost-persuaded non-Christian to the missionary, "If I could feel that you love me as much as you care for my soul, it might have been different."

"John said unto him, Teacher, we saw one casting out demons in thy name; and we forbade him, because he followed not us. But Jesus said, Forbid him not: for there is no man who shall do a mighty work in my name, and be able quickly to speak evil of me. For he that is not against us is for us." Mark 9:38-40.

(The closing quotation is from the findings of a study-group of Christian workers after a prolonged study of the subject.)

"The missionary of the past thought that it was his work to attack and break down Islam and his method was developed accordingly. He sought to prove to the Muslim by argument and controversy that Christianity was better and to force an intellectual assent. We believe that our primary aim for the world of Islam is so to live and work that people may follow Christ and find new life in Him."

To this we add another corollary; "It is realized that we have no power of ourselves to lead people to a new life, it being the work of the Holy Spirit to bring men to a new birth and so into a new life."

Our approach will be fusion of the *Christ of History* and the *Christ of experience*. We are called to teach the simple Gospel story of the life of Christ, making Him so to live by our presentation, coupled with our own and other Christian experiences, that He will leap out and into their lives.

We will be careful not to impose institutional religion and doctrine on the Muslim, it being understood that there is much in the ritual and dogma of the historic Church which is repugnant to him. Christian doctrines arose out of experience and it is unreasonable to expect the Muslim to understand them until he enters into that experience. Our message, like that of the early Christians, is simply a story. At a later stage in the presentation, when those facts are apprehended in terms of the eternal Christ, that is through experience, doctrines will inevitably arise out of them. Our aim is to present Christ, rather than His claims. The hearers, in their own way under the guidance of the Holy Spirit will come to a realization of His claims for Himself and upon them.

We believe, however, that there does come a time when the teaching out of experience has to give way to the teaching of authority. Obviously this will not be done except to one who is ready to unite with us in reverence and faith. In this connection we must keep before us the need of using the right terminology. Christian terms are meaningless to the Muslim until he comes into the experience for which they are symbols.

We believe, therefore, that we should encourage to the full all stages of witness within the Muslim community and not seek to detach the Muslim from Islam as a social unit. We will not raise the question of baptism unless applied for by himself. We look forward with expectancy to the time when the spirit of Christ will penetrate the existing form of the Islamic community.

Yet we believe that Christian experience cannot find its full expression in any other way than within the Christian Church. The full response to the call of Christ involves absolute surrender of everything that tends to keep men away from life with Him. Our teaching will therefore include Baptism and the Church as the Body of Christ, but the individual will be left to apply it to himself."

APPENDIX 2: A REFLECTION BY TIM LEWIS, THIRD GENERAL DIRECTOR OF FRONTIERS

Writing to the field workers…

Keeping a Holy Discontent

Along with many of you, I have a profound burden about the reality of progress of Christ's honor in the Muslim world. We've had decades of wonderful growth; numeric growth, financial growth, growth in the number of church-planting teams and sending bases, and most importantly, the number of people groups engaged. We've seen fellowships of MBBs where they haven't been in history (as far as anyone knows).

Yet, the overwhelming reality is that the state of the Kingdom across the Muslim world is far from what we (or the Lord) long for it to be, or what we understand from the Bible that IT WILL BE. Hopefully we all have an apostolic dissatisfaction and unease in our souls regarding what is… and what is NOT YET. It must bother us that still 86% of the Muslims on the earth have yet to connect with a follower of Jesus who cares for their state, both now and eternally.

Even if that's not our fault, we must be unhappy and dissatisfied with that reality. What will keep us driven by the Spirit to see that changed much more? What can we do to see God change that? I rejoice with the significant increase of disciple-makers far beyond what it was when we launched in 1982, but I long for so much more. We must not let up.

Strategic tools are being developed every day to this end. They take the best of what God's servants have learned over the decades and assist us in reviewing, reflecting, and refocusing on the task God has assigned to us. If we commit to pushing ourselves to learn more, to growing in godliness and to spurring one another on, we will surely be more fruitful.

Let us increasingly be "iron sharpening iron" to keep each other focused in faith and eager of greater understanding that will lead to upgrading and the goal of our Lord Jesus being loved as Lord and Savior by all Muslim peoples.

APPENDIX 3: THE CONVERSION OF SA'EED KURDISTANI (1863-1942)

As told in his biography: *Dr. Sa'eed of Iran*

The son of a mullah and named after the Prophet of Islam, Muhammad Sa'eed was born in western Persia in 1863. His father was a seventh generation mullah and Sa'eed attained this honorable title at the age of 13, which was an unprecedented honor for such a young boy. As he grew into a young man he devoted himself to education, hungry for knowledge and holiness. "During this time a copy of the New Testament in Persian came into his hands through a pupil. He read it from mere curiosity, found much in it that was unintelligible, and cast it aside in disgust." However, unable to satisfy the spiritual cravings that gnawed at him, he sought help from Islamic mystics and for a brief time, he found contentment in their arduous rites and continual chanting.

At the age of 17, Sa'eed met a Syrian Protestant pastor named Yohanan, who was traveling through Persia preaching the Gospel of Jesus Christ. However, his Persian was inadequate for his needs so Yohanan requested a tutor and Sa'eed obliged. The tutor was impressed by the humility of Yohanan and his two colporteurs, especially when they would pray for their enemies. Yohanan gave Sa'eed a Syriac Bible and began to study it with him. As they spent more time together, Sa'eed found within himself a change happening: "From day to day I found myself more drawn to the pastor. His love, his truthfulness, his pious life, his meekness, and his honesty affected me deeply... his life was a decisive witness to what he said."

For the first time in his life, Sa'eed was aware of his own shortcomings and this frightened him. He soon started to have doubts about the legitimacy regarding Muhammad as a true prophet of God and determined to never again let Christian blasphemy pass by his ears. He sent word to Yohanan, informing him that they could no longer meet. He later wrote: "But as time went on, I was brought to the sad realization that all my diligence in attempting to make my ways and works better was of no avail. The more I tried, the worse things became." Sa'eed resumed meeting with Yohanan and their studies in the Bible became more frequent and meaningful.

His brother Kaka became increasingly suspicious and began to openly mock Christianity in Sa'eed's presence. This only drove Sa'eed closer to Jesus. The words from Isaiah 60:1 echoed in his mind: "Arise, shine; for thy light is come, and the glory of the Lord is arisen upon thee." The power of God's words overwhelmed him.

This was ecstasy indeed after the months of doubt and bewilderment. All unknown to him, his inward rapture was mirrored in his face. Kasha Yohanan perceived the transformation and gently asked the cause. When Sa'eed had told of his new joy, they both knelt and thanked God. "My dear boy," said the pastor, "rejoice, for you have found grace with God."

Sa'eed was publically baptized, with Muslims present, on April 10, 1887 and a year later, he was married. He received advanced medical training and became a doctor: "Medicine and evangelism went hand in hand: this was his life purpose." With his Muslim patients, Sa'eed would regularly talk about his own Christian faith and every Thursday and Sunday afternoon he held Bible readings in his home, which a few brave Muslims would attend. He was especially eager to defend Christianity to Muslim religious leaders, seeing as he used to be one, and garnered respect from many of these encounters. "He found great encouragement in the opportunities he found for bearing straight forward witness to his Christian faith before influential leaders of Islam and their willingness to listen to him." He even encouraged Persian Christians to send evangelists out into their own country to spread the Gospel, as he himself was doing.

The following is a hymn penned by Dr. Sa'eed:

In joy and in sorrow
Christ satisfies me;
Tis Christ who from bondage
of sin set me free.
In all times of sickness
Christ is my Health;
In want and in poverty
Christ is my wealth.

BIBLIOGRAPHY

Why did the Church go to the Muslims last?

Leonard, Delavan. *A Hundred Years of Missions: The Story of Progress Since Carey's Beginning*. New York: Funk & Wagnalls, 1905.

Turkey

Addison, James T. *The Christian Approach to the Moslem*. New York: Columbia Univ. Press, 1942.

Anderson, Rufus, *History of the Missions of the American Board of the American Board of Commissioners for Foreign Missions to the Oriental Churches: In Two Volumes*. Boston: Congregational Publishing Society, 1872. *Archive.org*. Accessed 23 June 2016. https://archive.org/details/historyofmission01ande.

Beaver, Robert Pierce. *Ecumenical Beginnings in Protestant World Mission*. New York: Thomas Nelson & Sons, 1962.

Greene, Joseph. *Leavening the Levant*. New York: The Pilgrim Press, 1916.

Hamlin, Cyrus. *My Life and Times*. Boston: Congregational Sunday School and Publishing Society, 1893. *Archive.org*. Accessed 23 June. 2016. https://archive.org/stream/mylifetimes00haml#page/n7/mode/2up.

Pikkert, Peter. *Protestant Missionaries to the Middle East: Ambassadors of Christ or Culture?* Thesis. University of South Africa, 2006. http://uir.unisa.ac.za/bitstream/handle/10500/722/thesis.pdf?sequence=1.

Prime, EDG. *Forty years in the Turkish Empire: Memoirs of Rev. William Goodell.* New York: Robert Carter and Brothers, 1876. *Archive.org.* Accessed 20 June. 2016. https://archive.org/stream/fortyyearsinturk00good#page/n0/mode/2up.

Privratsky, Bruce G. *A History of Turkish Bible Translations.* Publication. Apr. 2014. Accessed 17 June 2016. https://historyofturkishbible.files.wordpress.com/2014/03/turkish-bible-history-version-sin-preparation.pdf.

Persia (Iran)

A Century of Mission Work in Iran (Persia), 1834-1934. Beirut: American Press, 1936.

Campbell, J. McLeod. *Christian History in the Making.* The Press and Publication Board of the Church Assembly, 1946.

Henry, B.V. *Forsaking All For Christ: A Biography of Henry Martyn.* London: Chapter Two, 2003.

Hopkins, Hugh. *Sublime Vagabond: The Life of Joseph Wolff.* Worthing: Churchman, 1984.

Miller, William. *My Persian Pilgrimage.* Pasadena: WCL, 1989.

Miller, William McElwee. *Tales of Persia.* Philadelphia: Dorrance, 1979.

Pakizegi, Zarin. *History of the Christians in Iran.* Oklahoma City: Sooner Printing, 1992.

Perkins, Justin. *A Residence of Eight Years in Persia.* Andover: Allen, Morrill & Wardell, 1843. archive.org. Accessed 8 Apr. 2016. https://archive.org/details/aresidenceeight00perkgoog.

Rasooli, Jay and Cady Allen. *Dr. Sa'eed of Iran.* Pasadena: William Carey Library, 1957.

Richter, Julius. *A History of Protestant Missions in the Near East.* New York: Fleming Revell, 1910.

Sargent, John. *Life and Letters of the Rev. Henry Martyn*. London: Steeley & Co, 1885.

Simpson, John. *Parading Persian History at Persepolis: Glimpses into the Rediscovery of Iranian Cultural Heritage and the Role of the Reverend Norman Sharp*. academia.edu. Accessed 20 June 2016. https://www.academia.edu/4037078/Parading_Persian_history_at_Persepolis_Glimpses_into_the_rediscovery_of_Iranian_cultural_heritage_and_the_role_of_the_Reverend_Norman_Sharp.

Stock, Eugene. *The History of the Church Missionary Society: Its Environment, Its Men and Its Work*. Vol. 3. London: Church Missionary Society, 1899. *Archive.org*. Accessed 8 Apr. 2016. https://archive.org/details/churchmissionary03stocuoft.

Twenty-Ninth Annual Report of the American Board of Commissioners for Foreign Missions. Boston: Crocker & Brewster, 1838. Google Play. Web. Accessed 12 Apr. 2016. My Book.

VanderWerff, Lyle. *Christian Mission to Muslims: The Record*. Pasadena: William Carey Library, 1977.

VanGorder, A. Christian. *Christianity in Persia and the Status of Non-Muslims in Iran*. Lanham: Lexington, 2010.

Wishard, John. *Twenty Years in Persia*. New York: Fleming Revell, 1908. *Archive.org*. Accessed 24 June. 2016. https://ia802607.us.archive.org/22/items/twentyyearsinpe00wishgoog/twentyyearsinpe00wishgoog.pdf.

Wolff, Joseph. *Missionary Journal and Memoir*. London: James Duncan, 1824.

Wolff, Joseph. *Travels and Adventures of the Rev. Joseph Wolff*. London: Saunders, Otley, 1861. Google Books. Web. Accessed 16 June 2016. https://books.google.co.uk/books?id=GTCurVPPNOUC&printsec=frontcover&source=gbs_ge_summary_r&cad=0#v=onepage&q&f=false.

Mesopotamia (Iraq, Syria, Lebanon, and Jordan)

Addison, James T. *The Christian Approach to the Moslem*. New York: Columbia Univ. Press, 1942.

Blincoe, Robert. *Ethnic Realities and the Church: Lessons from Kurdistan.* Pasadena: Presbyterian Center for Mission Studies, 1998.

Dann, Robert. *Father of Faith Missions.* Waynesboro: Authentic, 2004.

Dann, Robert. *The Primitivist Missiology of Anthony Norris Groves.* Victoria: Trafford, 2007.

Davis, RJ. Letter to Abe Thiessen. 19 Dec. 1969. *Records of the International Christian Broadcasters - Collection 86.* Billy Graham Center for Evangelism, 18 July 2008. *Billy Graham Center Archives.* Personal photograph by author.

Groves, Anthony Norris. *Journal of a Residence at Bagdad.* London: J. Nisbet, 1832. *Archive.org.* Accessed 3 Feb. 2016. https://archive.org/details/journalofresiden00grov.

Oren, Michael. *Power, Faith, and Fantasy.* New York: Norton, 2007.

"Our Mission Task in Iraq : The Land of Ancient Civilizations." United Mission in Mesopotamia. *GlobalMinistries.org.* Accessed 5 Feb. 2016. http://www.globalministries.org/mee/partners/the-assembly-of-presbyterian.htm.

Reed, Don, and Elva Reed. "Letter to Friends in Christ." Dec. 1958. Records of the World Evangelical Fellowship: Collection 338. Billy Graham Center for Evangelism. *Billy Graham Center Archives.* Personal photograph by author.

Richter, Julius. *A History of Protestant Missions in the Near East.* New York: Fleming Revell, 1910.

"Roger Craig Cumberland: Martyr and Messenger to the Kurds in Northern Iraq." *Crescent* 3 (2015): 19-26.

Scott, Frances. *Dare and Persevere.* London: Lebanon Evangelical Mission, 1960.

Thiessen, Abe. Letter to Philip Booth. 18 July 1973 "Records of the International Christian Broadcasters - Collection 86." Billy Graham Center for Evangelism. *Billy Graham Center Archives.* Personal photograph by author.

VanderWerff, Lyle. *Christian Mission to Muslims: The Record.* Pasadena: William Carey Library, 1977.

The Arab Peninsula

Al-Tameemi, Abdul Malek. *The Arabian Mission: A Case Study of Christian Missionary Work in the Arabian Gulf Region."* Thesis. Durham University, 1977. Durham University, 31 May 2012. Web. Accessed 20 June 2016. http://ethe ses.dur.ac.uk/3601/.

Chamberlain, Eleanor. *Fifty Years in Foreign Fields.* New York: Reformed Church of America, 1925.

DeMayer, Jenny. *Adventures with God.* Toronto: Evangelical, 1948.

Harrison, Paul. *Doctor in Arabia.* New York: Van Rees Press, 1940.

Harrison, Paul W. *The Arab at Home.* New York: Thomas Y. Crowell, 1924.

Kidd, Thomas S. *American Christians and Islam.* Princeton: Princeton UP, 2009.

Mason, Alfred DeWitt, and Frederick Jacob Barny. *History of the Arabian Mission.* New York: Board of Foreign Missions, 1926.

Mott, John R. *The Evangelization of the World in This Generation.* New York: Student Volunteer Movement for Foreign Missions, 1901.

Scudder, Lewis III, *The Arabian Mission's Story,* Grand Rapids: Eerdmans, 1998.

Shahîd, Irfan. *The Martyrs of Najrân: New Documents.* Vol. 49. Brussels: Soc. Des Bollandistes, 1971.

Thompson, Andrew. *Christianity in the UAE: Culture and Heritage.* Dubai: Motivate, 2013.

VanderWerff, Lyle. *Christian Mission to Muslims: The Record.* Pasadena: William Carey Library, 1977.

VanEss, Dorothy. *Pioneers in the Arab World.* Grand Rapids: Eerdmans, 1974.

Wilson, J. Christy Sr. *Apostle to Islam.* Grand Rapids: Baker, 1952.

Woodhead, Bevan. *A Grain of Mustard Seed.* U.K.: Christian Focus, 1998.

Zeigler, H. Conway. *A Brief Flowering in the Desert: Protestant Missionary Activity in the Arabian Gulf 1889-1973.* Thesis. Princeton University, 1977. Princeton: Princeton U, 1977.

Zwemer, Samuel M. *Sketch of the Arabian Mission*. New York: Arabian Mission, 1907.

Palestine

Addison, James T. *The Christian Approach to the Moslem*. New York: Columbia Univ. Press, 1942.

Bachmann., E. Theodore. (1939), *Mission Frontier in Palestine*. The Muslim World, 29: 275-284. doi:10.1111/j.1478-1913.1939.tb00406.x

Forder, Archibald. (1923), *Evangelism in Palestine*. The Muslim World, 13: 70-73. doi:10.1111/j.1478-1913.1923.tb01933.x

Forder, Archibald. *Ventures Among the Arabs*. Boston: W.N. Hartshorn, 1905. *Archive.org*. Accessed 23 June 2016. https://archive.org/stream/venturesamon gara00ford#page/n7/mode/2up.

Register, Ray. *Back to Jerusalem*. Enumclaw: WinePress Publishing, 2000.

Richter, Julius. *A History of Protestant Missions in the Near East*. New York: Fleming Revell, 1910.

Sunquist, Scott W., and Caroline N. Becker, eds. *A History of Presbyterian Missions 1944- 2007.* Louisville: Geneva, 2008.

Thorne, Dale. Email to the author. March 9, 2016.

VanderWerff, Lyle. *Christian Mission to Muslims: The Record.* Pasadena: William Carey Library, 1977.

Egypt

Cragg, Kenneth. *The Call of the Minaret*. New York: Oxford UP, 1956.

Douglas Thornton: Pioneer in Egypt and the Wider Muslim World. Crescent 1&2 (2012): 21-28.

Hutton, J.E. (1924), *Moravian Missions in Moslem Lands*. The Muslim World, 14: 125-130. doi:10.1111/j.1478-1913.1924.tb00504.x

McCague, Lydia (1919), *Egypt in 1857-1861*. The Muslim World, 9: 363-368. doi:10.1111/j.1478-1913.1919.tb01785.x

"Missionary News." *The Muslim World* 1.1 (1911): 92-96. *Wiley Online Library.* Accessed 4 Aug. 2015.

"Missionary News." *The Muslim World* 2.3 (1912): 332-336. *Wiley Online Library.* Accessed 4 Aug. 2015.

Mott, John R. *The Evangelization of the World in This Generation.* New York: Student Volunteer Movement for Foreign Missions, 1901.

Richter, Julius. *A History of Protestant Missions in the Near East.* New York: Fleming Revell, 1910.

Sharkey, Heather. *American Evangelicals in Egypt.* Princeton: Princeton University Press, 2008.

Swan, George. *"Lacked Ye Anything?": A Brief Story of the Egypt General Mission.* London: Egypt General Mission, 1932.

VanderWerff, Lyle. *Christian Mission to Muslims: The Record.* Pasadena: William Carey Library, 1977.

North Africa

Collins, George W. *Missionaries and Muslims: The Gospel Missionary Union in Morocco, 1895-1912.* Wichita: Wichita State U, 1975.

Douglas, Elmer. (1942), *Methods of Work in Algeria.* The Muslim World, 32: 212-218. doi:10.1111/j.1478-1913.1942.tb02004.x

Falk, Peter. *The Growth of the Church in Africa.* Bukuru: ACTS, 1997.

Heggoy, Willy N. *Fifty Years of Evangelical Missionary Movement in North Africa, 1881-1931.* Thesis. The University of Virginia, 1960. U Microfilms, 2009.

Hutton, J.E. (1924), *Moravian Missions in Moslem Lands.* The Muslim World, 14: 125-130. doi:10.1111/j.1478-1913.1924.tb00504.x

"In Memory of Margaret Chipperfield." Records of the Interdenominational Foreign Mission Association: Collection 352. Billy Graham Center for Evangelism. *Billy Graham Center Archives.* Personal photograph by author.

Isaacs, Albert. *A Biographical Sketch Relative to the Missionary Labors of Emma Herdman in the Empire of Morocco.* S.W. Partridge & Co: London, 1900.

Latourette, Kenneth S. *The Great Century: North Africa and Asia*. Grand Rapids: Zondervan, 1980.

Lundy, David, Gary Corwin and Gail Martin. *The Desert is Alive*. Bletchley: Authentic, 2006.

"Missionary News." *The Muslim World* 2.4 (1912): 436-442. *Wiley Online Library*. Accessed 4 Aug. 2015.

Missionary Review of the World. New York. Funk & Wagnalls. 1890. *Archive.org*, 2015. Web. Accessed 20 June 2016. https://archive.org/stream/missionaryreview1310unse/missionaryreview1310unse_djvu.txt.

"Missions to Morocco." *The Muslim World*. 2.3. (1912). 258-262. *Wiley Online Library*. Accessed 4 Aug. 2015.

St John, Patricia. *Patricia St John Tells Her Own Story*. Shoals: Kingsley Press, 1993.

St. John, Patricia. *Until the Dawn Breaks*. Franklin: Authentic, 1990.

Steele, Francis R. *Not in Vain: The Story of North Africa Mission*. Pasadena: William Carey Library, 1981.

Steven, Robert. (1917), *The Bible in Morocco*. The Muslim World, 7: 362-365. doi:10.1111/j.1478-1913.1917.tb01569.x

Stewart, Ruth. "Letter to Supporters August 1962." Records of the Interdenominational Foreign Mission Association: Collection 352 . Billy Graham Center for Evangelism. *Billy Graham Center Archives*. Personal photograph by author.

Stewart, Ruth. "Letter to Supporters June 1964." Records of the Interdenominational Foreign Mission Association: Collection 352. Billy Graham Center for Evangelism. *Billy Graham Center Archives*. Personal photograph by author.

Thornton, Douglas M. *Africa Waiting*. New York: Student Volunteer Movement for Foreign Missions, 1902.

Trotter, I. Lilias. (1924), *The Outlook in North Africa*. The Muslim World, 14: 131-135. doi:10.1111/j.1478-1913.1924.tb00505.x

Wiley, J. A., ed. *Life and Missionary Travels of the Rev. J. Furniss Ogle*. London: Longmans Green, 1873. *Archive.org*. Princeton Theological Seminary. Web. Accessed 22 June 2016. https://archive.org/details/lifemissionarytr00ogl.

General Missions History

Glover, Robert and Herbert Kane. *The Progress of World-Wide Missions*. New York: Harper & Row, 1960.

Goddard, Hugh. *A History of Christian-Muslim Relations*. Edinburgh: University Press, 2000.

Neill, Stephen. *A History of Christian Missions*. Harmondsworth: Penguin, 1986.

Tatford, Frederick A. *The Restless Middle East*. That the World May Know. Vol. 1. Bath: Echoes of Service, 1982.

Tatford, Frederick A. *The Muslim World*. That the World May Know. Vol. 4. Bath: Echoes of Service, 1983.

Tejirian, Eleanor and Reeva Simon. *Conflict, Conquest and Conversion*. New York: Columbia University Press, 2012.

Don McCurry, ed. *The Gospel and Islam: A 1978 Compendium*. Monrovia: MARC, 1979.

Tucker, Ruth. *From Jerusalem to Irian Jaya*. Grand Rapids: Zondervan, 1983.

Walls, Andrew. *The Missionary Movement in Christian History*. New York: Orbis, 2000.

General Christian History

Badr, Ḥabīb, Souad Abou El-Rousse Slim, and Jūzīf Abū Nahrā. *Christianity: A History in the Middle East*. Beirut: Middle East Council of Churches, Studies & Research Program, 2005.

Marty, Martin. *A Short History of Christianity*. New York: Meridian Books, 1959.

Moffatt, Samuel. *A History of Christianity in Asia*. Vol. 1. New York: Orbis Books, 1998.

Moffatt, Samuel. *A History of Christianity in Asia*. Vol 2. New York: Orbis Books, 2005.

Oden, Thomas. *Early Libyan Christianity*. Downers Grove: InterVarsity Press, 2011.

Wheatcroft, Andrew. *Infidels*. London: Penguin Books, 2003.

NOTES

1. Why did the Church go to the Muslims last?

1. Delavan Leonard, *A Hundred Years of Missions: The Story of Progress Since Carey's Beginning* (New York: Funk & Wagnalls, 1905), 281.

2. Turkey

1. EDG Prime, *Forty Years in the Turkish Empire: Memoirs of Rev. William Goodell* (New York: Robert Carter and Brothers: 1876), 112, https://archive.org/stream/fortyyearsinturk00-good#page/n0/mode/2up.
2. Ibid, 118-119.
3. Ibid, 148.
4. Ibid, 170-172.
5. Ibid, 175.
6. Peter Pikkert, *Protestant Missionaries to the Middle East: Ambassadors of Christ or Culture* (University of South Africa, 2006), 63, http://uir.unisa.ac.za/bitstream/handle/10500/722/thesis.pdf?sequence=1.
7. Prime, *Forty years in the Turkish Empire: Memoirs of Rev. William Goodell*, 489.
8. Ibid, 46.
9. Ibid, 46.
10. Ibid, 47.
11. Bruce Privratsky, *A History of Turkish Bible Translations*. Publication (April 2014), https://historyofturkishbible. files.wordpress.com/2014/03/turkish-bible-history-version-s-in-preparation.pdf.
12. Prime, *Forty years in the Turkish Empire: Memoirs of Rev. William Goodell*, 425.
13. Ibid, 425-426
14. Ibid.
15. Cyrus Hamlin, *My Life and Times* (Boston: Congregational Sunday School and Publishing Society, 1893), 436.
    https://archive.org/stream/mylifetimes00haml#page/n7/mode/2up.
16. Addison, *The Christian Approach to the Moslem*, 94.
17. Robert Pierce Beaver, *Ecumenical Beginnings in Protestant World Mission* (New York: Thomas Nelson & Sons, 1962), 23.
18. Pikkert, *Protestant Missionaries to the Middle East: Ambassadors of Christ or Culture*, 96.
    * outside the boundaries of orthodoxy
19. Ibid, 83.
20. Rufus Anderson, *History of the Missions of the American Board of the American Board of Commissioners for Foreign Missions to the Oriental Churches*: *Vol. 2* (Boston: Congregational Publishing Society: 1872), 483-484,
    https://archive.org/details/historyofmission01ande.
21. Joseph Greene, *Leavening the Levant* (New York: The Pilgrim Press, 1916), 157.
22. Ron Coody (Personal Communication, 2 April. 2016).

23. Ibid.

3. Persia (Iran)

1. A. Christian Van Gorder, *Christianity in Persia and the Status of Non-Muslims in Iran* (Lanham: Lexington, 2010), 123.
2. J. McLeod Campbell, *Christian History in the Making* (The Press and Publication Board of the Church Assembly, 1946), 213.
3. Joseph Wolff, *Missionary Journal and Memoir* (London: James Duncan, 1824), 46.
4. Joseph Wolff, *Travels and Adventures of the Rev. Joseph Wolff*, (London: Saunders, Otley, and Co: 1861), 221-222, https://books.google.co.ukbooksid=GTCurVPPNOUC&printsec=frontcover&source=gbs_ge_summary_r&cad=0#v=onepage&q&f=false.
5. Wolff, *Missionary Journal and Memoir*, 128.
6. VanGorder, *Christianity in Persia and the Status of Non-Muslims in Iran*, 122.
7. VanderWerff, *Christian Mission to Muslims: The Record*, 100.
8. Ibid, 116.
9. Van Gorder, *Christianity in Persia and the Status of Non-Muslims in Iran*, 137.
10. Ibid, 139.
11. *A Century of Mission Work in Iran (Persia), 1834-1934* (Beirut: American Press, 1936), 156.
12. *Twenty-Ninth Annual Report of the American Board of Commissioners for Foreign Missions* (Boston: Crocker & Brewster, 1838), 80, http://play.google.com/books/reader?id=YH81AQAAMAAJ&printsec=frontcover&output= reader&hl=en&pg=GBS.PP1.
13. Richter, *The History of Protestant Missions in the Near East*, 302.
14. VanderWerff, *Christian Missions to Muslims: The Record*, 116.
15. Richter, *The History of Protestant Missions in the Near East*, 301.
16. Justin Perkins, *A Residence of Eight Years in Persia* (Andover: Allen, Morrill & Wardell: 1843), 509, https://archive.org/details/aresidenceeight00perkgoog.
17. Eugene Stock, *The History of the Church Missionary Society: Its Environment, Its Men and Its Work: Vol. 3* (London: Church Missionary Society: 1899), 125, https://archive.org/details/churchmissionary03stocuoft.
18. VanGorder, *Christianity in Persia and the Status of Non-Muslims in Iran*, 131.
19. Vander Werff, *Christian Missions to Muslims: The Record*, 134-135.
20. Ibid, 135.
21. Ibid, 133.
22. John Wishard, *Twenty Years in Persia* (New York: Fleming Revell: 1908), 247, https://ia802607.us.archive.org/ /22/items/twentyyearsinpe00wishgoog/twentyyearsinpe00wishgoog.pdf.
23. *A Century of Mission Work in Iran (Persia), 1834-1934*, 157.
24. William McElwee Miller, *Tales of Persia* (Philadelphia: Dorrance, 1979), location 152.
25. *A Century of Mission Work in Iran (Persia), 1834-1934*, 158.
26. William Miller, *My Persian Pilgrimage* (Pasadena: WCL, 1989), 35.
27. Ibid, 51.
28. Ibid.
29. Ibid, 53.
30. Ibid, 63.
31. VanderWerff, *Christian Missions to Muslims: The Record*, 136.
32. Miller, *My Persian Pilgrimage*, 76.
33. Ibid, 96-97.
34. Ibid, 104.

35. Ibid, 118.
36. Ibid, 159.
37. Ibid, 181.
38. Ibid, 171.
39. Ibid, 193.
40. Ibid, 232.
41. Ibid, 238.
42. A first-hand account of his conversion is contained in Appendix 3.
43. Ibid, 252.
44. Ibid, 350.
45. Ibid, 184.
46. John Simpson, *Parading Persian History at Persepolis: Glimpses into the Rediscovery of Iranian Cultural Heritage and the Role of the Reverend Norman Sharp* (2011), https://www.academia.e-du4037078Parading_Persian_history_at_Persepolis_Glimpses_into_the_rediscovery_of_Iranian_cultural_heritage_and_the_role_of_the_Reverend_Norman_Sharp.

4. Mesopotamia (Iraq, Syria, Lebanon, and Jordan)

1. Michael Oren, *Power, Faith and Fantasy* (New York: Norton, 2007), 338.
2. Anthony Norris Groves, *Journal of a Residence at Baghdad* (London: J. Nisbet: 1832), 2, https://archive.org/ details/journalofresiden00grov.
3. Robert Dann, *Father of Faith Missions* (Waynesboro: Authentic, 2004), 163.
4. Julius Richter, *A History of Protestant Missions in the Near East* (New York: Fleming Fleming Revell, 1910), 187-188.
5. James Addison, *The Christian Approach to the Moslem* (New York: Columbia Univ. Press, 1942), 115.
6. Source unknown.
7. VanderWerff, *Christian Missions to Muslims: The Record,* 122.
8. Ibid, 127.
9. Ibid, 128.
10. The complete report is contained in Appendix 1.
11. VanderWerff, *Christian Mission to Muslims: The Record,* 131.
12. Addison, *The Christian Approach to the Moslem,* 125.
13. "Roger Craig Cumberland: Martyr and Messenger to the Kurds in Northern Iraq," *Crescent* 3 (2015): 25.
14. Ibid, 26.
15. "Our Mission Task in Iraq: The Land of Ancient Civilizations" (2016), *http://www.globalministries.org/mee/partners /the-assembly-of-presbyterian.html.*
16. Frances Scott, *Dare and Persevere* (London: Lebanon Evangelical Mission), 81.
17. The following can be found in the periodical *Under Syrian Skies,* from the years 1952-1954.
18. Records of the International Christian Broadcasters: Collection 86 (Wheaton: Billy Graham Center for Evangelism, 2008), http://www2.wheaton.edu/bgc/archives/GUIDES/086.htm.
19. R.J. Davis, Letter to Abe Thiessen, 19 Dec. 1969, Records of the International Christian Broadcasters: Collection 86 (Wheaton: Billy Graham Center for Evangelism).
20. Abe Thiessen, Letter to Philip Booth., 18 July 1973, Records of the International Christian Broadcasters: Collection 86 (Wheaton: Billy Graham Center for Evangelism).
21. Don and Elva Reed, Letter to Friends in Christ, Dec. 1958, Records of the World Evangelical Fellowship: Collection 338 (Wheaton: Billy Graham Center for Evangelism).
22. Ibid.

5. The Arab Peninsula

1. John R. Mott, *The Evangelization of the World in this Generation* (New York: The Student Volunteer Movement for Foreign Missions, 1901), 3.
2. Lyle VanderWerff, *Christian Mission to Muslims: The Record* (Pasadena: William Carey Library, 1977), 171.
3. Abdul Malek Al-Tameemi, *The Arabian Mission: A Case Study of Christian Missionary Work in the Arabian Gulf Region* (Durham University, 1977), 49. http://etheses.dur.ac.uk/3601/.
4. Alfred DeWitt Mason and Frederick Jacob Barny, *History of the Arabian Mission* (New York: Board of Foreign Missions, 1926), 127.
5. Dorothy Van Ess, *Pioneers in the Arab World* (Grand Rapids: Eerdmans, 1974), 2.
6. Ibid, 29.
7. Eleanor Chamberlain, *Fifty Years in Foreign Fields* (New York: Reformed Church of America, 1925), 187.
8. Al-Tameemi, *The Arabian Mission: A Case Study of Christian Missionary Work in the Arabian Gulf Region*, 58.
9. Ibid.
10. Ibid.
11. Ibid, 60.
12. Ibid, 61.
13. Ibid, 50.
14. Ibid, 161.
15. Ibid.
16. Ibid, 164.
17. Ibid, 167.
18. Ibid, 63.
19. Ibid, 64.
20. Ibid, 126.
21. Jenny deMeyer, *Adventures with God* (New York: Evangelical Publishers, 1942), 124.
22. Ibid.
23. Ibid., 135-136.
24. Ibid., 136-137.
25. Ibid., 138.
26. Ibid., 183.
27. Lewis Scudder, *The Arabian Mission Story* (Grand Rapids: Eerdmans, 1998), 27.
28. Ibid, 32.
29. Andrew Thompson, *Christianity in the UAE: Culture and Heritage* (Dubai: Motivate, 2013), location 982. Kindle Book.
30. Ibid, location 1014.
31. Ibid, location 1037.
32. Ibid.
33. Ibid.
34. Ibid, location 1062.
35. Ibid, location 1140.
36. Ibid, location 1332.
37. Ibid.
38. Al-Tameemi, *The Arabian Mission: A Case Study of Christian Missionary Work in the Arabian Gulf Region*, 168.
39. Ibid, 106.

40. Chamberlain, *Fifty Years in Foreign Fields*, 185.
41. Paul Harrison, *The Arab at Home*, (New York: Thomas Y. Crowell, 1924), 293.
42. Scudder, *The Arabian Mission's Story*, 217.
43. Ibid, 228.
44. Ibid, 208.
45. VanderWerff, *Mission to Muslims: The Record*, 174.
46. Thomas Kidd, *American Christians and Islam* (Princeton: Princeton UP, 2009), 126.
47. Bevan Woodhead, *A Grain of a Mustard Seed,* (UK: Christian Focus, 1998), 181.
48. Scudder, *The Arabian Mission's Story*, 221.
49. Mason, *History of the Arabian Mission*, 101.
50. Samuel Zwemer, *Sketch of the Arabian Mission* (New York: Arabian Mission, 1907), 35.

6. Palestine

1. Ibid, 159.
2. Ibid, 159.
3. Richter, *A History of Protestant Missions in the Near East,* 243.
4. Ibid, 244.
5. Ibid.
6. Ibid, 250.
7. Ibid, 250-251.
8. Archibald Forder, *Ventures Among the Arabs,* (Boston: W.N. Hartshorn: 1905), 122-123, http://archive.org/stream/venturesamongara00ford#page/n7/mode/2up.
9. Richter, *A History of Protestant Missions in the Near East,* 253.
10. Ibid, 254.
11. Ibid.
12. Ibid.
13. Ibid.
14. Addison, *The Christian Approach to the Moslem*, 318.
15. Ibid.
16. Archibald Forder, "Evangelism in Palestine," *The Muslim World* 13 no. 1 (1923): 70-71.
17. Ibid, 72.
18. Theodore Bachmann, "Missions Frontier in Palestine," *The Muslim World* 29 no. 3 (1939), 276.
19. Dale Thorne (Personal Communication, 9 Mar. 2016).
20. Ibid.
21. Ibid.
22. Ibid.

7. Egypt

1. J. E. Hutton, "Moravian Missions in Moslem Lands," *The Moslem World* 14 no. 2 (1924): 125-30.
2. Lydia McCague, "Egypt in 1857-1861," *The Moslem World* 9 no. 4 (1919): 363-368.
3. Ibid.
4. Ibid, 363-364.
5. Ibid, 364.
6. Ibid.
7. Ibid.
8. Ibid.

9. Ibid, 365.
10. Ibid, 366.
11. Ibid, 367.
12. Ibid, 367-368.
13. VanderWerff, *Christian Missions to Muslims: The Record,* 145.
14. Ibid, 151.
15. Ibid.
16. Richter, *History of Protestant Missions in the Near East,* 80.
17. "Douglas Thornton: Pioneer in Egypt and the Wider Muslim World." *Crescent* 1 (2012): 27.
18. Ibid, 27-28.
19. "Douglas Thornton: Pioneer in Egypt and the Wider Muslim World." *Crescent* 2 (/2012): 26.
20. Ibid, 27.
21. Ibid, 28.
22. George Swan, *"Lacked Ye Anything?": A Brief Story of the Egypt General Mission* (London: Egypt General Mission, 1932), 12.
23. Ibid, 20.
24. Ibid, 22 & 25.
25. Mott, *Evangelization of the World in this Generation,* 114.
26. Ibid, 28.
27. Ibid, 28 & 31.
28. Ibid, 34.
29. Kenneth Cragg, *The Call of the Minaret* (New York: Oxford UP, 1956), 304.
30. Mott, *Evangelization of the World in this Generation,* 37.
31. Ibid, 45.
32. Ibid, 51-52.
33. Ibid, 61.
34. Ibid, 62.
35. Ibid, 76.
36. "Missionary News." *The Moslem World* 1 no. 1 (1911): 92-96.
37. "Missionary News." *The Moslem World* 2 no. 3 (1912): 333.
38. Ibid.

8. North Africa

1. Willy Heggoy, *Fifty Years of Evangelical Missionary Movement in North Africa, 1881-1931* (The University of Virginia, 1960), 5.
2. Ibid, 14.
3. Ibid.
4. Kenneth Latourette, *The Great Century: North Africa and Asia* (Grand Rapids: Zondervan, 1980).
5. Francis R. Steele, *Not in Vain: The Story of North Africa Mission* (Pasadena: William Carey Library, 1981.
6. Heggoy, *Fifty Years of Evangelical Missionary Movement in North Africa, 1881-1931,* 80.
7. Steele, *Not in Vain: The Story of North Africa Mission,* 27.
8. Heggoy, *Fifty Years of Evangelical Missionary Movement in North Africa, 1881-1931,* 82.
9. Ibid, 82-83.
10. Ibid, 93.
11. Ibid, 173.

12. *Missionary Review of the World* (New York: Funk & Wagnalls: 1890), 776, https://archive.org/details/missionaryreview1310unse.
13. Steele, *Not in Vain: The Story of North Africa Mission.*
14. Albert, Isaacs, *A Biographical Sketch Relative to the Missionary Labors of Emma Herdman in the Empire of Morocco* (London: S.W. Partridge & Co, 1900), 16.
15. Ibid, 30.
16. Ibid, 36-37.
17. Most of the non-footnoted material in this section is taken from George W. Collins, *Missionaries and Muslims: The Gospel Missionary Union in Morocco, 1895-1912* (Wichita: Wichita State U), 1975.
18. Ibid., 3.
19. Ibid.
20. Steele, *Not in Vain: The Story of North Africa Mission*, 68.
21. Collins, *Missionaries and Muslims: The Gospel Missionary Union in Morocco, 1895-1912*, 7.
22. Ibid, 8.
23. Ibid, 8-9.
24. Ibid, 12.
25. "Missions to Morocco," *The Moslem World* 2 no. 3. (1912): 260 & 262.
26. Heggoy, *Fifty Years of Evangelical Missionary Movement in North Africa, 1881-1931,* 181.
27. Robert Steven. "The Bible in Morocco." *The Moslem World*. 7 no. 4 (1917): 362-365. *Wiley Online Library*, 4 Aug. 2015. 362-363.
28. Robert Steven, "The Bible in Morocco," *The Moslem World* 7 no. 4 (1917): 364.
29. Ibid, 365.
30. Heggoy, *Fifty Years of Evangelical Missionary Movement in North Africa, 1881-1931,* 249.
31. Steele, *Not in Vain: The Story of North Africa Mission.*
32. Ibid.
33. Patricia St John, *Patricia St John Tells Her Own Story* (Shoals: Kingsley Press, 1993), 129
34. Ibid.
35. In Memory of Margaret Chipperfield, Records of the Interdenominational Foreign Mission Association: Collection 352 (Wheaton: Billy Graham Center for Evangelism).
36. J. E. Hutton, "Moravian Missions in Moslem Lands," *The Moslem World* 14 no. 2 (1924): 125-26.
37. J.A. Wylie, *Life and Missionary Travels of the Rev. J. Furniss Ogle* (London: Longmans Green: 1873), 194, https://archive.org/details/lifemissionarytr00ogl.
38. Ibid, 242.
39. Steele, *Not in Vain: The Story of North Africa Mission.*
40. Heggoy, *Fifty Years of Evangelical Missionary Movement in North Africa, 1881-1931,* 24.
41. Steele, *Not in Vain: The Story of North Africa Mission.*
42. Heggoy, *Fifty Years of Evangelical Missionary Movement in North Africa, 1881-1931,* 26.
43. Steele, *Not in Vain: The Story of North Africa Mission.*
44. Heggoy, *Fifty Years of Evangelical Missionary Movement in North Africa, 1881-1931,* 56.
45. Douglas M. Thornton, *Africa Waiting* (New York: Student Volunteer Movement for Foreign Missions, 1902), 34.
46. Steele, *Not in Vain: The Story of North Africa Mission.*
47. Heggoy, *Fifty Years of Evangelical Missionary Movement in North Africa, 1881-1931,* 61.
48. Ibid, 214.
49. Steele, *Not in Vain: The Story of North Africa Mission.*
50. Ibid, 247.
51. Ibid, 254.
52. Ibid, 338.

53. Patricia St. John, *Until the Dawn Breaks* (Franklin: Authentic, 1990), 19.
54. Ibid, 23.
55. Ibid., 24.
56. Ibid, 26.
57. Ibid., 31.
58. Ibid., 33.
59. Ibid., 39.
60. Ibid., 42.
61. Ibid., 83.
62. Ibid., 94.
63. Ibid., 100
64. Ibid., 101.
65. Ibid., 104.
66. Ibid., 105.
67. Elmer Douglas, "Methods of Work in Algeria," *The Moslem World* 32 no. 3 (1942): 212 & 214.
68. Ruth Stewart, A Letter to Supporters, August 1962, Records of the Interdenominational Foreign Mission Association: Collection 352 (Wheaton, Billy Graham Center for Evangelism).
69. Ruth Stewart, A Letter to Supporters, June 1964, Records of the Interdenominational Foreign Mission Association: Collection 352 (Wheaton: Billy Graham Center for Evangelism).
70. Ibid.
71. Ibid, 155.
72. Ibid, 256.
73. Most of the non-footnoted material in this section is taken from Steele, *Not in Vain: The Story of North Africa Mission.*
74. "The Outlook in North Africa," *The Moslem World* 14 no. 2 (1924): 135.
75. Thornton, *Africa Waiting*, 33.
76. Most of the non-footnoted material in this section is taken from "Missionary News," *The Moslem World.*
77. Kenneth Latourette, *The Great Century: North Africa and Asia* (Grand Rapids: Zondervan, 1980), 20.
78. "Missionary News." *The Moslem World* 2 no. 4 (1912): 439.

CPSIA information can be obtained
at www.ICGtesting.com
Printed in the USA
JSHW011600300123
36929JS00002B/5